D1095737

HEAR THE TRAIN BLOW

HEAR THE TRAIN BLOW

A PICTORIAL EPIC OF AMERICA IN THE RAILROAD AGE

Lucius Beebe

and

Charles Clegg

WITH TEN ORIGINAL DRAWINGS
By E. S. HAMMACK
AND 860 ILLUSTRATIONS

GROSSET & DUNLAP, Publishers

New York

Copyright, 1952, by E. P. Dutton & Co., Inc.
All Rights Reserved. Printed in the U.S.A.

BY ARRANGEMENT WITH
E. P. DUTTON & CO., INC.

No part of this book may be reproduced
in any form without permission in writing
from the publisher except by a reviewer
who wishes to quote brief passages in con-
nection with a review written for inclusion
in magazine or newspaper or radio broadcast.

Library of Congress Catalog Card Number: 52–8254

Down in the meadow
Meadow so low
Late in the evening
Hear the train blow.

Contents

Foreword

THE BIBLIOGRAPHY of railroading is both extensive and comprehensive, ranging in the variety of its authorship from Charles Francis Adams to Colonel Robert S. Henry and from the technicians and experts of the Corps of Engineers assigned "to ascertain the most practicable and economical route for a railroad from the Mississippi River to the Pacific Ocean" to Oscar Lewis whose specialty is the Big Four of Central Pacific and Gilbert Kneiss, an authority on railroads to bonanza.

The cross references under the head of railroading in the Library of Congress occupy thousands upon thousands of reference cards and scores of index files. They include books on the surveying and location of railroads, their construction and financing, internal economy and operating technique, tariffs, legislation and vital statistics, and to a certain extent their social implications. Nowhere, however, to the best knowledge of the authors of this essay is there available in pictorial form a record of the folklore of railroading, its consequences to the national way of life and its place in the fabric of existence in the United States during the century and a quarter that railroads have been in operation.

There have been intimations of such appraisals in the corporate histories of individual railroads where they have been written by chroniclers not too inhibited by the advertising, operations or legal departments, notably James Marshall's *Santa Fe Trail* and Lloyd Lewis' and Stanley Pargelis' *Granger Country,* the story of the Burlington. But the over-all consequences of railroading, told predominantly in pictures, and the place the locomotives and the cars have come to assume in the American consciousness have not yet been recounted.

For a period of one hundred and twenty-five years American life, thinking, history and economy have been conditioned by the flanged wheel riding the steel rail. During that period a variety of other modes of transportation: canal boats, river steamers, toll roads and horse-drawn coaches, have been almost entirely eliminated by the cars. The pattern of the industrial East was predominantly determined by the location and destination of twin ribbons of metal running parallel to each other precisely four feet, eight and a half inches apart. The seemingly illimitable West was eventually bounded, populated and given its character by the smoking locomotive. Deep buried in the subconscious of four entire generations of Americans has been the image of a steam locomotive engine.

It is, therefore, with the subjective aspects of railroading, its overtones and by-products that the authors of this book have concerned themselves. They have attempted, in their selection of pictures and narration of story, to show what railroads have meant and how they came to make America the most mobile, within its continental limits, of the civilizations of history.

That universal transportation affected the national economy and social pattern is obvious. Less obvious, for instance, is the circumstance that Pullmans and dining cars had no small effect upon the general manners, or that a large portion of the world has come through the agency of the cars to regard the West as the essential and typical America, and that around the railroads and their destinies have been evolved a national body of legend and folklore as tangible and well defined as the body of mountain folklore of Tennessee. It is interesting to realize that for several generations of Americans, the ultimate hallmark of wealth, importance and social achievement was the private railroad car. Neither yachts, stables, mansions nor any other cachet of distinction were the equal of the privately owned Pullman riding grandly at the end of the varnish trains of the land. The balladry, art and language of the high iron have become inextricably entwined in the fabric of American usage. The railroad depot is the nation's cathedral, and the single sound which symbolizes America in the general imagining is probably not the eagle scream, which very few have ever heard, but the lonely locomotive whistle in the country night.

To a generation in which the practice of rail transport has been reduced to the regimented estate of any major industry, characterized by a universal sameness and paralyzing magnitude; it is difficult to comprehend that for a full century in the American record the steamcars were possessed of a compelling beauty and wonderment in the consciousness of an entire nation.

Joaquin Miller spoke for uncounted millions when he wrote that "there is more poetry in the rush of a single railroad train across the continent than in all the gory story of burning Troy." Edna St. Vincent Millay expressed an almost universal urge when she proclaimed that there wasn't a train she wouldn't take no matter where it was going.

During the greater part of their life span the locomotives and cars were individualistic, possessed of character, and railroad travel exercised a charm upon the human spirit. The rails running to the horizon were indeed a royal road to romance. The cars were palaces in microcosm and a whole people rode them to far places and happy destinations in fact and in fancy, both literally and metaphorically. Manifest destiny lay around the curves and down the tangents.

To the amateur of the rich overtones of the national saga these footnotes to the record are characterized by a singular and compulsive fascination, and to those readers who may share their pleasure in the depiction of vanished times the authors commend this book.

L. B.
C. C.

Virginia City, 1952.

LIBRARY OF CONGRESS

"A ROUND TRIP TO ROME HAUL WE'LL GO
AND BACK AGAIN TO BUFFALO."

The Erie Canal

A freight train on Horace Porter's New York, West Shore & Buffalo Railroad casts a shadow of portent
as it crosses the Erie Canal in upper New York State.

I

Cars Along the Canals

With the First Train Brigades Came an End to a Serene Way of Life, to the Barge Canals and Dusty Toll Roads, the Old Days and the Tranquil Times

THE COMMANDING and transcendent fact in the conquest of the American continent and the evolution of the United States as a nation is that water heated into steam occupies one thousand six hundred times as much space as it did in liquid form.

There are other and more complex factors. Probably the rifled gun is one. Samuel Colt's repeating firearms certainly are. So eventually were the principles of the internal combustion engine, but the dominant scientific fact that made possible the

10

change and, in some cases progress, was the coefficient of expansion of heated water.

The fact had been established for centuries. Internal expansion engines were in use in a number of forms as far back as the eighteenth century, but when the theory of steam power was applied to the coupled wheel and continental transportation, a new force was harnessed only inferior in its universal importance to the invention of explosives.

America came into maturity riding on the railroad. It achieved its geographic entity on iron and later on steel rails. Its entire economic structure is predicated on railroading. It has fought four wars to their conclusions riding behind the lineal descendants of *The Best Friend of Charleston* and *The Stourbridge Lion*. The history of the United States from 1830 to the present time has been more than it is anything else the history of the flanged wheel on the steel rail.

It is therefore one of the ironies of history that almost all the first, essential contributions toward the conception, evolution and eventual operation of steam locomotive power for railroads had their origins in England, a country which less urgently required railroads than almost any other on the then drawn map of the world. The margin of time between the first primeval origins of railroading technique in England and their translation to America was a slight one. Speaking roundly, because of the impossibility of arbitrarily determining what constitutes a "first" in any field of history, it required less than five years for steam railroading to cross the Atlantic. Simply, as has been remarked, it was ironic that the passage should have been a westbound one instead of in the other direction.

Throughout historic times the commerce of England had been water-borne. With Britain surrounded by seas, its commerce had floated over them and in the early nineteenth century was still voyaging over them toward imperial destinies. Within the British Isles themselves there is no single point that is farther than seventy-five miles removed from the sea, and the nation's inland waterways and highways, the latter following in many cases the chariot roads of the Romans, were well adapted to its social and economic life.

Yet the germ of the railroad found its first expression in a succession of English minds; its first dawn-impulse was in the intelligence of a nation of seafarers.

For many decades, perhaps as long as a hundred years prior to the emergence of steam locomotive power, coal miners in Cornwall, ancestors of the "Cousin Jacks" who later emigrated to every mining community of consequence in the United States, had made a practice of hauling their coals in horse-drawn wagons whose wheels were fitted to ride over rails. The rails were wood, in some cases shod with strap iron; the horse followed a towpath between them and was able to haul up to ten times the burden of which he was capable in a conventional cart.

It is worth noting that the first railroad authorities in the United States thought also in terms of animal power but in an improved form. Writing in Philadelphia, in 1830, Thomas Earle, an engineer of fair repute in his own age, said:

> If the power of horses or oxen can be advantageously applied to a carriage *in which they ride,* it will probably supersede the use of steam because the former can be applied profitably on roads requiring, because of their undulation, no power exerted for the greater portion of the distance. The loads may be light and consequently the rails and their foundation cheap, while the tendency of the heavy weight of the steam engine requires expensive rails and expensive foundations.

Steam motive power for railroads in England had a number of "fathers." As remotely as the year 1700 Thomas Newcomen and Thomas Savory had evolved a working steam engine for pumping water from the shafts of deep coal mines. To this day Newcomen's memory is kept green in England and America by a Newcomen Society composed of railroad men and engineers. Sixty-nine years later James Watt, a Scot, had patented a number of improvements on this engine. It remained for Richard Trevithick, a Cornishman, to build the first steam engine designed to replace horsepower on railroads, and it actually functioned when in 1804 it hauled, for the Merthyr-Tydvil Railroad in South Wales, a load of bar iron "in as many carriages as contained ten tons." Also, this Eohippus of the rails hauled them for a distance of nine miles at a rate of five miles an hour and up a slight grade.

The stage had been set for the first practical railroad as we know it today, available to public traffic in freight and passengers, maintaining regular schedules and operating between two terminals of general social, economic or geographic importance.

The actor who walked onto the stage was named George Stephenson and the title of his drama was the Stockton & Darlington Railroad.

On the historic date, September 27, 1825, with Stephenson on "the engineer's side" for the first time in human experience, the engine *Locomotion No. 1* moved away under its own motive power across the startled English countryside. Behind it rode thirty-four "carriages" weighing, with their loads, the amazing total of ninety tons. This is about the weight of an all-steel Pullman Standard sleeping car of the mid-twentieth century. Ahead of this fearsome cavalcade and waving a red flag, a boy rode mounted on a saddle horse, a type of warning of a train's approach which was still required by New York City law until 1937 when the last New York Central train rolled through a public street in Manhattan.

Now, and for the first time in public, commercial and practical operation the steam locomotive engine was a demonstrated success. On both sides of the Atlantic interest quickened. Toll-road operators shook their heads and canal promoters took a dim view of the new science. It could end in nothing good. But men of imagination and resolution saw the future open down almost illimitable avenues of potentiality.

Between 1812 and 1837 private capital and public funds to the extent of more than $60,000,000, a fantastic sum for the times, was expended on the construction of canals in the regions north of Richmond and east of Chicago. Capital in the Deep South was largely absorbed in the purchase of plantations and the slaves to work them, but the East and Middle West were swept by a compulsion to build canals which was, in its time, comparable to the railroad fever which followed it.

In New England there were the great Middlesex Canal and the Blackstone between Worcester and Providence as well as the New Haven & Northampton. In the middle states the canal scene was, of course, dominated by the Erie but there were also the Delaware & Hudson, the Chesapeake & Ohio (names prophetic of railroads to come), the Delaware & Raritan and the James Canal between Lynchburg and Richmond. The Ohio Territory boasted the Ohio & Erie running from Portsmouth to Cleveland, the Miami from Toledo to Cincinnati, the Wabash & Erie and the Illinois & Michigan Canal between the Illinois River and Lake Michigan at Chicago. To an astronomical observer from another planet they might not have rivaled the putative canals of Mars, but they were impressive achievements in a young country pushing resolutely westward.

CULVER SERVICE

"IF THE PRESENT GENERATION SHALL ADOPT CANALS
THE NEXT MAY TRY THE RAILWAY."

Oliver Evans, 1819

BROWN BROS.

In the 1820s the pastoral progress of passenger packets such as this along the Morris Canal, "length 100 miles 64 chains," between Jersey City and Easton, Pennsylvania, was part of a fixed and orderly pattern of life which the noisy and fearsome monsters of the rail threatened overnight to destroy. Soon grass would grow along the towpaths, the friendly boatman's horn would not again roll over the meadows and farmsteads and the comfortable floating life of the canawlers would be at an end. No wonder the railroad was feared and hated. The industrial age with all its evils and corruption would be the first freight aboard the cars. Below: A vignette of Canal Life, "Sunday Morning."

CULVER SERVICE

THE OLD DAYS, THE QUIET WAYS

An artist on the staff of *Leslie's* drew this Morris Canal pastoral with the moralistic title "Drones and Workers." Below is a scene on the historic James River Canal just outside of Richmond as a gay excursion was setting out to celebrate Fourth of July. The rails of the Richmond & Alleghany Railroad, now the Chesapeake & Ohio, when it was built followed the canal for many miles. Piles of ties in background dates the picture. Insert shows "Wash-day on a Canal Boat."

CHESAPEAKE & OHIO RR.

CULVER SERVICE

"THE FRENCH FOUR AND THE PIGEON WING"

Life on the canals was gusty and good and the canawlers lived well and merrily in an age innocent of urgency. The atmospere of the place and period are admirably recreated in Walter Edmonds' classic "Rome Haul," the story of the building of the "Erie Ditch." Canal-side taverns (*above*) were notoriously profane places where one could come to no good if one took a dram too many, and from Rome to Buffalo there were many of them. Less boisterous was dancing on deck to the music of a yaller-backed fiddle playing "Old Zip Coon" as George Caleb Bingham's "Jolly Flatboatman" danced the French Four and the Pigeon Wing.

CULVER SERVICE

The canal fever was definitely on the decline by 1837. The great financial panic of that year abruptly dried up the sources of investment capital in the United States and frightened potential foreign investors. By then the railroads were clearly in the ascendancy in the field of transportation everywhere in the land. Traffic on these early canals continued in ponderable volume throughout the entire nineteenth century but their financing and construction were fairly well defined by the years mentioned.

Even the epochal *Locomotion No. 1* was not, however, to be Stephenson's masterpiece. Four years after its dramatic run on the Stockton & Darlington, the directors of the Liverpool & Manchester Rail-Road offered a prize of £500 in a sort of engine fair, and Stephenson won it, hands down, with an engine that has since become a part of history, *The Rocket*. At the trials *The Rocket* first ran at the rate of fifteen miles an hour with a pay load of thirteen tons. The next day it covered seventy miles, an amazing distance for the time and even later, without a breakdown or what would now be called "engine failure," and later it achieved an average speed of fourteen miles an hour with a revenue load of forty-two tons. The Liverpool & Manchester directors rocked on their heels, double-checked the records and statistics, and promptly ordered four engines of identical pattern with the design of *The Rocket*. The first big order for motive power had been placed by an operating railroad.

Across the Atlantic the first railroad in America to run a steam locomotive in a "train brigade," as well as the first to inaugurate and maintain regular freight and passenger service as what would now be known as a public utility, was the South Carolina Railroad running north and east out of Charleston in the general direction of Augusta, Georgia. When, in 1833, it achieved this objective—135 miles from Charleston—it was the world's longest railroad, and the long fiber cotton of inland Georgia began traveling out over the iron rails instead of floating down to Savannah aboard river boats. By this date the railroad was in open competition in the South with inland waterways and was preparing to compete with them in Massachusetts, Connecticut and New York.

The South Carolina Railroad opened for business in December 1830, quite literally with a bang. Its fine new locomotive, *The Best Friend of Charleston* built in New York from the designs of C. E. Detmold and E. L. Miller, was ready to go into the first scheduled service of any locomotive built this side of the Atlantic. The first run was, one gathers even at this remote date, a hilarious success. The coaches tied to the drawbar of *The Best Friend of Charleston* carried a military brass band, a detachment of artillerymen who discharged a small fieldpiece at frequent intervals from a car window, and a delighted group of stockholders, directors and otherwise forensically inclined dignitaries. It was a day of feasting, toasts and oratory and set a pattern for the opening of scores and scores of railroads across the American continent in the next three-quarters of a century. Regular train service was inaugurated out of Charleston the next day.

Although not strictly the concern of this book save as antecedent or background material, it is notable that the opening to service of the South Carolina Railroad was marred by no such melancholy event as had occurred earlier in the year when the Liverpool & Manchester, England's first railroad of any magnitude, commenced operations. The occasion was a gala one with many notables, including the Duke of Wellington, and the train was drawn behind eight engines decorated with flags and bunting.

"The accident to Mr. Huskinson, the distinguished statesman, appears to have arisen from the irresolution of the unfortunate gentleman," said a contemporary account. "He was standing close to the carriage that contained the Duke of Wellington, for the train having stopped at Park-side Bridge, several of the passengers, against the advice of the company's servants, got out of the carriages and among them was Mr. Huskinson. If he had stood up close to the carriage he was near another train might have passed without injuring him; but unfortunately the moment before *The Rocket* passed he caught hold of the door of the ducal car which was struck by the passing engine and, being thrown on the line of rails on which *The Rocket* was moving, his right leg came in contact with the engine and was completely crushed. So severe were the injuries he received that death put an end to his suffering."

Mr. Huskinson must go down in history as the first fatality on record in the history of steam railroading.

The Best Friend of Charleston was destined, a few months later, to achieve another "first" when it perished noisily in the first boiler explosion on an American railroad. The South Carolina at once replaced it with the equally successful *West Point,* but not before its directors had ordered a "barrier car" loaded with baled cotton to be carried behind the engine and ahead of the passengers as a precaution against temperamental boilers.

TRANQUILLITY IN UPPER YORK STATE

The pastoral quietude of the era of canals, as is suggested by this old-time engraving of the locks of the Erie Canal at Lockport, New York, was of short duration, for the sound of the engine whistle and the whooshing of its exhaust were just across the hills.

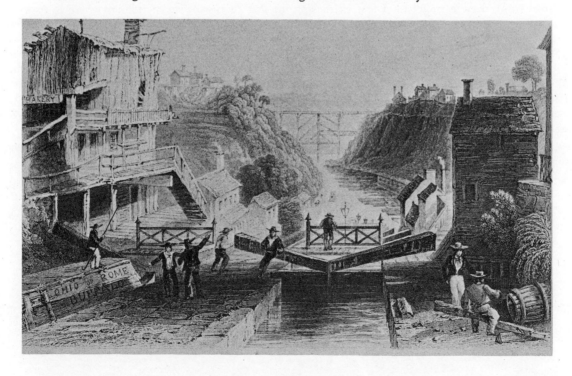

17

(THREE PICTURES) ASS'N OF AMERICAN RAILROADS

Boatmen along the Savannah River decided that the world was going to hell in a hack when on Christmas morning 1830 *The Best Friend of Charleston*, the fine new locomotive engine of the South Carolina Railroad *(top)*, drew a trainload of first citizens on the first successful steam ride anywhere in America. A squad of artillery fired a cannon from a flatcar, frightening the countryside cruelly, and everyone agreed the occasion was bang-up. A few months later the *Best Friend*, still ahead of the field, scored another first by producing the first boiler explosion in the land and was immediately replaced in service by the *West Point (center)* which trailed a "barrier car" loaded with cotton to protect passengers against any similar contingency. Still another first was credited to the South Carolina when, in the middle thirties, increasingly dense traffic made night operations, and hence illumination of the rails, a necessity. Horatio Allen, the company's chief engineer solved the problem by pushing a flatcar *(below)* on which a brisk bonfire burned ahead of the engine.

LIBRARY OF CONGRESS

Still another "first" and one which was not appreciated by the management was when unidentified miscreants fired upon a passenger train of the South Carolina a few years after it was placed in regular service. A Mr. Sears of Baltimore was unfavorably impressed with Southern hospitality when a rifle slug punctured his expensive beaver hat and *Leslie's,* in an editorial which accompanied the above drawing, remarked that such uncouth practices should be abated. Below is the original *Best Friend of Charleston* restored as good as new after its boiler explosion.

SOUTHERN RAILWAY

In the three years following the opening to traffic of the South Carolina Railroad, events in the world of steam transportation followed hard upon one another's heels. In 1831 a fine new locomotive, the *DeWitt Clinton,* went into service on the Mohawk & Hudson Railroad in New York State. In the same year there arrived from England the celebrated *John Bull* destined for eventual service on the newly chartered Camden & Amboy in New Jersey. Henry Clay presided at a meeting at which was organized the Lexington & Ohio, first railroad west of the Alleghanies, and the first locomotive of Matthias Baldwin, a Philadelphia jeweler and watchmaker, *Old Ironsides,* was outshopped for the Philadelphia, Norriston & Germantown Railroad, now the Reading. And last but not least it was in this epochal year that Horatio Allen and John Jervis devised the first swivel or bogie wheels mounted in a truck for guiding the frames of locomotives around curves.

The year following saw the second railroad of the Deep South, the Pontchartrain out of New Orleans, and the chartering of the New York & Erie Railroad whose completion a decade later was to be hailed as "the work of the age" and whose history extending down to the immediate present was to be the stormiest in the legend of transportation.

Railroading in the early thirties was very much of a trial-and-error venture. Strap iron rails which frequently came loose and speared up through the cars in "snakeheads" were still commonplace. The coaches which composed the rolling stock of a "train brigade" were largely patterned after the horsedrawn road stagecoaches they were supplanting and were coupled together with chains so that the cars snapped together and apart with the inequalities of the roadbed and starting and stopping were accomplished with a prodigious amount of jerking and crashing.

Motive power was unreliable. For several years it was doubted if steam engines could be operated in wet weather and the Philadelphia, Germantown & Norriston would not let their fine *Old Ironsides* out of its barn when it rained. As late as 1834 the Philadelphia & Columbia Railroad advertised that in inclement weather horses would be substituted for its locomotive engine. Many communities refused to allow steam engines within the municipal limits for fear of sooting up the windows; the Rensselaer & Saratoga and many another was towed into Troy by teams of horses maintained at the town limits for this purpose.

Encounters with livestock were commonplace and led to great indignation among farmers and rural folk generally who were forever suing the railroads for damage to cattle and pigs—often winning substantial judgments from antirailroad magistrates. The canawlers, the teamsters and stagecoach drivers were, of course, archenemies of the railroads and often had the sympathy of substantial citizens of conservative leanings. Municipal indignation in those times had a low boiling point and the avoidance of a community when a railroad was located or the erection of its depot contrary to the interest of real estate dealers led to hideous denunciations in the public prints and legislatures.

Particularly vexatious in its early days of operations were the farmers along the right of way of the Long Island Rail Road whose meadows and pastures occupied what are today the city blocks of Hempstead, Mineola and Hicksville. Railroad property was burned, trains derailed and railroad employees attacked by angry agriculturalists who foresaw, quite correctly, the time coming when their rolling farmsteads would be sacrificed to the progress of metropolis.

Dawn-Horses of the Iron Highroad

1831 DeWITT CLINTON

1832 OLD IRONSIDES

(FOUR PICTURES) ASS'N OF AMERICAN RAILROADS

The year 1830, on the threshold of the railway age, found a total of twenty-two railroads planned or functioning in the United States, most of them on paper. The next half decade was to see tremendous progress in the technique of rail transport, especially steam motive power. The *De Witt Clinton* and *Old Ironsides (above)* were locomotives of railroads that were eventually to become the New York Central and the Pennsylvania, respectively. In the *John Bull* and the *Pioneer (below)* are visible the first traces of the steam locomotive that was to be the symbol of American railroading for more than a century to come.

1833 JOHN BULL

PIONEER 1836

The Glory of the Erie Was Short-Lived

BROWN BROS.

THE ELEGANT KEG

Even in an age that rejoiced in civic ceremony, the opening of the Erie Canal was a notable commotion. In the presence of a monster aquacade De Witt Clinton poured a barrel of Lake Erie water into New York harbor from an "elegant keg." Guests of honor were presented with "elegant medals" and entertained at an "elegant collation." Twenty-five years later the canal locks at Schenectady, shown below, were paralleled by three railroads, the Central, the Delaware & Hudson and the Fonda, Johnstown & Gloversville. The Civil War saw the last boom in canal traffic on the Erie.

BROWN BROS.

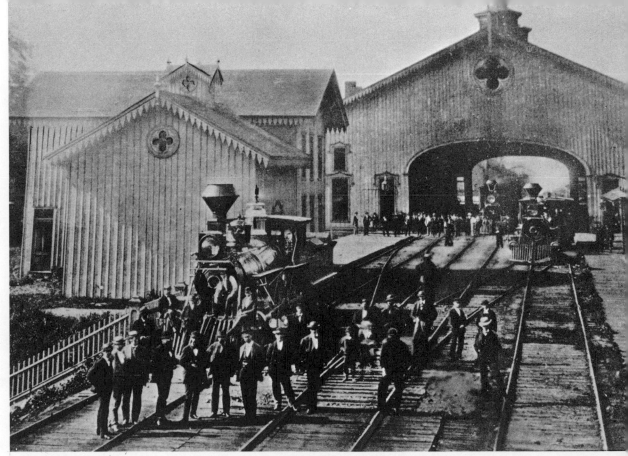

ERIE RR.

To many simple folk, countrymen in particular, the dawning of the industrial age was a thing of terror and the railroad locomotive a monster freighted with destruction. Nothing to allay these fears can be found in a contemporary drawing of an early Erie engine "coming along the Susquehanna Station." In terms of the switchman beside it, this locomotive would have been thirty-five feet high with eight-foot drivers and a mansion for cab. For such a Leviathan of the rails even the Erie's original six-foot gage wouldn't have been too wide. An early photograph of the Meadville, Pennsylvania, depot shows the six-foot track before it was relaid to standard.

ERIE RR.

Following the Lead of the Deep South

BALTIMORE & OHIO RR.

A race between Peter Cooper's diminutive engine *Tom Thumb* and a horse-drawn rail car on the Baltimore & Ohio near Relay, Maryland, in 1830 ended in victory for the older motive power and the little engine was shelved. Two years later, however, the *Atlantic* (*center*) was purchased by the B. & O. and remained in actual operation for sixty years. Behind the "grasshopper" engine are two Imlay double-decker coaches. The Mt. Clare depot of the B. & O. was the first railroad station in the world (*below*) and from it the first train departed for Washington in 1835.

Rails Come to Maryland and Pennsylvania

PENNSYLVANIA RR.

The mighty Pennsylvania Railroad system, like the B. & O., had its inception in the 1830s, not in the form of a single main line, but as a number of separate and often disconnected short lines. It wasn't until the middle forties that the Pennsylvania Central was organized to divert traffic from the Erie and the B. & O. to Philadelphia from Pittsburgh and the West. A poster of one of the Pennsy's early component roads operating in 1833 is shown above together with a picture of *Old Ironsides,* first engine of the Philadelphia, Germantown & Norristown Railroad and its builder, Matthias Baldwin. Below is the *John Bull* of the Camden & Amboy, built in 1831 and shown in rebuilt form and with coaches of a later period. The Pennsylvania in a few years embraced all these railroads in its far-flung network.

Canal and Turnpike Alike Bowed To The Cars

CHESAPEAKE & OHIO RR.

Old timers grieved but railroaders rejoiced to see rails following the towpath of the historic James River Canal, near Richmond, after the construction in 1882 of the Richmond & Alleghany Railroad. Thirty years later the Chesapeake & Ohio's train No. 9 runs over the same route. Another casualty, along with the inland canal, to the railroad was the turnpike or toll road. Shown below is the toll gate house at Distler's Park near Metropolitan Avenue in Brooklyn after a suburban trolley line had been run through the carriage gate. As far back as 1852 Eli Bowen had written prophetically:

And the steam king rules the travelled world
And the pike is left to die.

LIBRARY OF CONGRESS

At Port Carbon, Pennsylvania, (*above*) the coal docks were once busy loading the canal barges for shipment to industrial centers over a network of inland waterways and barge canals, but only a few years later the canal locks everywhere (*center*) were millponds innocent of all traffic. By the end of the century the tracks of the Lehigh Valley Railroad and the Erie Railroad ran on either side of the Erie Canal at Rochester (*below*) while traffic in the canal locks at the left of the picture is non-extant.

GEORGE EASTMAN HOUSE

LIBRARY OF CONGRESS

Slowly, Even

The

Erie Canal

Yielded

To The

Steamcars

CULVER SERVICE

For half a century a flood tide of commerce flowed almost undiminished along the great Erie Canal joining Lake Erie with the Hudson River and New York. On the opposite page is shown the grain trade with the East in the seventies, loading at the elevators in Chicago, being towed across Lake Erie and, at the bottom, sailing the placid inland reaches of the canal itself. On this page (*top*) the grain barges have left the canal at Troy and are being towed down the Hudson. But by the time of these scenes, both banks of the Hudson itself were paralleled by railroads, the West Shore and the Central, and the New York & Erie, the Lehigh Valley and the Lackawanna had been completed or were building toward Buffalo. A smoky locomotive of the great Vanderbilt line, the Central (*below*) symbolized an end to the great days of the Erie and its connecting waterways.

CULVER SERVICE

A ride on the cars in those days was a great adventure. Samuel Hopkins Adams remembers that in the middle thirties his grandfather, a confirmed patron of the Erie Canal by preference, had been forced by untoward circumstances to take a trip from Ballston to Troy aboard the Rensselear & Saratoga Railway and that the trip of twenty-six miles was a "parlous" one accomplished in just under six hours.

There were two cars in the train richly upholstered in crimson morocco with coach-lace trimmings. One had a panel picture, "The Wounded Tiger" painted on its side. The other was similarly ornamented with a genuine oil painting of "Napolean Crossing the Alps." Grandfather took the latter. "The rear car was advised to be safer."

When it was time for the train's departure the engineer made a round of the passengers on the platform, offering them snuff, raising his beaver hat politely to the ladies, reassuring them as to the train's safety and generally exuding confidence. The conductor, in a puce surtout, blew five blasts on a small horn, assumed a graceful stance on the running board of one of the cars, waved his top hat at the engineer and they were off.

At every curve in the forest the train stopped and the fire boy was sent ahead to reconnoiter the track. The week before a she bear with two cubs had attacked the locomotive and tried to bite the machinery, spreading great alarm among the passengers and delaying the train half an hour. When the train, the day grandfather rode it, achieved a speed of twenty-five miles an hour on a downgrade, the lady next to him said her prayers.

When the locomotive was unable to haul the cars up the railroad's ruling grade a committee was dispatched to a farmhouse two miles away to borrow a span of oxen and these, together with the assistance of all the male passengers pushing from behind, finally got the train over the hump. Samuel Hopkins Adams' grandfather caught a severe quinsy from exposure while waiting for the oxen and was confined to his room at the Troy House for a week. He traveled by canal the rest of his days.

The age of the canals had been the age of a pastoral America, of casual commerce and leisurely expansion toward the beckoning West. But the dawn of the industrial era was at hand and the slow and easy traffic of the waterways would not suffice for its demands. The beaver hats were giving way to silk top hats; Madeira was losing ground to champagne, and travel aboard the canal barges could no longer compete with the lurching car behind the clamorous locomotive engine.

By the beginning of the eighteen-forties it was apparent to informed persons that the day of canal building was over, but inland waterways, canals in particular, continued to transport tremendous quantities of passengers and merchandise all through the nineteenth century. In 1863, for example, due to the wartime boom in manufactures in the North and the resulting flow of merchandise, the Erie Canal actually moved more tonnage through its locks than the combined carloadings of the Erie and New York Central railroads. Passenger traffic on the canals was, however, largely eliminated at a much earlier date as a result of the far greater speed of the railroads. Samuel Hopkins Adams' grandfather was persuaded to take the cars of the Rensselear & Saratoga Railway for the twenty-six miles between Ballston and Troy because he could not spare the two days required by the passenger packet on the Erie Canal. Five years after the railroads came into being the traffic of the canals was already declining.

THE CARS COME TO STAY ALONG THE CANALS

By the closing years of the nineteenth century the supremacy of rail transport over the canals, which had had its beginnings when first the *Best Friend of Charleston* rolled through the cotton plantations of South Carolina, was complete. Symbol of this supremacy is the freight train of the Belvidere-Delaware Railroad hauling half a mile of merchandise cars beside a deserted canal near Trenton, New Jersey, in 1889. The canal is the Delaware, originally known when it was built in 1830 as the Delaware & Raritan and connecting Trenton and New Brunswick. Only slightly more than half a century later its towpath was weed-grown, its locks neglected and the commerce that had once floated on its surface rolled smokily along its banks aboard the steamcars.

N. Y. PUBLIC LIBRARY

Two of Boston's earliest railroads had their intersection, as shown here, within sight of the gilded dome of the State House, the Common and the spire of Park Street Church. The Providence train, in the foreground, came in over Roxbury flats, the Worcester cars, at the left, skirted the Back Bay.

II

Spokes of the Hub

Spreading Fanwise From the Boston Stone, a Network of Gleaming Rails Snared Yankee Commerce in an Iron Noose and Soon Reached Westward Toward the Richer Land

B Y THE middle thirties of the nineteenth century, only six years after *The Best Friend of Charleston* had powered the first "brigade of train coaches" over the South Carolina Railroad, New England had taken leadership away from the South and Central Atlantic States and was established as the center of the American railroading scene with Boston as its spectacular focal point.

32

Not without grievous trial and error had this preeminence been achieved, and the technique of railroading, a science virgin and without precedent, had been painfully evolved. Horse power had been discarded in favor of steam. Stone sills, expensively laid in the New England earth, had had to be almost as expensively uprooted and replaced by wooden crossties. The early theory that the railroad was only a short-haul artifice to span distances between waterways and interested communities gave way to the concept of rails as the major medium of transport over distances as great as those embraced by the national economy and geography of the time.

The year 1835 found no fewer than three proved and successful steam railroads in operation, radiating from Boston—now literally The Hub—to the three available points of the New England compass and terminating at Lowell to the north, Worcester to the west, and Providence, with through connections for New York by steamer, on the south.

The "Loco Motive engines" of these three pioneer railroads, some imported from England, some from the new erecting shops of William Norris in Philadelphia, some from the Mill Dam Foundry in South Boston, were the wonder of the engineering world and an occasion for outrageous pride among the Yankee citizenry. The operations of the roads, which already included train movements over double tracks, the distinction between various classes of trains, the dispatching of separate passenger and "burthen" consists and a close adherence to employee's time cards, were studied by transportation experts from all over the United States.

The railroads had not yet by any means overcome the opposition of conservative opinion. Farmers generally favored it as an obvious facility for the expeditious shipment of their produce to centers of consumption and distribution, but townsfolk were shy of the terrifying locomotive engines and many a New England hamlet was at first by-passed at its own insistence, later to be joined to the main line by a branch, often enough constructed, as a sort of penance, at the public expense. In some cases towns which had at first rejected the railroad began expanding in the direction of the tracks and even removing bodily to secure their advantages.

There were, too, aristocratic old sirs who believed that the horse was intended by God for human transport and pointed out that coaches took them to their very doors instead of depositing them in sooty depots with common persons all around. The canal sympathizers, particularly along the Lowell route—where the Middlesex Canal faction was so vehement that the railroad promoters had to retain Dan'l Webster to silence them—still reared threats and objections.

But the newspapers and intelligent businessmen were unanimously for the railroad and, most powerfully of all, it was established in the hearts and imaginations of the great New England public.

Great was the rejoicing when first the railroad came to town. There was oratory and bunting and free rides for the directors and first citizens from terminal to terminal. There was champagne for the members of the Great and General Court (the Massachusetts legislature is still so called) and Stone Fence, a remarkable arrangement of hard cider laced with Medford rum, for the potential shippers and passengers. There were railroad banquets and railroad balls, thundering panegyrics by the ever helpful Dan'l Webster and flowery editorials in the *Boston Transcript* and *Boston Advertiser*. To this day antiquarians cherish whisky flasks with the delightful inscription blown in the glass "Hoorah for the Railroad" and china pitchers with locomotives and cars for decoration as testimony to the hold exerted by the wonderful railroad on the public imagination.

Sometimes the festive trains, loaded with celebrants far gone in Stone Fence, were delayed and limped back into town after dark, a perilous maneuver in an age innocent of headlights or even running lamps. When the Boston & Worcester's prideful engine *Meteor* broke a coupling chain, the equivalent at the time of pulling a drawbar, the engine crew didn't notice for a distance of a mile and a half that there was no train behind them, and the event was considered hilarious by all concerned. When a group of New York financial editors came up to inspect the Boston & Providence, one of William Norris' Philadelphia engines broke down, but the failure was politely overlooked and the newsmen wrote that "the application of horses afforded us a most fortunate opportunity for inspecting the grand structure over which we passed."

As was inevitable, the establishment of reliable and tolerably fast freight and passenger service over these first "trunk" lines—the Worcester road was forty-four miles long, the Lowell twenty-five and the Providence forty-one—encouraged their extension at their suburban terminals and the construction of feeder lines and branches with which to augment their traffic. By the summer of 1835 the new Long Island Sound steamer *Lexington*, built by Commodore Vanderbilt and destined for a calamitous end by fire, was connecting with the Boston train at Providence and it was thus possible to dine in Boston (dinner was then a noon meal) embark at Providence at four in the afternoon and be in New York before the Exchange opened next morning.

After enjoying the hospitality of Boston's famed Tremont House, Dwight Boyden proprietor—a Manhattan editor achieved his own desk in the amazing time of sixteen hours from terminal to terminal. "The railroad," he wrote, "is a work which in days of yore might have done honor to the enterprise of an emperor."

A few years later, when the railroad had been extended to Bristol and Stonington and steamer service was also provided out of those ports to New York, the rivalry with the Providence boat line became intense. The Providence captains contrived to maintain their supremacy however by a promotion campaign which included a free band concert every afternoon on the pier at sailing hour. Free tea and cakes were dispensed and the general manager of the line presided as master of ceremonies. The signal for departure was indicated when this elegant functionary peeled off his expensive white kid gloves and tossed them overside into the water. Such magnificence for years filled the Providence steamers to capacity with awed and enchanted patrons.

The Boston & Providence was to be the scene in 1837 of one of the first railroad accidents involving a fatality. One of the cars of what must have been a mixed train, since it evidently consisted of both freight and passengers, became derailed and ditched its load of lumber, "on the top of which were a number of passengers, two of whom, Dennis Condor and William Kervin, Irishmen, were killed." The speed of trains in the thirties was seldom in excess of twenty miles an hour, but "this great speed and irresistible momentum of the machines" combined with an almost total absence of brakes to make them dangerous enough to scare the wits out of the public.

To Stage-Line Operators the Railroad Seemed Chimerical

BAKER LIBRARY

Before the coming of the railroads, Boston's Haymarket Square (*above*) within a few city blocks from the Boston Stone itself, from which all distances in New England were measured, was the center of the coach and teaming network which radiated into the Yankee countryside. At the right is the Old Quincy Market, in back of which stood and stands Peter Faneuil's Hall with its grasshopper weather vane of song and legend. From here stage wagons rolled (*below*) Down East to Maine, west to Worcester and southward to the Rhode Island Plantations where Roger Williams cried "What cheer!" and Providence was founded.

When Boston financiers began applying to the Great and General Court of Massachusetts for charters to run rails to outlying communities, a storm of protest arose from the already existing canal operators, tollroad proprietors and wagon freighters. To plead their cause the proposers of the Boston & Lowell Railroad retained the greatest orator of the age and so pursuaded him in their cause that Daniel Webster seldom addressed a public meeting thereafter without finding a good word for railroads in general. Far from being wild and fanciful, said Webster, railroads in the foreseeable future might even extend fifty and a hundred miles from the slopes of Beacon Hill.

BAKER LIBRARY

CULVER SERVICE

Tranquility Rode The Horse-Drawn Stages

At Medford, on the Mystic River, famed for its rum and as Paul Revere's first stop on his ride to alarm Lexington and Concord, travelers in coaching times descended at the Fountain House (*above*) to sample the spirits distilled by the Lawrence family, which also produced bishops, merchant princes and college presidents. Further afield, at Northampton, they set down at the inn (*center*) maintained by J. B. Vinton, from whose porch a cheerful view of the village green was available.

The Roxbury-Boston stage, shown at the bottom of the page traversing Tremont Road on its way to town, lasted well into the fifties, running beneath the looping wires of the new magnetic telegraph. Through Roxbury Flats, too, ran the cars of the Boston & Providence Railroad which even operated on Sunday to the scandal of the ministers of its many churches.

(THREE PICTURES) BAKER LIBRARY

The Rails Followed the Rivers, Crowded the Canals

CHARLES O. EGERTON

Crossing a stone arch over the Middlesex Canal, whose owners were indignant about the whole thing, a Stephenson locomotive of the Boston & Lowell Railroad (*above*) hauls six coaches on its way from Boston to the mill city. In the lower drawing by Charles O. Egerton, an authority on early New England roads, Ross Winans' "crab engine" *Maryland* of the Western Railroad, later the Boston & Albany, heads a long train of "burthen cars" through the Berkshire Hills of Western Massachusetts. Alarming as they were, the railroads seemed actually to be functioning.

CHARLES O. EGERTON

ALBANY TO BOSTON IN A SINGLE DAY

CULVER SERVICE

In December of 1841 "the Boston city government in a body" headed by the august Josiah Quincy and several trainloads of other notables journeyed to Albany to celebrate the completion of the Western Railroad, the first true trunk line in the United States. There was, of course, a state banquet at which "Quincy the inimitable" kept the head table in a roar with his flashes of urbane wit and Judge VanBergen made an address in Dutch. Afterward there was the equally inevitable grand ball (*above*) where Yankees and Patroons mingled in the stately and commemorative measure.

The party at Albany achieved such momentum that, at its conclusion, a number of New York legislators accompanied their guests back to Boston, via the cars, where the flags were run up and bunting displayed and the military paraded (*right*) in the shadow of the Old State House where only a few years previous doings of revolutionary import had been toward.

CHARLES O. EGERTON

THROUGH THE BERKSHIRES
IN STEAM

Although "even the most sanguine of its
friends doubted whether enough freight
would ever be offered to test the real capacity of its motive power," the Western Railroad prospered from the beginning. Crossing the Berkshires in Western Massachusetts
three engines were required for its freights
(*above*) and the artist has here shown the
Whistler engine *Bristol* and an early American Standard type eight-wheeler as helpers
to the road engine, a Winans crab type.
Passengers on the Western rode in the type
of car shown in the center of the page
which was now generally coming into use
to displace the coaches mounted on railroad
trucks (*bottom*) which had been universal
only half a decade previous, this one on the
Boston & Providence.

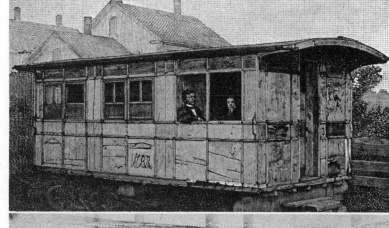

N. Y. PUBLIC LIBRARY

Venerable and Mellow: "The Old Fall River Line"

NEW HAVEN RR.

When, after ninety years of continuous and unbroken operation, it suspended service, the Fall River Boat Train to Boston was the longest-lived train in American history, according to Alvin F. Harlow, dean of New England railroad historians. Inaugurated in 1847 by the Old Colony Railroad and continued by the New York, New Haven & Hartford after the merger of the two roads, the Boat Train left Boston, decade after decade, at six in the afternoon and departed from Fall River after the New York boat had docked in the morning. The steamers with which it made connections, the *Pilgrim,* the *Puritan* and the *Priscilla,* were among the first to boast electric lights and their cuisine was world-famous. The photograph (*above*) shows the Boat Train in the early years of its operation, its primitive equipment drawn by the Old Colony locomotive *Randolph.* The grand stairway of the Fall River steamer *Bristol,* shown below, was accounted elegant in the stately sixties. The *Bristol* carried 1,000 passengers nightly and its dollar dinner ran to ten courses.

LIBRARY OF CONGRESS

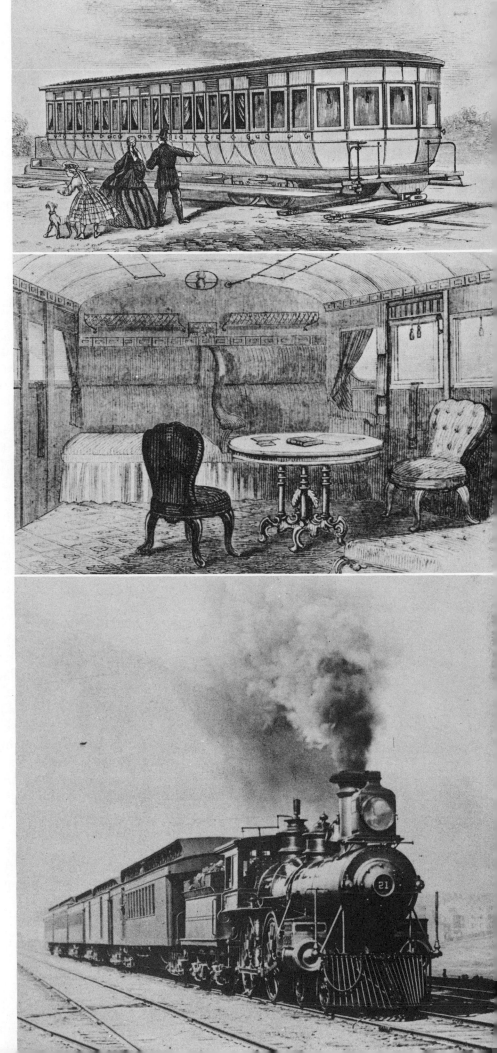

THE BOAT TRAIN
WAS A TRADITION

Presidents of the United States in succession, Fillmore, Grant, Arthur Cleveland, Harrison and two Roosevelts rode the Fall River Boat Train. Long a New England institution of codfish-cake dimensions, the Fall River steamers and their Boat Train achieved national celebrity when Harry von Tilzer wrote the popular sing hit, "The Old Fall River Line." Asa R. Porter, conductor of the Boat Train, was for many years the most famous train captain in America and when the cars pulled up to the dock at Fall River he personally shook hands with Choates, Lowells and Frothinghams and other passengers of distinction and wished them a good trip. Presidents were careful to call him "Mister Porter." At one time during the sixties English type coaches (*top*) were briefly introduced on the Boat Train but failed of popularity. Impressed by their luxuriously upholstered compartments, a contemporary publication remarked editorially: "We are rapidly approaching that time in the luxuriance of travel when we shall step into our suite of rooms aboard the cars in New York and have no occasion to leave them until we reach New Orleans." During the nineties, after the Old Colony had been leased to the New Haven the Boat Train (*bottom*) was drawn by such beautiful, high-stepping eight-wheelers with capped stacks as the New Haven's No. 21 on its trip from South Station in Boston to pierside at Fall River.

N. Y. PUBLIC LIBRARY

NEW HAVEN RR.

A road to connect with the Boston & Worcester at its mid-state terminal, the Western, was almost at once organized to reach Albany and the regions of Upper New York State by way of Springfield and Pittsfield. A survey was also made for a branch railroad running south out of Springfield to Hartford and New Haven with its implications of eventually connecting New York and Boston by an overland railroad without recourse to the Providence-Long Island Sound connection. This, although the Providence steamer and later connection with the New York, New Haven & Hartford Railroad, existed as a sturdy New England institution for almost a century longer.

To the north, out of Lowell, arrangements were speedily perfected to convey freight and passengers into deepest New England.

Lowell Railroad and Steamboat Lines For New Hampshire and Vermont (read the advertisement in the papers). The cars for these lines will leave the depot at Boston at 9 o'clock A.M. after Monday, June 29th. On their arrival at Lowell the carriages will take passengers free of charge immediately on board The Steamer which will convey them to Nashua, New Hampshire, where stages in connection with the Amherst and Francestown lines will be in readiness to take them forward. The passengers will dine on board The Steamer while she is passing up the river.

At the Boston end a similar carriage service was inaugurated to "call at almost any part of the city for passengers and take them to the depot free of charge." This was definitely a bid for the patronage of the aristocratic old sirs whose faith was pinned in the horse, and constituted a pickup and delivery service a full century before the phrase was ever invented.

Thus to the north, south and west, wherever the land lanes beckoned, the railroads of New England began their march out of Boston toward what was in a few years time to become a vast network of interdependent and interlocking lines covering the countryside in a complex of carriers extending from the Canadian border to New York and from Massachusetts Bay to the margins of the Middle West itself.

Later it will be seen how, having their origins in the first railroads of New England in the thirties and forties, a succession of generations of Yankee railroad men were to flow outward over their radiating rails to dominate the greater part of railroading in the entire United States. New England, for almost a century, was the mother of railroading and railroad men throughout America.

Most important of the early railroads to be built as extension of the Boston lines, both in its implications of the westward course of empire and in the fact of its construction, was the Western Railroad, completed from Worcester to Albany in 1841. Its location through Springfield, Pittsfield and the Berkshires was almost precisely that of the later Boston & Albany, now part of the New York Central System, and the possibilities of through connecting railroads integrated to each other's operations at once, upon the opening of the Western to traffic, became universally apparent.

The Western, like the railroads radiating out of Boston itself, fairly bristled with the names of proper Bostonians and was a very Yankee project indeed. Abbott Lawrence presided at the mass meeting which gave it birth. Edward Everett gave it his eloquent benediction. Josiah Quincy, Jr., was its first treasurer, and the great George Whistler was its chief engineer and superintendent.

The completion of the Western in 1841 was the signal for a tumult of demonstrations which dwarfed almost to nothingness the joyous completion eleven years before of the South Carolina Railroad where a cannon was fired from a coach window as the first train rolled out of Charleston.

The celebration itself took the form of a three-day junket—whose personnel included the entire government of Boston and most of its prominent businessmen—which rolled over the new railroad to Albany for a veritable orgy of speechifying and starry eyed viewing of the future. At a banquet attended by bigwigs of both cities, candles made that same morning of whale oil in New Bedford were burned in silver candelabra, and when a numerous contingent of the celebrants decided the party was far too fine a thing to terminate and betook themselves and their guests back to Boston, they brought with them table salt which had only the previous day been 300 feet underground in the deep mines near Syracuse.

"Bring on your wooden nutmegs, gentlemen—and other knick-knacks, bring them on," thundered the editorial columns of the *Utica Daily News*. "Here is a western world now, open to Yankees, which all your ingenuity and industry cannot fill."

In connection with the early days of the Western and the Boston & Worcester Railroads it is interesting to note that, true to Yankee loyalty to the mother country in other matters, many of their first locomotives were English importations. The success of the two John Bulls, one on the Camden & Amboy and the other on the Mohawk & Hudson combined with the prestige of England as the original home of railroading combined to influence many mechanical superintendents, or "masters of machinery" as they were first known, to order their engines abroad. Invariably they came with English crews and equally invariably the crews considered that the mechanical details of their engines should be treated as Druidic mysteries. No Americans were allowed near, much less to operate thm. At night the crews slept with their charges as a trainer would with his race horse before Derby Day. The English were not going to have the thieving Yankees steal their secrets of construction, but in a few years American locomotives had so outdistanced the imported product in power, speed and operating efficiency that English importation was a thing of the past. For years New England railroads recalled the pretentions of the English engine crews with a mixture of scorn and amused tolerance.

New England in the early forties enjoyed the unhappy distinction of being the first section of the country to be overbuilt with railroads. They were financed, located, surveyed and graded in such florid abundance that a single tiny section of Massachusetts countryside near the New Hampshire line was served by four independent railroads: The Boston & Lowell, the Lowell & Nashua, the Andover & Wilmington and the Andover & Haverhill. It shortly became obvious that such a multiplicity of transport services would contrive to strangle each other while dying from lack of traffic, and eventually the entire pattern of railroading in eastern New England had to be reorganized and absorbed into the economy of what is today the far-reaching Boston & Maine-Maine Central System.

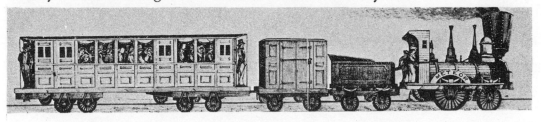

A Gallery of Yankee Yesterdays

(TWO PHOTOS) NEW HAVEN RR.

The pastoral vignettes on these two pages convey something of the charm and simplicities of early New England railroading. Above is the earliest known photograph of a car with a sort of primeval vestibule pictured somewhere between Seymour and Derby, Connecticut, behind the Naugatuck Railroad's engine *Jericho*. The little one-car train (*below*) on the Old Colony's Nantucket branch ran between Boston and Hyannis on Cape Cod where the Folgers, Backuses, Coffins and Starbucks as well as off-islanders took the steamer for Martha's Vineyard and Nantucket Island. The Hyannis depot, according to Harlow, boasted a Ladies Saloon, "a large, spacious room elegantly furnished and richly carpeted with luxurious sofa, chairs, rockers and a table·of costly style and structure. Another saloon so richly and luxuriously furnished cannot be found in any depot on Cape Cod." Nantucketers admired the convenience of breakfasting at home and having noon dinner at Parker's in School Street.

NEW HAVEN RR.

The engine *Barnstable* (*top*) of the Cape Cod Railroad had a guard to protect its drivers and valve gear and hauled a most primitive train when pictured in 1848. The photograph in the center from the collection of Beaumont Newhall shows where locomotive firemen acquired the name "tallowpot." Before the days of self-activating lubrication they climbed out on the running board while the engine was in motion to oil moving parts with mutton tallow. The Housatonic Railroad's No. 4 (*below*) with its fluted sand dome, the hallmark of its builder, Rogers, was heavy duty power in the Connecticut seventies.

NATIONAL LIFE INSURANCE CO.

THE STEAMCARS CARRIED AWAY NEW ENGLAND'S YOUTH

The Yankee exodus from the New England states began long before Horace Greeley, himself late of the New Hampshire Grants, began doing what Ralph Waldo Emerson characterized as "the thinking for the whole West at $2 a year for his paper." The going out began shortly after the turn of the nineteenth century so that by the middle fifties a Down East editor wrote in desperation that "more than 300,000 people of New England will leave before the end of 1857." The first homesteaders found their way to the Western Reserve, as the strip of land along Lake Erie was then known, by water routes before the age of steam. The favorite route was across New England by wagon, down Lake Champlain and Lake George by packet boat and thence westward via the Erie Canal. After 1840, however, as the steel network spread throughout New England converging upon Boston, young men with carpet bags in ever increasing numbers boarded the cars at North Hero, Vermont, Saco, Maine, or Concord, New Hampshire, to head over the Western Railroad for Iowa, Michigan and Nebraska. "The old men at the New England crossroads . . . could tell that the old order was passing," wrote Stewart Holbrook in his classic "Yankee Exodus." "You could see that the old cocked-hat men were now pitifully few—the survivors who still wore small clothes and hose and shoes with big buckles—the men who still took snuff and preferred that their women use the fireplace instead of the new and loathsome cooking stoves . . . who had shaken hands with General Stark or might even have been with Old Put in Mr. Bunker's pasture at Charlestown." The steamcars carried away the young men in thousands to the unknown, the irresistible Western Land.

E. S. HAMMACK

YANKEE GENIUS WAS RAILROADING'S BACKBONE

Throughout the nineteenth century New England produced the vast majority of the nation's railroad builders, operators, financiers and executives. They included Thomas Nickerson, W. B. Strong and E. P. Ripley of the Sante Fe; Collis Huntington, Grenville M. Dodge, Thomas Durant and Oakes and Oliver Ames of the Pacific Railroad; Daniel Willard of the Baltimore & Ohio, M. E. Ingalls of the Big Four and Henry B. Plant of Florida pioneering fame. There were John Murray Forbes and Thomas Elliott Perkins of the Burlington, Onslow Stevens, Ginery Twitchell and Charles Francis Adams, the historian of the entire industry. And right back home among the Yankees there were George Whistler who built the Western Railroad to Albany, one of the first engineers of his time, William Mason of Taunton, who brought to locomotive design its classic and enduring beauty, and Charlie Minot, superintendent of the Boston & Maine who made railroad history in New England and wherever else he went. It was Charlie Minot who, in 1848, arranged for the Boston & Maine's *Antelope* to cover the twenty-six miles between Boston and Lawrence in as many minutes and gave the world its first mile-a-minute run. Three years later as general superintendent of the Erie, Minot ordered the telegraph operator at Goshen whose name was Ezra Cornell and who later had a university named for him, to halt an opposing train at a station down the line so that Minot's special might go through. With Minot standing behind him in the drawing above, Cornell is handing the conductor the first telegraphic train order in history.

New England's Railroads Once Knew a Golden Age

The golden age of New England railroading lasted approximately from the early seventies until Charles S. Mellen wrecked the New Haven shortly after the turn of the century. Rails such as those of the Atlantic & St. Lawrence disputed with Chaos and Old Night for the mountain passes (*above*) of Vermont and New Hampshire, where the air was thick with snow and the plows rode through it as a sea. Rails bisected the industrial regions of Massachusetts and Connecticut in profitable profusion and the New Haven paid 10 per cent like clockwork. The lines reached westward, too, and a project was even chartered in the inclusive terms of the Portland, Rutland, Oswego & Chicago Railroad. All this time the great New England locomotive builders, McKay & Aldus, Hinkley & Drury, the Rhode Island Locomotive Works and the wonderful shops at Manchester, Portland and Taunton, were turning out the finest locomotives the world was ever to see. Most celebrated of them all was William Mason of Taunton whose *Highland Light* (*center*) built for the Cape Cod Railroad is considered by many authorities to be the handsomest locomotive ever outshopped in the history of steam. The motive power of the New Haven throughout the Periclean Age (*bottom*) was so beautifully maintained as to attract affection and admiration for the railroad wherever its lines extended.

And the White Train Was Its Most Upholstered Ornament

When executives of Boston's firm of Lee Higginson or members of the Somerset Club went "over" to New York in the nineties, they secured passage, if its late afternoon departure suited their convenience, on the New York & New England's *White Train* (*above*) the most luxurious daylight run luxury varnish in all the United States. Nothing before or since has ever even approximated the conspicuous niceties of its all-white painted, all-Pullman Palace Car consist, its parlor cars (*center*) with their velvet carpets and white silk curtains and chairs upholstered in old-gold plush, and its five hour and forty minute running time across the Connecticut countryside which inspired Rudyard Kipling, then a resident of Vermont, to write a short story called "007." The *White Train*, which inevitably acquired the popular name of "The Ghost Train" from its spectral appearance as it raced through the New England twilight, ran over the old Air Line from New Haven through Middletown and Willimantic. The wine lists in its club cars and diners (*below*) were the choicest within the selection of Boston's revered S. S. Pierce & Co., and its menus bristled with scrodded haddock, Cape Cod oysters and other regional fauna dear to the palates of a departed generation of the proper Bostonians.

NEW HAVEN RR.

CULVER SERVICE

For half a century "railroad meetings" swept the land with promises of prosperity and the assurance of good times to come when all America should ride the cars.

III

"The Panter From His Lair"

Junketings, Gold Spike Ceremonies, Banquets, Parades, Oratory, Bunting and Bond Issues Were Symptoms of a Rage to Build Which Swept the Land in the Years of Boom and Bust

WHEN, on July 20, 1876, the first locomotive to reach the sprawling and uninhibited cow town of Fort Worth shrilled its whistle at the milepost of the Texas & Pacific Railroad, the people went wild with joy and a local reporter wrote in *The Democrat* that the sound of the engine had "aroused the panter from his lair, the birds from their nests in afright and carried joy to many anxious hearts."

Presumably there were still panthers in the environs of Fort Worth and the joy that was brought to anxious hearts included the town's publicans who enjoyed boom times all day.

Fort Worth was but one of hundreds and indeed thousands of American communities where the arrival of the first train brought good cheer to the populace. A list of the ceremonial first trains, golden spike drivings, honorific oratory and exuberant gunfire would include the pioneer operation of almost every railroad in the land and there were hundreds of them. The railroad was religion. Its arrival was an act of faith and its traffic bore golden promise of prosperity and comforts beyond all dreaming of an earlier and less fortunate age.

But the story of the coming of the T. & P. to Fort Worth is so typical of the hopes and fears that arrived with the railroad, of the sacrifices made to bring it into being and of the national belief that along with freight and passengers would come the millennium that it is worth rehearsing in some detail.

Fort Worth first began dreaming of a railroad as far back as 1858 when a monster mass meeting was called together at the county courthouse for the purpose of formally inviting the Houston & Texas Central to enter town and bring with it the even then growing stockyard business which otherwise might be snatched by Fort Worth's deadly rival, Dallas. But before the railroad could be financed the Civil War intervened and it wasn't until 1872 that the finances of the Southwest were again sufficiently robust to consider such hazardous expenditures of hard come-by money.

In the years following the Civil War Texas had viewed with satisfaction the long trail herds wending northward toward the railhead of the Kansas Pacific. Indeed the most notable of all the cattle trails, the Chisholm, had passed through Fort Worth itself at the very point where today the rails of the Texas & Pacific cross over those of the Santa Fe at the South Tower in the yards. The hard money the trail bosses brought back to the land-rich cattle barons of Texas went into improving the longhorn stock until at one time, when Wyatt Earp was city marshal, as many as 200,000 head of Texas cattle arrived in Wichita in a single day.

But Texas, viewing the long overland drive to Kansas with its attendant perils, hardships and loss of stock to drought, Indians and thieves, would be pleased to have a railroad of its own. It sent lobbyists to Washington to woo Congress, for land grants such as had made the building of the Union Pacific possible and, indeed, profitable. The railroad announced that it was coming to Fort Worth and the cow town's population increased from 300 to 3,000 in a single year. Rents climbed, fortunes were made overnight in real estate. The Amon Carters of the seventies ballyhooed Fort Worth as the comingest city in all of up-and-coming Texas and the T. & P. began laying iron out of Dallas. It had got just six miles when the banking house of Jay Cooke & Co., failed in Wall Street. The date, September 18, 1873, has ever since been known as "Black Friday" and business houses and banks of issue all over the country crumbled into the dust of the ensuing panic.

The T. & P.'s finances were hard hit. Construction stopped in the middle of the plains out in the general direction of Grand Prairie and the fortune hunters, speculators and solid businessmen who had multiplied Fort Worth's population tenfold all went helling back to Dallas and safety where the railroad already was. Various other railroads with an eye on Fort Worth such as the Katy, the Houston & Texas

51

Central, the Red River & Rio Grande and the Fort Worth & New Orleans were just as broke as the T. & P. and not even as near Fort Worth as that road was.

It looked as though the panter would remain unmolested in his lair and the birds unfrightened on the wing.

But the men and women of Fort Worth, while dismayed were not despairing. They went to the Legislature at Austin and secured a promise of land grants, sixteen sections to a mile, if the T. & P. should reach the Fort Worth city limits by January 1, 1873. Two successive legislatures extended the time limit a year each, but finally that august body put its foot down and made the offer invalid "the date of the adjournment of the first legislature held under the new state constitution."

When the 1876 legislature convened Fort Worth knew that time was now really of the essence. The lawmakers might vote their sessions at an end any time and there would go the hope of the railroad all over again. In Austin the senate was getting restless. Crops had to be got in. Constituents had to be gentled and reassured on matters of state. A go-home bloc in the senate lacked one vote to close up shop. Tarrant County's senator was bedridden with a mighty fever, but every day for fifteen days he had himself carried into the senate on a litter to vote against the go-homers.

Fort Worth citizens swarmed out to the railhead which by this time had reached within twenty miles of the city limits. Volunteers located and began grading the right of way. They worked in twenty-four-hour shifts and the good women of the town brought hot food out to the workers in bucket brigades laden with stews and hot cakes. When a farmer's duck pond got in the way they didn't bother to bridge or fill it, they just went around, a practice which gave the railroad a peculiarly informal flavor. In one place the tracks were laid right down the middle of an already graded country road which was handy to the right of way. All the business houses of Fort Worth closed for a week so that clerks and accountants and junior partners could volunteer to work on the precious railroad.

In the middle of July the City Council of Fort Worth was hastily convened and voted to extend the city limits a half mile to meet the oncoming graders and track layers. Out in Nevada a few years later the bonanza town of Austin resorted to a similar stratagem to insure the meeting of a deadline by its arriving railroad.

On July 19th the legislature finally rose, but on that day, too, the T. & P. arrived within the new municipal limits and the land grants were safe. Fort Worth filled up with visitors as never before. Ranchers to whom a railroad was until then a mere myth brought their families in to view the wonder. The streets blossomed with bunting. A huge barrel of Savannah Artillery Punch was set up at East Lancaster and Main Streets and No. 20 with a T. & P. work train made its triumphal entry.

Nothing like it had ever happened in Texas before. The Fort Worth Cornet Band was noisily in evidence. No. 20 wabbled dizzily on the unballasted grade threatening at any moment to encompass its own destruction. Strong men paled and women drew back in alarm while the band rendered "Hail Columbia" and Major J.J. Javis and P.J. Bowdry smote mightily on anvils borrowed from Williams' blacksmith shop. The engineer pulled the whistle cord, the people roared with joy and the panter was well and truly roused from his lair.

The celebration, after the manner of its kind, went on far into the night. The contractors paid off their hands and the masculine element indulged in one of the highest, widest and handsomest benders in the long history of Texas whisky doings. "Our police officers should exercise discretion and leniency and drunk and disorderlies should be viewed with toleration" admonished the editor of *The Democrat*.

That was how the railroad came to Fort Worth where it was shortly joined by half a dozen others to make it one of the busiest rail centers in the land, but it had been a close thing. And it took some time to get the T. & P. on a footing of greater formality in the matter of its right of way.

The story of the T. & P. and its Fort Worth arrival is cited because of its dramatic qualities, but its theme, in various forms, was repeated many hundreds of times throughout the United States in the great age of railroad construction. It became an article in the national credo that nothing could stop the community that had its rail connection and, in time, it became apparent that if the railroad wasn't in itself a passport to instant and overwhelming prosperity at least its lack was a fairly sure indication that the life expectation of any town or city was a poor one indeed. The pattern of rail construction was often unsophisticated in the extreme. Lines were built from one remote township to another, practically from no-place to no-place, without the least consideration of main-line connections or other economic justification. The mere presence of a depot, water tank and line of light rails coming in over the prairie lent encouragement to a thousand communities. They had their railroad and the future was secure.

While the majority of the main-line railroads of the land were financed through conventional corporate organization and the agency of large-scale investment by capitalists and assistance from state and Federal governments, many were by more humble contributors who shared in the overwhelming urge of every community in the land for its own, its very own railroad. Some persons invested modestly from their savings in the securities of the promised railroads. Others donated valuable parcels of land or rights of way through their property for the passage of the line. In early times when wood-burning locomotives were universal, a favorite gift was a stand of wood or the right to cut it handily adjacent to the lengthening rails. Others, lacking tangible resources, made their contribution to the great project in the form of volunteer labor with the grading crews or track-laying gangs or the loan of a span of farm horses absented at great sacrifice from their accustomed duties.

Particularly touching is the record of the sacrifices which made possible the building in upper New York State of the Fonda, Johnstown & Gloversville to connect with the New York Central at the sleepy canal town of Fonda. A passionate advocate of the railroad, one Willard Heacock, assumed the function of circuit rider in the interest of obtaining the consent of the majority of local property holders as required by law before railroad bonds might be issued. For many weeks he visited the homes abounding in the rambling countryside, convincing canal advocates and die-hards of the advantages inherent in the railroad and finally taking their sworn affidavits of consent in the presence of a justice of the peace. So great was the excitement over the project that when Heacock was able to report a convert who had no more than promised not to oppose the railroad, a cannon was fired at Johnstown and there were wide-spread demonstrations of joy. When the Fonda was completed it maintained Gloversville in the estate of the glove capital of the world for three-quarters of a century.

Good Times Everywhere Rode into Town on the Cars

AT LAST.

THE DAY HAS COME.

HOPE ENDS IN FRUITION.

Yesterday morning at twenty-three minutes past eleven, Engine No. 20 of the Texas & Pacific railroad, Kelly engineer and Beale conductor, uttered its shrill scream within the corporate limits, arousing the "panter" from his lair, startling the birds from their nests in affright, and carrying joy to many anxious hearts who have waited

"FORT WORTH STAR TELEGRAM"

In the railroad age every printer had a stock symbol of a locomotive in his type case and the *Fort Worth Democrat* ran it amidst general jubilation when the Texas & Pacific came to town in 1876. The Goddess of Plenty was about to pour her riches on fortunate Fort Worth and, indeed, did just that. Below, in a scene typical of hundreds at the time, the Mayor of Cincinnati receives the guests of honor arriving in town for the celebration which opened the Little Miami Railroad to operations.

CULVER SERVIC

N. Y. PUBLIC LIBRARY

GROUND BREAKINGS AND REJOICINGS WERE ON EVERY HAND

BALTIMORE & OHIO RR.

When ground was broken for the Iowa Central Railroad at Cedar Rapids, Iowa, country bumpkins and city men of affairs alike rejoiced amidst oratory and optimism, and the band stand was trimmed with such sentiments as "Be Sure You're Right, Then Go Ahead," and "Not Dangerous to Stand on *This* Platform," an allusion to the familiar car door warning which delighted everyone. When the "first stone" of the Baltimore & Ohio Railroad was placed with Masonic ceremony near Baltimore in 1828 (*below*) Charles Carroll of Carrollton, last surviving signer of the Declaration of Independence, wielded the spade that turned the first sod.

Welcoming the Railroad Was a Municipal Convulsion

N. Y. PUBLIC LIBRARY

When in 1857 the lavishly financed Ohio & Mississippi Railroad was completed between St. Louis and Cincinnati thousands of celebrants traveled between the two terminals in a tidal wave of jubilation and excitement. The delegation from Cincinnati was received in St. Louis with a guard of honor and a monster parade lit with Greek fire after which they were put up for the night upon a score of river steamers (*above*) moored to the levee. The next day, augmented by a numerous delegation from St. Louis they all returned by rail to Cincinnati where they were greeted (*below*) by the mayor with appropriate sentiments and a great lifting of silk hats.

CULVER SERVICE

At Cincinnati a railroad banquet (*above*) and a railroad ball (*center*) proclaimed the glory of the completed Ohio & Mississippi Railroad for the elect and guests of honor. For the man on the street the next day witnessed a public demonstration by all the fire engines of the town, a trial which justified everyone's faith in the newly patented Amoskeag steam pumper shown in the foreground below.

N. Y. PUBLIC LIBRARY

The gold-spike ceremonies, railroad balls, firings of cannon and siroccos of oratory which swept the land during the era of rail construction and finance could in themselves constitute material for a learned monograph of extended dimensions. The railroad jollification took its place in the roster of American folk festivals along with barn raisings, hayrides, moonlight boat trips, Saturday ball games and the Fourth of July.

It may be profitable briefly to recount the details of one more triumphal entry of the cars, this at once earlier and more sophisticated than the panter-waking at Forth Worth.

In 1851 the New York & Erie Railroad, which had been chartered by the State of New York almost twenty years earlier, entered Dunkirk on Lake Erie, 446 miles from its eastern terminal at Piermont, a short distance up the Hudson from New Lork City. It was the longest railway in the world. It was the first rail connection between the East and the region that was then the American West. It was, in the words of New York's Board of Trade, which never spared a superlative, "The Work of the Age," and its completion was celebrated on continental dimensions and with a degree of hurrah that has echoed down the years from that day to this.

For the epic first train ride over the entire length of road, the Erie had as its guests of honor President Millard Fillmore and his entire Cabinet and Daniel Webster himself, at the time Secretary of State. There were also more than three hundred assorted dignitaries identified by their gold-headed walking canes, well-brushed beaver hats and the prosperous aroma of Lawrence's Medford Rum which pervaded the gathering and clung refreshingly to the cuffs and collars of fur-lined greatcoats.

The junket had really started two days previously when a special train had been run from Washington to New York over the rails of the Baltimore & Ohio and the Camden & Amboy, awash with dignitaries who paused at Barnum's Hotel in Baltimore for a six-hour breakfast, had spent the night happily splashing around in the refreshment parlors of Philadelphia and arrived in Manhattan slightly frayed at the edges but, all things considered, in fairly good repair. They had been met at South Amboy by Benjamin Loder, President of the Erie, a detail of 9,000 militia in dress attire, five platoons of police in charge of Captain Carpenter of the Fifth Ward, six bands and forty accomplished barkeeps or "manipulators" as they were known at the time. That night all drinks in the bars of two of New York's most famous hotels, the Astor House and the Irving, were cuffed by President Loder and a number of the beneficiaries of this philanthropy stayed up all night in order not to miss the steamer to Piermont which left the Battery at six the next morning.

At Piermont dock the steamer *Erie* was met at the more mature hour of seven-thirty by Dodsworth's Band, a salvo of artillery, and another corps of talented servitors bearing double bottles of champagne as a prelude to a light breakfast served on the pier and including beefsteak, roast fowl, spiced eels, broiled shad (the season was May), sausages and johnnycake. Two trains elaborately decorated with flags and bunting awaited the dignitaries, the first carrying President Fillmore and the second including a specially built flat car upon whose deck a rocking chair had been installed for the particular accommodation of Mr. Webster who wanted to see everything and liked the fresh air. A conveniently uncorked bottle of Medford, a steamer rug and a knitted scarf with which the Secretary of State secured his top hat completed the arrangements.

With a final salvo of cannon fire the trains headed westward. There were stops for speeches to the assembled crowds at Goshen and Middletown and a long pause for luncheon at the home of Major Fields at Narrowsburg. There was further oratory at Cohocton, Callicoon and Deposit and more refreshment while the notables admired the "combined handiwork of God and man," the phrase is Edward Hungerford's, at Cascade Bridge and the great Starucca Viaduct. At Susquehanna the conventional artillery salute was augmented by the whistles of sixteen locomotives drawn up in military array at the roundhouse. At Binghamton President Fillmore addressed 4,000 listeners, quoting poetry and Scripture.

By the time the cavalcade put up at Elmira for the night where there was a seven-hour banquet at Brainard's Hotel, the spirit of oratory sat powerfully on the company. There were speeches by President Fillmore, President Loder and Daniel Webster. "It was an extraordinary occasion," says Edward H. Mott, the historian. "Great liberty and license were permitted everyone. Everybody was celebrating and making merry. Men who were known as staid and strict men were more than unbent and dallied perhaps overmuch with the help of the good cheer which prevailed everywhere without money and without price."

Groggy but game, the party started on the next day and repeated previous splendors at Corning, Hornellsville and Alleghany. At Dayton there was a brief contretemps when an enthusiastic citizen who had mounted a fieldpiece dating from the War of 1812 beside the right of way overcharged the gun and blew off both arms as the trains roared past. A collection was hastily taken up for his reassembly and the cortege pressed on to Dunkirk.

Dunkirk was, in the language of a century later, the pay off. A pleasant town on the shore of Lake Erie, Dunkirk had been brought into being by DeWitt Clinton of steamboat fame who had indulged a native whim by naming the various streets after a variety of birds, animals and snakes. Clinton himself was on hand for the occasion. There was a triumphal arch of flowers over the railroad tracks and in mid-harbor the U.S.S. *Michigan* swung at anchor ready to discharge her cannon on the least provocation. Added fire power was provided by the Sixty-Fifth Regiment's mounted artillery and the numerous church bells of the town started a tremendous tolling as the Presidential train hove in sight. Even in an age accustomed to proclaiming satisfaction through the agency of gunpowder, brass bands, anvil-smiting and carillons the din was generally acknowledged to be gratifying.

All previous excursions into the realm of oratory along the Erie's right of way paled by comparison with the ensuing forensics. For the state dignitaries a sumptuous banquet had been prepared at the Loder House, newly built and named for the railroad's president. For plainer folk there was an immense pavilion running from Deer Street to Lion Street along Railroad Avenue where, on a single table more than 300 feet in length, were provided "chowder, a yoke of oxen roasted whole, beef *a la mode*, corned beef, buffalo tongues, bologna sausage, beef tongues both smoked and spiced, roasted fowls, coffee" and etceteras. The etceteras mostly came in square-faced bottles of reassuring design and content.

During the course of the festivities the cookhouse in which the oxen were being roasted caught fire and burned to the ground amidst great municipal enthusiasm. The oxen were a little overdone but pronounced delicious. Bread appeared in loaves two feet square and ten feet long. An unidentified scoundrel insinuated a quantity of high-proof French cognac into the general coffee urn and deacons and wardens of the church were observed to be behaving peculiarly. Everyone had a fantastically good time.

59

Erie's First Run Was the Grandest of All

Probably the most epic of all railroad celebrations was the cross-country jollification which marked the completion in 1851 of the New York & Erie Railroad, "The Work of the Age" as it was universally hailed, between New York City and Dunkirk on the shores of Lake Erie. The great excursion began at "Washington City" where President Millard Fillmore, Daniel Webster and numerous other dignitaries boarded a special train for New York, pausing all day for what was termed "breakfast" at Barnum's Hotel in Baltimore. Some of the less inhibited delegates (*above*) were sketched as they emerged from Barnum's by an artist for *Leslie's* who was providentially on the scene. At Elmira there was the usual banquet (*center*) which progressed through twenty-four courses at Brainard's Hotel and the next day the special trains arrived at Dunkirk. "Hospitality was unbounded," wrote a contemporary. "Men who were known as staid and strict were more than unbent and dallied perhaps overmuch with the help of the good cheer that prevailed." During the evening the shanty where oxen were being barbecued burned to the ground and the happy citizenry cheered the firemen (*below*) on their way to the blaze.

And Dan'l Webster Was the Starred Performer

E. S. HAMMACK

Although President Millard Fillmore and most of his Cabinet were along and other notables and dignitaries past counting, the star performer on the Erie's epic first train to Dunkirk was the aging Dan'l Webster, elder statesman, Secretary of State and wielder of the mightiest oratorical measure of any living man. For Webster's convenience in seeing the countryside of the Southern Tier a platform rocker was stoutly secured on an open flatcar. His nether limbs were wrapped in a warm shawl and a reassuring flagon of Lawrence's rum from Medford, Massachusetts, was set handy. "It is a beautiful country," proclaimed the great man in mellow mood during one of the seven speeches he made that day. "May God bless you and enable you to enjoy all of its blessings."

ASS'N OF AMERICAN RAILROADS

A best-selling lithograph in the 1880s was this busy scene depicting a depot platform of the Chicago & Alton Railroad. To the nineteenth century imagination the railroad was implicit at once with romance and material prosperity.

The Erie celebration was not without its political aspects of national significance. Of the distinguished guests aboard the two specials it was reported that every single one, Benjamin Loder excepted, was a political candidate for the Presidency of the United States. Present, too, was Stephen A. Douglas whose day of celebrity was yet to dawn, ex-Governor Seward of New York and, of course, the godlike Webster. Politics in the age of Erie was unthinkable in any atmosphere devoid of whisky and oratory and this midst the Erie supplied in quintessential form.

When the Northern Pacific at a somewhat later date ran no fewer than four "last spike" trains across the continent to solemnize its completion at Gold Creek, Montana, the beneficiaries of its hospitality included ten United States senators, three former senators, twenty-six congressmen, nine governors and four ex-governors, nine army generals, twenty-five judges and mayors and, last but by no means least, fifty newspaper reporters.

The greatest of all gold-spike ceremonies was, of course, on the desolate and windy Utah upland at Promontory Point, where on May 10, 1869, the locomotives of the Union and Central Pacific Railroads met, "pilots touching head to head," to unite a continent. But for nearly a century there were lesser occasions everywhere in America where hopes were high and good cheer abounded because of the coming of the railroad which was to mean prosperity and a good way of life for everyone.

WESTERN COLLECTION

When, in 1888, the Denver, Texas & Gulf Railroad was completed to give Colorado and the Mountain States direct access to the Gulf Ports of Texas and Louisiana, a huge parade in Denver celebrated the occasion. The paraders in the attire of traveling salesmen carrying Japanese parasols were explained as symbolizing American trade with the Orient now available through sea routes. Other paraders in carriages (*below*) welcomed the Lone Star State to direct rail communication with the Rocky Mountains.

Henry Villard's Day Of Days

NORTHERN PACIFIC RR.

When the Northern Pacific Railway, "Main Street of the Northwest," was completed between St. Paul and Portland in 1883, the citizens of Minneapolis thought enough of Henry Villard, its builder, to erect a triumphal arch (*above*) and toss posies at the financiers as they rode through the streets. To celebrate the driving of the N. P.'s last spike at Gold Creek, Montana, four special trains like the one below were run across the country with guests including ten United States senators, twenty-six congressmen, nine governors, nine generals of the Army, twenty-five judges and mayors and fifty newspaper reporters. A few years later control of the N. P. was acquired by Jim Hill, the tiger-eating man of railroading, but for the moment all was well with Henry Villard.

Last

To

The Coast

There was dancing on the depot platform at Elko, Nevada, (*above*) when the first train of the Western Pacific Railroad, last of the transcontinentals, was run from Salt Lake to Oakland in 1908. This was probably the last spontaneous outburst of enthusiasm for the coming of the cars in the United States and much of it derived from the fact that the W. P. promised to break the hitherto absolute monopoly west of Salt Lake of the powerful Southern Pacific. At the bottom of the page the first W. P. train is welcomed at Oakland. In the center Arthur W. Keddie, a California pioneer and the first to discover the railroad's route down the spectacular Feather River canyon, speaks at the last spike ceremonies. Connecting at Salt Lake with the Denver & Rio Grande Western Railroad which in turn tapped Chicago via the Burlington, the W. P. provided the first competition over the Central Overland route since the completion of the Pacific Railway forty years previous.

WESTERN PACIFIC RR.

BROWN BROS.

IV

Away You Rolling River

Along the Levees the Smoking Locomotive Spelled Doom for the Floating Palaces and the Stately Way of Life That Once Followed the Great Rivers of the Continent

THE COMING of the railroads brought their own legend of romance to the nineteenth-century United States, the swift passage between distant points, the opening of almost illimitable vistas of continental destiny, the rich appointments of the cars, and the locomotives, at once wonderful and terrible, which drew them. The rails also spelled destruction of three other modes of travel in themselves implicit with glamor and enchantment in the American consciousness.

66

The first to know its doom was the leisured life of the canals, although the canawlers never really disappeared until the turn of the century. The next victim was the Concord coach, imperishably the symbol and for many years the essential fact of the venturesome, hard-riding West. Last were the river packets which, since the beginnings of steam, had so grandly dominated the traffic of the Mississippi and the Ohio, the Missouri and Yellowstone.

For more than three centuries before the coming of the railroad the Mississippi and its valley had possessed identity and been part of a recorded human epic. They had resounded to the war whoop of the Choctaw Nation, the clash of body armor worn by the doomed followers of Hernando de Soto, the psalms of Pere Marquette, the proclamations of the Sieur de Bienville and the smooth bore muskets of Canadian *voyageurs*, trappers and *couriers du bois*. And finally, briefly, the Mississippi and its allies and tributaries, the Yazoo and the Ohio, the Tennessee, the Missouri, Arkansas, Platte, Kanawha, the Red, the Yellowstone and the Tallahatchie resounded to what must have been the mellowest trumpeting in the American symphony, the now forgotten tooting of the river steamers and their leit-motif, the gentle whooshing of exhausts.

Of the breed of river packets, the floating palaces of the great tradition on the Mississippi were by far the grandest, the most breath-fetching, the most beloved. Their personnel: pilots, planters, gamblers, rich Southern merchants and vast landholders, were the free-wheeling, free-spending, powder-burning aristocracy of the American mid-continent. Their properties, the towering crenelations of cabins and Texas, pilot houses and monstrous smokestack, the crystal and mirrors of grand promenades, Turkey carpets, rare woods, stupendous vistas of luxury, represented the sophisticated tastes of a rich and ostentatious civilization.

In comparison to the serene nobility of the river steamers the first railroads in the Mississippi Valley were white trash of the poorest, *arivistes* too debased to be acknowledged.

When it first came the Mississippi River steamer arrived with such a prodigious tooting that it was audible all over the Western world. The first self-driven packet was built by Nicholas Roosevelt, a partner of Robert Fulton, in 1811 at Pittsburgh and in it he descended the Ohio and the Mississippi to New Orleans in fourteen days. His steamer, the *New Orleans*, was driven by side paddles and definitely established the supremacy of steam over the pole boats and barges which had previously monopolized the river traffic. In 1815 a notable pioneer named Henry Shreve first successfully negotiated the uphill run all the way from New Orleans to Louisville, and in the next decade it is estimated that more than 500 river steamers were built along the banks of the Ohio and Mississippi alone. By 1842 Pittsburgh conveyed more steamboat tonnage than the seaports of Baltimore, Charleston and Philadelphia combined, and by the mid-century more than 1,000 packets of all classes and tonnage were in service on the Mississippi runs.

By 1832, twenty years after Nicholas Roosevelt's first Mississippi steamer, St. Louis had grown from a shanty-boat river settlement of traders and trappers to a metropolis of 7,000 persons and the great entrepot of the upper river. By 1880, in the last splendid decade of the supremacy of the Mississippi freight and passenger packet, it had reached 350,000. New Orleans boasted by mid-century five miles of docks which bristled with the masts and funnels of the river trade and resounded with the shouts of roustabouts, the music of colored minstrels and the escape of steam from low-pressure boilers. Front Street in Memphis became the cotton capital of the universe. Sugar was a prodigious crop in the fields above New Orleans. Still later the factories of Natchez and the oil refineries of Baton Rouge were to augment the incalculable resources of the Mississippi Valley, but the river packets with their bales of cotton tiered in ramparts as high as the Texas have disappeared forever. The cotton goes out of Memphis now on half a score of railroads of continental dimensions: the Frisco, the Gulf Mobile & Ohio, the Illinois Central, the Louisville & Nashville and the Cotton Belt. Only the oil continues to move on the River in appreciable quantities in the slow barge hauls up to Illinois, Indiana and Missouri.

Packets running on such rivers as the Cumberland and the Tennessee were known in the nineteenth century as "mountain boats" and boats that owned the Mississippi as their home waters ran as far west as Fort Benton, Montana, and east to Olean, New York. The first white woman to arrive in Dakota Territory in 1847 came aboard the steamer *Martha*. The first complete and accredited exploration of the Yellowstone was accomplished on the *Josephine* in 1875. The survivors of the Custer debacle at the Little Bighorn were brought down the Yellowstone by river packet.

On the Mississippi the gingerbread and crystal palaces running between Cairo, St. Louis, Memphis, Natchez, Vicksburg, Baton Rouge and New Orleans were in themselves a self-contained way of life. Planters and their families from down river en route for fashionable amusements made the trip annually to St. Louis aboard the *Great Republic*, the *Robert E. Lee* or *Queen City* year after year. Dangerous gamblers in skirted frock coats with Remington derringers hidden in their lace cuffs contributed a gaudy chapter to the saga of the river. The financial destinies of the great landholders and cotton nabobs of the Deep South rode with their annual crops of cotton and sugar to the levee at New Orleans.

Mark Twain, greatest of the chroniclers of the Mississippi whose river legends have passed into the body of American folklore, was by no means the only celebrity to be associated with "The Big Sluice," as it is known to rivermen. Abraham Lincoln got a job chopping wood at Foy's Point opposite Memphis after he had been rolled of his savings on an upriver packet. Presidents McKinley, Cleveland and Theodore Roosevelt knew the Mississippi at firsthand. On the Cumberland the Marquis de Lafayette fell overboard and had to be rescued by a deckhand when the *General Pike* was snagged at the mouth of Deer Creek.

Fleeing an embezzlement charge and on the way to Central America, O. Henry paused briefly to earn pocket money working on the levee at New Orleans and used to suspend his labors to watch the towering floating palaces as they headed in to tie up at the end of the run from Louisville or Memphis.

Nor was the race between the *Robert E. Lee* and the *Natchez* immortalized by Currier & Ives the only great race between river steamers. There were contests on which fortunes in gold eagles passed hands in the river ports between the *Diana* and the *Baltic*, the first *J.M. White* and the *Shotwell* and the *Eclipse* and the *Ruth*. The record is filled with accounts of catastrophes in which boilers exploded and packets were lost due to the desire of their masters to carry more steam than they were able. When the *Sultana* blew up near Memphis in 1865 the death toll reached more than three hundred persons.

Like the canawlers before them, the Mississippi rivermen were unable to perceive that their own destruction rode the iron rails which by the mid-nineteenth century were reaching across the river itself and beginning to parallel its banks and levees with a highroad over which passenger service and commerce alike would soon be flowing in an ever denser stream. Almost as though they were contemptuous of it, river captains carried the seed of self-destruction in their cargo manifests when they ferried the first railroad engines to the westerning railheads at St. Joseph, Cincinnati and Council Bluffs.

The advent of the railroads spelled the end not alone of the floating palaces of the Mississippi and Ohio, but of an entire way of life which had been built around their traffic. Wharfs and warehouses along the waterfront fell into decay. The Negro roustabouts sought other and less colorful employments. The boat owners and pilots became a dying race and great mansions in such river towns as Keokuk and Burlington that had provided wealthy owners with a view from the bluffs of the source of their wealth and commerce became vacant. At Natchez the girls and the gamblers who had made the lower city the wickedest port west of Cairo drifted to new centers of free wheeling, many of them railroad terminals and shops, but the railroad man was never the profligate spender or hearty carouser of the river tradition and the red lights burned low indeed. At Maysville, once one of the busiest of all Ohio River ports, the beautiful wrought-iron balconies of mansions that had fronted on lawns to the river fell into disrepair and the curtains of new and less genteel owners were sooted by the locomotives of the Chesapeake & Ohio whose rails soon ran along the river bank.

"I suppose New Orleans and St. Louis have not suffered materially from the change," lamented Mark Twain in *Life on the Mississippi,* "but alas for the wood-yard man. He used to fringe the river all the way . . . and he sold uncountable cords of it every year for cash on the nail. . . . Where now is the wood-yard man?" This was written in 1874, but Clemens need not have been so grieved, for the woodyard man sold fuel to the railroads along the Mississippi for three quarters of a century after that. The last wood-burning railroad in the Deep South, the Mississippi & Alabama, only closed its books in 1950.

Turpentine knots fueled railroads in the South for nearly a century and a quarter.

CHARLES CLEGG

It's Golden Years Rode to St. Louis on the River

(ALL PICTURES) BROWN BROS.

Until the coming of the cars, all its wealth arrived at St. Louis via the levee (*above*) and in the great spring morning of the western continent, St. Louis, already a city of a thousand memories, queen of the waters, gateway to the future land, was entrepot for the fur trade of the Rockies and all the trade routes beyond the wide Missouri. Its levee teemed with river-borne commerce and St. Louis in the person of Stephen Foster, gave the nation a singer whose songs became the ballad-lore of a continent in the making. Below, the *City of Cairo* proudly flies the pennant of the U.S. Mail while at the bottom of the page the second *Natchez* rolls splendidly upstream, a tangible repository of the legend and tradition of the River's spacious days.

And Spacious Times to New Orleans by Steamer

Fifteen years after the close of the Civil War the levee at New Orleans (*above*) throbbed to the pulse of America's ever crescent commerce. Five miles of water front were crowded with river shipping from up-river plantations whose cotton was bound for Manchester, Liverpool, Lowell and Lawrence. The last great boom in river traffic in the eighties was typified (*center*) by New Orleans before the disappearance of the passenger trade. Five years later Charles Dudley Warner was to write: "The change from river to railroad transport has made her levees vacant," but still as in the old days a packet sometimes carried a deckload like that of the *Katie Robbins* (*bottom*) approaching 10,000 bales.

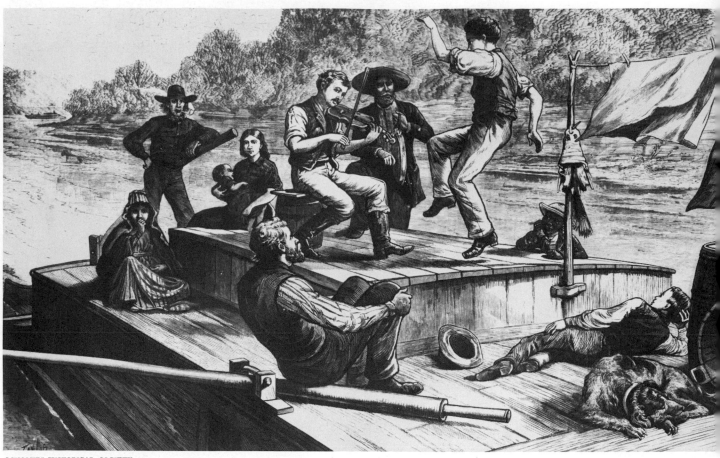

MISSOURI HISTORICAL SOCIETY

Passengers on the great river packets looked down on the decks of passing flatboats and keel boats (*above*) where the boatmen danced daylong and into the night to the music of yaller-backed fiddles and now forgotten folk harmonies. The romance of life on the river steamers entered into the national consciousness and score upon scores of songs (*lower right*) testified to the wondrous romance of the steamers. From the time of the first of all Mississippi side-wheelers, the *New Orleans* (*below left*) the life of the river was part of the American profile of commerce, expansion and "manifest destiny." In far-off Dakota the river steamer *Far West* assumed military significance (*bottom*) when it brought out the survivors of Custer's ill-starred campaign which ended at the Little Big Horn.

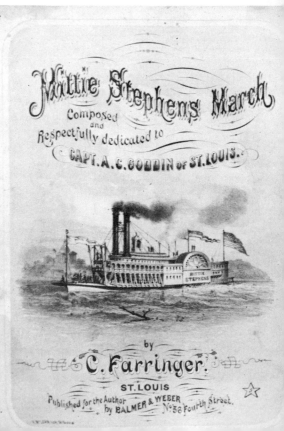

"THE BUCKWHEAT CAKE WAS IN HER MOUTH"

In an age which took abundant table fare for granted and delighted in twenty-course dinners sluiced with Niagaras of Madeira, claret, champagne and the spirits of Bourbon County Kentucky, dining on the Mississippi packets was in keeping with the luxury pattern of river life. There were no game laws and antelope, venison, partridge, sage hen, bear meat and other wildlife were almost too commonplace to mention. There were no labor unions and passengers ate to the limit of their capacity while singing darkies ran up a profusion of boiled, roast and cold dishes, relishes, puddings and desserts, and the gentlemen smoked Havana-rolled panatellas over crystal sniffers of the finest Bourbon ever to emerge from Frankfort at the luxury price of a dollar a bottle. Four years before the Civil War this menu of the *Wm. M. Morrison,* John Bofinger commanding, on the St. Louis-New Orleans run, listed connections with the North Missouri, the Pacific Mail Road, the Iron Mountain and the Illinois Central railroads. Twenty years later the connections were to increase tenfold and the doom of river passenger service was foretold in the steel rails that ran beside Old Man River every mile of the way.

MISSOURI HISTORICAL SOCIETY

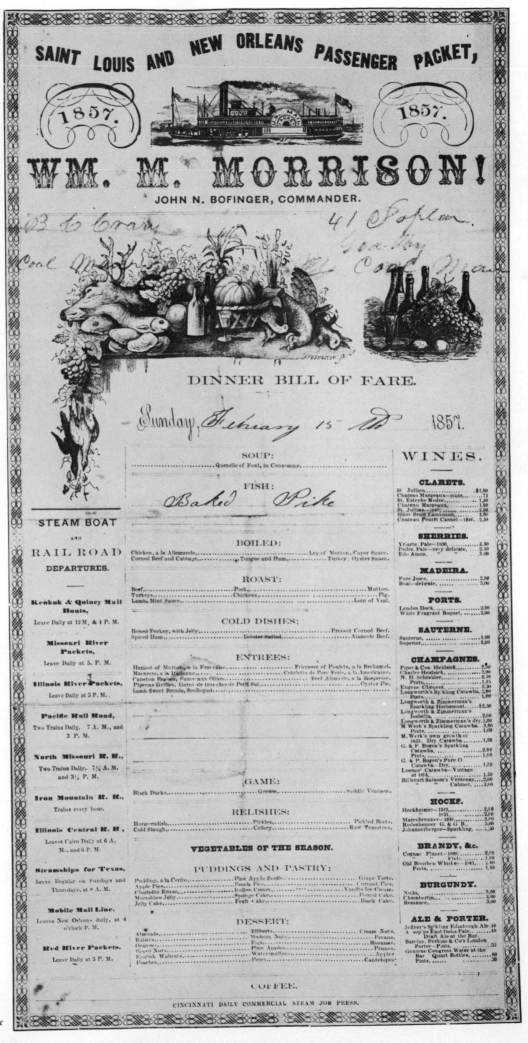

In Their Bright Noontide the River Packets Glittered

(FOUR PHOTOS) MISSOURI HISTORICAL SOCIETY

At a time when the palace cars of the railroads were also achieving a florid peak or ornamentation, the river steamers of the Mississippi rejoiced in flowered carpets, marble-topped tables, gilded wall trim and eighteen-foot ceilings such as those depicted on this page aboard the *J. M. White* built for the St. Louis–New Orleans run in the early eighties. Its main salon (*upper left*) boasted a grand piano and a thousand coal-oil lamps; its ladies' retiring room or parlor (*upper right*) a French mirror of monster dimension. Its turreted water cooler (*lower left*) was solid silver and its wheelhouse was a miracle of ornate trim and wedding cake cream and gold.

Luxury and Ostentation Delighted Their Patrons

CULVER SERVICE

For a generation that admired to promenade, the grand salons of the river steamers presented an almost limitless vista of balconies, aisles and grand stairways for the parade of wealth and fashion. Staterooms opened off the salon itself and gas and coal-oil lamps in countless hundreds lent splendor to the scene and a continuous peril of holocaust. Private apartments such as the one shown below were as sure a clue to the taste of the era as though General Grant himself had supervised their decor.

CULVER SERVICE

Mighty Inland Cities Lived by the River Traffic

LIBRARY OF CONGRESS

The forest of booms, smokestacks, gangways and exhaust pipes that rose beside the levee at Memphis tell the story of its supremacy as the cotton capital of the world in the years of its greatness. In the picture at the lower left two famous packets the *Robert E. Lee* and *Great Republic* tie up at Cairo to do business for their owners, while at the lower right coal barges await a tow on the Ohio well into the twentieth century at Pittsburgh. In 1842 Pittsburgh had more steamboat tonnage than Baltimore, Charleston and Philadelphia combined.

In 1855 the cars were just across the Mississippi from Davenport, Iowa, and in that year the first railroad bridge of the Rock Island Railroad spanned the river itself and the cars headed west.

Still deeper in the continent at Omaha, Nebraska, on the banks of the Missouri the river steamers *Colorado* and *Denver* sowed the seeds of their own destruction when they unloaded material for the construction of the Union Pacific Railroad for loading aboard the freight cars shown at the extreme left.

As the westering rails crossed the Mississippi and spread out from Omaha, the prophetic iron and a woodpile for its locomotives appeared beside the river in Front Street, Sacramento. This was the track of the Central Pacific which was soon to meet the Union Pacific at Promontory. Traffic on the rivers of California still had a long time to live and only disappeared completely during the Second World War.

DAVENPORT PUBLIC MUSEUM
UNION PACIFIC RR.
CALIFORNIA HISTORICAL SOCIETY

Traffic on the River Was Perilous in the Extreme

LIBRARY OF CONGRESS

Fire, boiler explosion and navigational mischance ended the careers of most of the great floating palaces on the Ohio and Mississippi Rivers, and the burning of the second *Robert E. Lee* at Yucatan Plantation in Louisiana in 1882, shown at the top of the page, was but one incident in a long chapter of holocausts. Below is shown the conflagration which destroyed the *Grand Republic* and *Carondelet* at the St. Louis levee a few years later. At the bottom of the page the *River Eagle* goes to its death. Between 1817 and 1850 boiler explosions alone destroyed 235 packets on the Mississippi with the loss of 2,500 lives so that insurance companies charged as high as 15 per cent on river steamers and often refused policies entirely. Pilots in the early eighties estimated that between St. Louis and Cairo alone there were the hulks of 5,000 river steamers lost through accident.

LIBRARY OF CONGRESS
CULVER SERVICE

ESTERN COLLECTION

Sometimes river boats such as the one shown above on the Red River were caught by forest fires, and in this case the passengers appear to make a good thing of the opportunity to shoot wildlife fleeing the flames before seeking safety on a barge. Below is the wreck of one of the last packet tourist steamers, the *Golden Eagle*, snagged on the way from St. Louis to Cairo in 1947, while at the bottom of the page the *Aurora* burns with great loss of life at Memphis in 1879. "Seeing the great body of fire that rages beneath the frail pile of painted wood with its machinery not warded off or guarded in any way, the wonder is that any journey should be so safely made," wrote Charles Dickens. Even the matchbox construction of the early railway cars which rolled along the riverbank seemed safe by comparison and the railroads were not slow to point out their advantage to life and limb.

ACME
CULVER SERVICE

The Railroads Flourished As The River Died

CHARLES CL.

Mark Twain's lament for the wood-yard man facing oblivion with the passing of the river steamers was groundless in vast areas of the Deep South where wood continued to be the fuel for many railroads some of which, like the Mississippi & Alabama (*above*) flourished in old-time simplicity down to the middle of the twentieth century. Woodpiles along the track (*below, left*) were familiar sights in Dixie Land long after the crescent of the New Orleans water front (*lower right*) had bade farewell to the last of the packets bound for Cairo and Memphis, St. Louis and wicked Natchez-Under-the-Hill.

LUCIUS BEEBE

N. Y. PUBLIC LIBR.

BROWN BROS.

RAILS ALONG THE RIVERS ENDED THE PACKET RUNS

This photograph, taken at Houston in the eighties in the yards of the Houston & Texas Central Railroad, tells the story of the decline of the river packets. When shippers turned to the cars for the transport of cotton in the Deep South the day of the river steamer was done. As the steamboats disappeared from the rivers, so did the rich, lusty life of the river towns sink into twilight tranquility. In some places entire townships disappeared leaving only rotting pilings and weed-grown streets that had once been instinct with life and movement. The river was no longer the life stream of the nation and the smoking locomotives took trade to inland cities that had been impervious to commerce in the age of packets. But the grand way of life aboard the steamers remained a romantic chapter in the American epic and the river packet clutched at the heart of the beholder as few human contrivings have ever done. The light of its crystal lamps upon the water, the fiddle music of its orchestra remained over the years and will be a part of the national consciousness forever.

N. Y. PUBLIC LIBRARY

The Civil War saw the first emergence of railroad armor in the form of this armored car built to protect the tracks of the Philadelphia & Baltimore Central Railroad after rebel sympathizers had burned its trestles in Maryland.

V

War Rides the Cars

The Civil War for the First Time Saw Troop Movements by Rail, and the Science of Logistics Made Possible the Closing Campaigns of Grant and Sherman for the North

THE American Civil War was notable for a number of firsts in the history of armed conflict. It was the first war in which breech-loading weapons of precision and repeating firearms were used to any appreciable extent. It was the first war to achieve photographic record, and the collodion plate pictures of Mathew Brady and Alexander Gardner, to name the two best-known photog-

82

raphers of the time, have preserved its every detail except that of action, a technique not to become practicable for another thirty years. It was the first war in which the now universally recognized science of logistics, the supply, transportation and distribution of materiél, began to be appreciated and, concurrently with this circumstance, it was the first railroad war. And, more or less incidentally, it was the first war in which a chief of state in the person of President Lincoln commonly and frequently traveled by railroad in the execution of his function as commander in chief.

A good many reasons ranging from the superior quality of General Grant's brand of whisky and the replaceable parts of Sam Colt's firearms to the firepower of the Union artillery at Shiloh have been advanced for the ultimate defeat of the Confederacy. Only a comparatively small group of historians, among them Charles Francis Adams and Stewart Holbrook, have ventured the hypothesis that the Union triumph in arms was in heroic measure attributable to the fact that Northern industrial supremacy extended into the field of railroading and that this supremacy was recognized, organized and commanded by an officer of remarkable parts.

Few Americans to whom the names of Grant, McClellan, Sherman and Sheridan are household words so much as recognize the mention of General Daniel Craig McCallum, commander of the United States Military Railroad, and yet it was he who very demonstrably highballed the Union cause to victory around the curves and down the tangents of the iron highroad.

In addition to having been a former general superintendent of the Erie in a day when Erie's operations if not its finances were accorded widespread professional respect, McCallum had the distinction of being the only general in the Union Army to be something of a popular poet, and his philosophical verses in *The Water Wheel* were widely admired during the latter nineteenth century although now almost wholly forgotten.

But it was McCallum's claim to lasting fame that he was the first commander in military history to demonstrate that, under conditions of continental warfare, the railroad could be a deciding factor in almost any campaign.

He first became convinced of the war potential inherent in railroads when the Rebel General Longstreet, an astute tactician, moved an entire army corps from the Army of Northern Virginia to Georgia in time to participate in the Battle of Chickamauga on its second fateful day. Eighteen thousand men were moved by Longstreet by way of Charlotte, Columbia and Augusta and thence through Atlanta to Ringold, Georgia, over a variety of Southern railroads, and thenceforth McCallum never underestimated the importance of the cars either as a line of supply or for the actual expeditious movement of large bodies of troops. Nashville, captured by Union forces in 1862, was the headquarters in the West of the United States Military Railroads and from this central position McCallum directed a series of extensive railroad movements which culminated in Sherman's advance upon Atlanta from the Ohio River over the rails of the Louisville & Nashville and the Nashville, Chatanooga & St. Louis roads: "The Atlanta campaign would have been an impossibility without those roads," Sherman wrote in his memoires.

For four months Sherman's army of 100,000 men and 35,000 horses and mules was serviced with food, ammunition and replacements to equipment over 473 miles of the single track of the L. & N. from Louisville to Atlanta. The rail artery made possible the decisive campaign of the entire Civil War.

Most of the railroads within the borders of the Confederacy such as the L. & N., the N.C. & St.L., the Mobile & Ohio, the West Point Route, the Norfolk & Western and the southern reaches of what is now the Illinois Central were wrecked by the war either through the agency of continual use without maintenance or repair or destruction at the hands of Union armies. Of the Northern roads only the Baltimore & Ohio which operated extensively through Virginia suffered appreciably from raids by General Stonewall Jackson's men.

Railroads provided the materiél of war in more ways than one. John W. Thomason, Jr., in his *Lone Star Preacher* recalled that when a regiment of Texans was encamped south of Richmond in the early months of 1863, their uniforms, although fairly complete, were lacking in headgear of any kind. Resourceful infantrymen lay in wait along the line of the Petersburg Railroad until a passenger train came into sight. Delegated specialists with strong lungs then made a tumultuous demonstration by the right of way and the unwary passengers, to see what was toward, popped their heads out the windows, whereupon the soldiery knocked off their hats with fishpoles procured for the purpose. All sorts of headgear was secured in this manner: planters' hats with broad brims, the beavers of politicians, soft felts of city fellows, whatever the traveling public was wearing. After a few days the regiment was at least protected against the elements even if not in a very military or uniform manner.

Along with the technique of operating railroads to military advantage, there inevitably was evolved a technique for their destruction. Sherman's bummers on their march through Georgia made a fine art of the already established practice of delaying pursuit by heating rails over a bonfire and then twisting them around a convenient tree. On numerous occasions munitions trains were cut loose by both sides to run headlong into the enemy lines, but the results were generally more spectacular than factually destructive. "Word can scarcely convey the awful grandeur of the ensuing holocaust," wrote a correspondent for a New York newspaper after Union engineers had driven a trainload of ammunition against advancing Rebels in Virginia but the military achievement was probably less than notable.

The most publicized railroad episode of the Civil War and one which is occasionally retold to this day was entirely devoid of military significance or consequence. The so-called "Andrews Raid," in which a group of Northern soldiers in disguise attempted to wreck the Western & Atlantic Railroad by stealing the locomotive *General* and a train of boxcars with the intention of burning the bridges between Atlanta and Chattanooga, has been dramatized because of the chase it involved by Confederate troops with the engine *Texas*. The Andrews raiders were captured before they could accomplish any damage of importance and several were hanged as spies, since they were in civilian attire. Andrews himself, in fact, wore a silk top hat throughout most of the exploit, but, aside from its colorful details, it had less significance than scores of less celebrated exploits in steam.

Along with almost all the rest of the industry of the South, its railroads were reduced to rolling scrap heaps before the war was over. The Confederacy had neither the material nor the manpower to replace communications lines whose rails and trestles had been destroyed by enemy action or worn out by military traffic. As soon as the times afforded, patriotic and farsighted Southerners, of whom General Lee was the foremost, set about rehabilitating their railroads and planning new ones. A portion of the Chesapeake Western running between Harrisonburg and Staunton, Virginia, in whose construction the former Confederate leader was influential, is still known as "General Lee's Railroad."

Curiously enough many influential men of the South, particularly in Georgia, were bitterly opposed to railroad construction even with the example of the industrially booming North before them. To former slaveholders and the feudal aristocrats brooding in their ruined estates the locomotives and the cars were symbols of the Union victory and of the encroachments of modernity. They brought in new ideas and new ways, gave the Negroes notions and frightened the horses. As a result of this attitude many main-line railroads in the Deep South were forced to avoid important towns and cities when they were built. Later, when the folly of this hostility became apparent, scores upon scores of Southern communities were forced, usually at their own expense, to build connecting branches and spurs with the result that, more than three-quarters of a century after the first railroad war, the South remained the home of the short-line railroad. Usually these souvenirs of feudal hatreds had more character than the main lines ever possessed. Often they were still functioning reminders of the elsewhere vanished Old South and an individualistic way of life that a regimented generation well may envy.

THE YANKEES RIDE THE CARS TO WAR

The opening phases of the Civil War in 1861 saw the first recorded movement of troops by rail to military destinations by both armies. Here the Sixth Massachusetts Volunteers entrain at Jersey City for Washington aboard the cars of the New Jersey Railroad, connecting with the Pennsylvania at Philadelphia.

N. Y. PUBLIC LIBRARY

Destruction

Appeared

Mounted

On

The Rails

N. Y. PUBLIC LIBRARY

Front-line artists for *Leslie's* early in the conflict lost no time in sending home the stirring scene depicted above when Union troops sent a loaded ammunition train to destruction amidst Southern troops firing a bridge across the Chicahominy. In the war's early stages, too, appeared cannon mounted on railroad trucks capable of being pushed into position and withdrawn after firing. This howitzer in Grant's army (*lower left*) mounted a shield to protect it gunners. "The Dictator" (*lower right*) was a thirteen-inch mortar used by Federal troops before Petersburg. It fired a 200-pound shell with a charge of twenty pounds of black powder.

ASS'N OF AMERICAN RAILROADS

The war was not without its preposterous aspects. Northern cartoonists liked to imagine Southern gentlemen going to war in upholstered ease. The flunkied warrior in this picture is supposed to have arrived at the front lines "aboard a parlor coach of the Richmond & Petersburg Railway" with his entourage of servants, a rocking chair for combat duty and plentiful supply of bottled courage of high proof.

In an age when military dignity was represented by the man on a battle charger, the *New York Illustrated News* poked mild fun at General Ambrose Burnside, whose whiskers were already a national institution, when he directed operations from a handcar during a campaign in North Carolina. "Riding in state," the *News* called it.

Preposterous, too, was the Winans steam rifle which General Butler's troops captured from its Confederate builders near the Relay House early in the war. Yankee technicians proposed its removal from the steam fire-engine carriage on which it was mounted and its adaptation to railroad use where steam for its operation would be supplied by the locomotive. Experts claimed it would sweep all before it.

N. Y. PUBLIC LIBRARY

The Tide of War Rolled Relentlessly on the Rails

N. Y. PUBLIC LIBRARY

When a Confederate masked battery (*above*) opened fire on a company of Union troops advancing by train over the rails of the thirty-eight mile long Alexandria, Loudon & Hampshire Railroad near Vienna, Virginia, a staff artist attached to McDowell's command was on the scene to send back his impressions. During the course of hostilities hundreds of engines and cars were destroyed (*center*) by the military while others were impressed into the service of the opposing armies. Below is shown a trainload of Union troops on the Louisville & Nashville Railroad passing General Buell's army on the Louisville and Nashville Turnpike, a demonstration of the superiority of railroad transport in wartime.

With Intimations of Civilian Shortages to Come

N. Y. PUBLIC LIBRARY

As Southern economy fell apart every effort was made to ship cotton, resin and turpentine from the interior to seaports still open to trade with England before the Union blockade could be established. The scene shows a vessel being loaded from the cars at Wilmington, North Carolina. As in more recent wars, civilian travel became troublesome in the South where old equipment (*center*) was overcrowded as the star of the Confederacy declined. In far better shape, the U.S. Military Railroad once moved an entire railroad, engines, rolling stock and rails, in a single movement ninety miles up the James River (*below*) for strategic reasons.

Logistics Had Their Beginnings With McCallum

N. Y. PUBLIC LIBRARY

AN ARCHITECT OF VICTORY, McCALLUM WAS A RAILROADER

ERIE RR.

The installations of the United States Military Railroad at Vicksburg after the city fell into Union hands July 4, 1863, with its important resources of motive power (*above*) were part of a comprehensive pattern of organized supply of Federal armies in the field created by General Daniel McCallum, a former Erie superintendent elevated to command of the entire Union army railroad. McCallum (*below*) who was known as one of the few Civil War generals who wrote poetry, evolved the technique of military supply by rail in an age that had not heard the word "logistics," and was credited by Grant and Lincoln as being one of the decisive architects of Union victory. The first train across Bull Run bridge after the second Battle of Manassas (*below*) was a military train whose consist included cars from the Pennsylvania Railroad whose nearest approach to the scene was Baltimore, seventy-five miles to the north.

PENNSYLVANIA RR.

N. Y. PUBLIC LIBRARY

During the closing campaigns of the war in 1863, Falmouth Station on the Richmond, Fredericksburg & Potomac Railroad (*above*) became the chief supply depot for the Army of the Potomac, and the troops, food, clothing, arms and ammunition unloaded here and dispatched to the front by team supported Burnside and Hooker along the Rappahannock. At Manassas Junction (*below*) two important railroads, the Manassas Gap Railroad and the Orange & Alexandria, converged and it was over the Manassas Gap that engines stolen from the Baltimore & Ohio at Harper's Ferry brought in Kirby Smith's brigade which effected the rout of the Union Army at First Manassas.

LIBRARY OF CONGRESS

Destruction of Materièl Included the Railroads

Destroying rails by heating them over a fire of ties was a technique practiced by both armies. "Sherman's Bummers" improved it by tying the red-hot rails around trees from which they could never be unbent.

Sometimes Confederate gunlayers got a sight on a moving Union locomotive. Here a frock-coated conductor points to the dent of a cannonball on the eight-wheeler named the *Fred Leach*. Engines of the Military Railroad often bore names.

When the Confederate Army evacuated Richmond it left behind it such scenes of desolation as this in the roundhouse of the Richmond, Fredericksburg & Potomac Railroad, to be photographed by Mathew Brady.

LOUISVILLE & NASHVILLE RR.
ASS'N OF AMERICAN RAILROADS
LIBRARY OF CONGRESS

Burning of the wooden railroad bridges of the time was an obvious strategy in obstructing enemy movements. Here the Rebels are firing a bridge on the Tennessee Central Railroad. Their purpose was to cut off General George B. Thomas in charge of Federal forces at Nashville from communication and supplies from Grant's army in the North.

The span of the Louisville & Nashville Railroad across Bacon Creek in Hart County, Kentucky, was destroyed by Confederate engineers early in the campaign of 1861. Even such a short span caused delay until it could be replaced.

Lincoln was fond of remarking that McCallum's engineers built their railroad trestles out of "string and beanpoles," but this lofty and complicated wooden span served to permit operations of an essential nature over the Richmond, Fredericksburg & Potomac in the last months of the war.

LOUISVILLE & NASHVILLE RR.
LOUISVILLE & NASHVILLE RR.
N. Y. PUBLIC LIBRARY

Hospital Trains First Appeared in the Civil War

After the Battle of Fair Oaks, the Union wounded were brought in field ambulances to Fair Oaks Station of the Richmond & York River Railroad and loaded on the available cars for removal to base hospitals in the North. In the absence of specially fitted hospital cars, flatcars and boxcars were pressed into service.

Later, specially built and fitted hospital trains were ordered by the Sanitary Commission, predecessor of the Red Cross, such as this on the Nashville, Chattanooga & St. Louis Railroad drawn by the military engine *Frank Thompson.*

This temporary tent hospital was built·by the U.S. Military Railroad at City Point, Virginia. In the background are the engines *General Dix* and *General McClellan,* both built for the government after the outbreak of hostilities.

N. Y. PUBLIC LIBRARY
LOUISVILLE & NASHVILLE RR.
ASS'N OF AMERICAN RAILROADS

And the Telegraph Speeded Mars and the Railroads

The first president to require a communications chief for his exclusive service was Lincoln who, at the start of the Civil War, hired a Western Union telegraph operator to fill this post which had been part of the President's entourage ever since. Already in wide, although not universal use by the nation's railroads for the transaction of official business, the telegraph was speedily adapted to the uses of war. Field telegraph stations (*above*) were set up on the scene of battle and field operators (*lower left*) speedily relayed dispatches to the headquarters operator (*lower right*). Thus the White House was in constant touch with the tide of war.

Lincoln's Funeral Train Was Seen by Millions

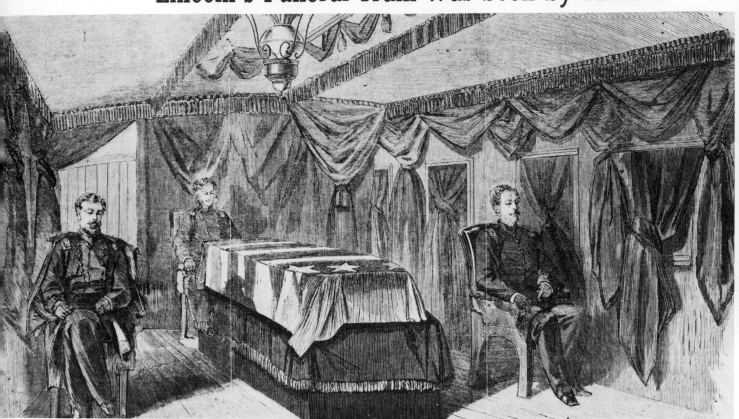

N. Y. PUBLIC LIBRARY

After the assassination Lincoln's body was carried to his native Springfield, Illinois, over a variety of railroads by way of Baltimore, Philadelphia, New York, Albany, Buffalo and Cleveland, passing beneath shrouded arches in mourning cities while bands played dirges and cannon thundered on country hilltops. Over the final stage on the Chicago & Alton Railroad Mrs. Lincoln's party rode behind the funeral coach in George Pullman's sleeping car *Pioneer,* thus giving the invention incalculable publicity. With the coffin (*above*) rode a guard of honor representing the three branches of the military service. The exterior of the car (*below*) through which thousands passed to pay their last respects was fringed in black draperies. In New York harbor (*bottom*) it was ferried to the Manhattan shore aboard a steam lighter while the usually noisy whistles of the harbor traffic were muted.

Reconstruction Set the Cars Rolling Once More

N. Y. PUBLIC LIBRARY

Not so badly battered as the railroads of the South, which required a full generation for their rehabilitation, the Baltimore & Ohio was able two years after the close of hostilities to run this inspection train filled with top-hatted officials over its West Virginia divisions. Rails were already heavily ballasted and at this junction point night and day semaphores were operated from a centralized switch tower.

To prevent their falling into the hands of the Rebels, large numbers of engines of railroads radiating out of Alexandria had been run across the Potomac and stored at Washington in the shadow of the Capitol. With the coming of peace they were restored to their owners to assist the program of reconstruction.

ASS'N OF AMERICAN RAILROADS

WELLS FARGO BANK

"Oh, then we went life's flowery ways
That ended with our staging days."

VI

Plains Without Rails

Before the Railroads There Was the West of the Mountain Men, the Long Hunters, the Buffalo Grass, the Swaying Stagecoaches and the Long Wagon Trains Rolling Out of Kansas

THE PHRASE "the American West" is not a very precise or definitive geographic locale. There was a time when the frontier was upper York State and Ohio and the dark and bloody ground of Kentucky. After the American Revolution and just before the turn of the nineteenth century the frontier had receded to a strip along the shores of Lake Erie known as New Connecticut or the Western Reserve. By the time the nineteenth century was achieved on Christian calendars, the character and personality of the Mississippi Valley which had been described by Alexis de Tocqueville as "the most magnificent dwelling place prepared by God for man's abode" had been incorporated in the established precincts of civilization. And in 1810 the publication of the diaries of Lieutenant Zebulon Pike describing the wonderments of the Santa Fe country and what was to become Colorado gave the first impetus to what, three-and-a-half decades later, was to be the most compulsive item in the national creed, that of "manifest destiny."

All these places were, in turn, the frontier West. But the place and the time as well as the character and time-spirit suggested most widely by the phrase "the old West" is the region comprehended by another spacious phrase "across the wide Missouri" and its date, again in the popular conception, is roughly the span from the rise of the Rocky Mountain fur trade in the early thirties to the driving of the gold spike at Promontory in Utah, in 1869. These forty years embrace, chronologically and geographically, the Texas of the Alamo, the Colorado of the Pike's Peak excitements (which didn't follow the Lieutenant himself for half a century) the splendid legend of the Santa Fe trade, the overland immigration to California after the discovery of gold and the only slightly less stirring bonanzas of Nevada, Arizona, New Mexico and South Dakota. They enfold, too, the Mormon exodus, the saga of the Oregon Trail and the establishment of a network of overland communications through the agency of the great staging companies which culminated with the identification, through the advertising of the Pony Express, of the Great Central Overland Route which became the carotid of Western travel through which coursed and still courses the heart's blood of the nation.

All of these agencies and occasions contributed to the coming of the railroads, yet all of them existed before the actual advent of the cars. The various oriflammes of the age bore the legends "Remember the Alamo," "Pike's Peak or Bust," "Oh, Suzanna," "Darling Clementine," "Gold on the American River," "Glory to Washoe," and the faith of the Latter Day Saints: "All Is Well."

That the hallmarks and identifications of civilization were discernible in varying densities in various times and places goes without saying, and only the most naive and uninstructed visualize the old West in its entirety as an uncouth and unsanitary farrago of Bowie knives, buckskin shirts, Indian massacres, sod houses and buffalo hunts. At the time—the year was 1838—that Captain Samuel Walker of the Texas Rangers was persuading Samuel Colt of Hartford, Connecticut, to perfect the five-shot repeating revolver that was to be the greatest single artifact of the American frontier, invalids from the East were traversing the Santa Fe Trail in Newburyport-built carriages in search of health in the Colorado uplands. Evening attire was a commonplace in the de luxe restaurants of San Francisco when the first longhorns were being driven to the Kansas railheads over the Chisholm Trail, and in Virginia City, Nevada, scene of the greatest of the later bonanzas, gentlemen were drinking vintage Madeira in the barroom of the exclusive Washoe Club a full decade before George Armstrong Custer came to grief at the Little Big Horn. The West before the coming of the iron horse was a fascinating study in contradictions. It all depended whether the observer viewed it from the vantage point of the St. Francis ballroom on the slope of what was eventually to be known as Nob Hill or from the board sidewalk of Tough Nut Street in Tombstone.

Long Before the Cars the Fur Trade Held the West

The Mountain Men and the Long Hunters such as Jim Bridger shown in this old-time picture were almost the only white men west of the Great Plains until the Pike's Peak gold rush in the late fifties. The Mountain Men knew steamboats, for the American Fur Company operated two of them out of St. Louis and as far afield as Fort Clark, sixty miles above Bismarck, North Dakota, as early as 1833. But none of the great names of the fur trade lived into the age of the railroad West, except Dick Wootton whose love affair with the Santa Fe Railroad is described elsewhere. When you said Mountain Man you may have meant Kit Carson or Milton Sublette or William Ashley or Captain Benjamin Louis Eulalie de Bonneville, but archetype of the craft was Old Gabe, Jim Bridger, as mighty a scout, trapper and killer of Indians as the West was ever to know.

The last great summer rendezvous, shown below, the fur trade institution at which the Mountain Men, traders, trappers, Indians and representatives of the fur companies met to barter and plan the next year's hunting, was held at Horse Neck Creek in the Ute Country in 1839. The rise in popularity of the silk top hat and consequent decline of the beaver trade gradually eliminated the Long Hunters until by the time the first railroad was built west of the Mississippi, they were only a memory and the stage was set for the Westward rush in search of precious metals.

WESTERN COLLECTION

CULVER SERVICE

The Oregon fur trade was dominated by the haughty Hudson's Bay Company whose *engages* and *voyageurs* frequently ranged into what are now Idaho and Wyoming to come into conflict, as shown above, with representatives of John Jacob Astor's American Fur Company. These two rich factions and a third, the Rocky Mountain Fur Company, and the so-called "free hunters" held sway over the entire American West, but by the forties the fur trade was a thing of the past and the Rocky Mountains knew the camps (*below*) of non-commercial hunters and amateur sportsmen.

WESTERN COLLECTION

The fur traders had scant use for wheeled vehicles, but the emigrants who followed left Westport and Independence in covered wagons drawn by oxen and built like boats in order to float across streams. The old Santa Fe Trail divided at Cimarron Crossing, the safe northern route achieving its goal via Bent's Fort and the Raton Pass, the dangerous southern alternate, the Cimarron Cutoff, being also known as the Jornada del Muerta because of its scarcity of water holes. Thirty years after the flood tide of the Taos and Santa Fe trade, white-topped wagons were still following the old trails Westward parallel to the railroad (*below*), but now the way was safe; forts and townships dotted most of the route.

CULVER SERVICE

(FOUR PICTURES) N. Y. PUBLIC LIBRARY

Life on the Santa Fe Trail possesses a romantic charm for the American imagination. Sometimes the white tops set out across the seemingly endless sea of buffalo grass in groups which enjoyed a common evening campfire under the Kansas stars (*upper left*). Others went it alone with only a little dog for company as above at the right. All slept under their buffalo robes dreaming of heady Spanish wines and wild fandangos. A few perished by the wayside from Indians or other mischance and their bones whitened the trail (*lower left*) for years, but the rutted tracks of the Santa Fe Trail in Kansas were still visible a century after its great days (*lower right*), a trace of the American version of the Golden Journey to Samarkand.

The Look of the West Before the Rails Were Laid

Chicago's first public school, erected a full decade before the first railway locomotive whistled into town, was located on the southeast corner of what are now Madison and Dearborn Streets. Having two floors it was considered a monster edifice by the bull-whackers who passed its portals.

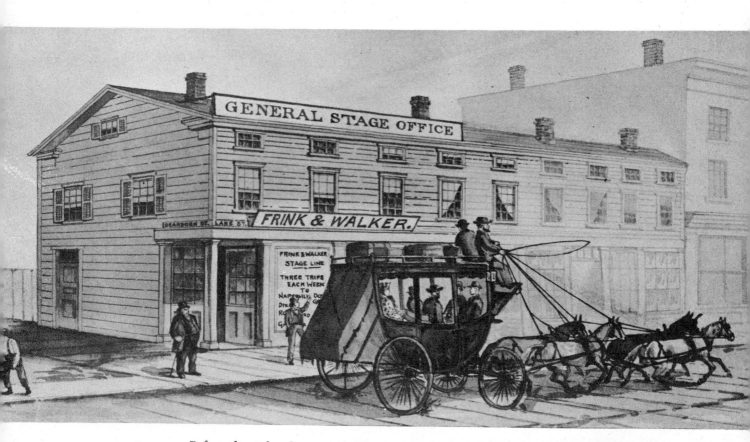

Before the railroads came to Chicago, the future hub of the steamcar universe, John Frink and Martin Otis Walker in 1838 undertook to furnish transport by stage between Chicago and Rockford over the Galena highway, a *jornada* which required twenty-four hours in clement weather, imponderably longer if the roads were muddy. Their office was at the corner of Dearborn and Lake.

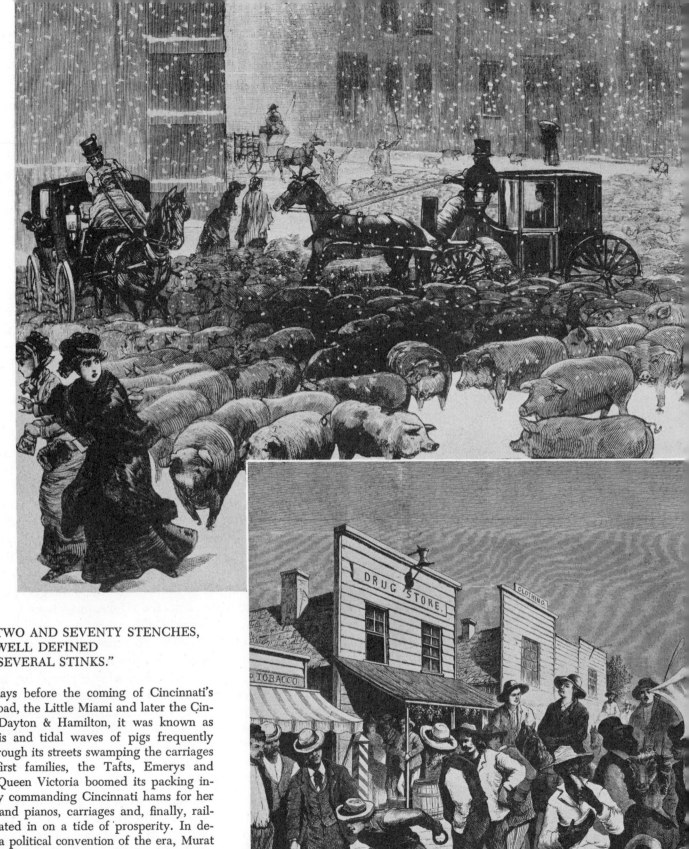

". . . TWO AND SEVENTY STENCHES, ALL WELL DEFINED AND SEVERAL STINKS."

In the days before the coming of Cincinnati's first railroad, the Little Miami and later the Cincinnati, Dayton & Hamilton, it was known as Porkopolis and tidal waves of pigs frequently rolled through its streets swamping the carriages of the first families, the Tafts, Emerys and Storers. Queen Victoria boomed its packing industry by commanding Cincinnati hams for her table; grand pianos, carriages and, finally, railroads floated in on a tide of prosperity. In describing a political convention of the era, Murat Halstead wrote: "Imagine all the hogs ever slaughtered in Cincinnati giving their death squeals together." The Missouri-Kansas-Texas Railroad, first into Texas, didn't come to Denison (*below*) until 1872 and until the Katy's gun-packing special officers brought a measure of tranquility it was a roughneck frontier town populated largely by gamblers, easy girls and municipal riff-raff generally. This pastoral vignette of Denison is on the optimistic side.

There were, however, certain properties and characteristics which were almost universal in the old West of our definition whether they figured in the daily life of the silk-hatted and tail-coated banker of Montgomery Street, the mule skinner guiding the ever crescent immigrant trains out of Kansas or the Texas cowhand waging deadly and continuous warfare against drought, cattle thieves, Mexican renegades or the more warlike members of the Nations. They were a universality of drinking whisky, a common reference to firearms, and dependence upon the stagecoaches and express companies which brought in the mail, carried out the dust, nuggets and bullion and in time diminished the almost incalculable distance between the Missouri River towns and railheads and the cosmopolis of San Francisco to commensurable proportions.

The span of life of staging in the West was from the year after the discovery of gold in California when the gold-and-crimson Concords first supplanted the mounted traveler and the Spanish carreta as a superior means of transport until the coming of the automobile. They lasted long after the railroads had reached their maximum extent and diversity of routes, serving regions impervious to rails and as feeders of the main lines just as they had originally fanned out from earlier railheads at St. Joseph, Denver and Sacramento. Long before Leland Stanford smote valiantly at the golden spike at Promontory (and missed it most unprofessionally) the hallmarks of the American West were what they have remained to this day in the general imagining; the Colt's or Remington repeating revolver, the Henry or Winchester rifle, the distilled spirits of Bourbon County, Kentucky, and the durable coaches made by Abbot Downing & Co., in far-off Concord, New Hampshire.

The rise of staging is in itself one of the major and most stirring epics of the nation's progress westward. Having its inception in California three years after the arrival of the Argonauts, the greatest of the express and banking firms and one whose name was to become a household word for more than half a century, was the business started in San Francisco and the Mother Lode diggings by Henry Wells and William George Fargo. From the beginning they banked the dust, nuggets and bullion of the placer miners, transported it to their vaults for safekeeping, issued letters of credit for its shipment to the East and supplied Californians with mail in a time and place where the Federal mails were practically nonextant. Cautious and conservative and pledged to make good any losses of valuables in transit, a pledge which was scrupulously maintained in an age of almost universal irresponsibility in such matters, Wells Fargo & Co., in a few years time had absorbed scores of smaller express lines in California, taken over the business of Adams & Co., their predecessors and chief rivals in the field, and had made the name of the firm synonymous with swift communications, irreproachable honesty and insuperable enterprise. In the counting rooms of Montgomery Street, Wells Fargo's broadcloth-coated cashiers were the sage and aristocratic overlords of the banking world. In the firm's outland agencies the Wells Fargo manager and route agent were the proconsuls of every mining community in California, Nevada, Arizona and Montana. On the unguarded highroads of the old West, Wells Fargo's stage drivers and shotgun messengers, fearful of aspect and terrible in their wrath against encroachment, were the representatives of law where it existed not, at once the furious Jehus and the tireless avengers of a world of speed and gunfire.

The affairs of the overland express companies operating between the Missouri and California, sometimes as independent agencies and sometimes in corporate association with Wells Fargo as precursors of the Pacific Railroad, constitute another galloping chapter in the Western narrative. One of the first great transcontinental mail routes was that established at the outbreak of the Civil War by George Chropenning and Absolom Woodward to carry the mails once a month on thirty-day schedule between Sacramento and Salt Lake. Another was the still remembered Butterfield Overland Mail Route and Emigrant Trail to California from Fort Dodge by way of the Cimarron Cutoff, Santa Fe, El Paso and Fort Yuma. For many years what amounted to a vast freighting monopoly was maintained throughout the Southwest by the firm of Russell, Majors & Waddell whose army of teamsters, hundreds of giant cargo vans, thousands of horses, mules and oxen and scores of relief stations, outposts and forwarding centers constituted an empire on wheels. The Leavenworth and Pike's Peak-Platte River Route provided mails and freight for a time to the hesitant residents of Denver City who, for some years, couldn't decide whether to become a ghost town or the Queen City of the Plains. And, last and most important of them all, because it indicated the location of the railroad which was shortly to follow, was the route of the Pony Express, the Great Central Overland from St. Joseph to Sacramento via Julesburg, Fort Laramie, Fort Bridger, Salt Lake, Carson City and Mormon Station, now Genoa, Nevada.

The life span of overland staging was a brief one of only two decades but it sought out and established the life lines of continental conquest, and the tourist today who rolls on cushioned wheels over U.S. 40 or U.S. 50, U.S. 66 or U.S. 80 is following the routes of the straining oxen, the covered white tops and the old bearded kings of distance who once followed the sun westward to California.

One of the most succinct records of the diminishing amenities of civilization as the traveler went westward was furnished by Horace Greeley. In 1859 Uncle Horace was momentarily weary of national politics and even of the editorial chores of the *Tribune* and he wanted to see at firsthand the growing agricultural and mineral promise of Colorado, the reportedly verdant valley of the Latter-day Saints, the Comstock Lode and the surely exaggerated wonders of California whose publicists were even then straining the general credulity. Greeley wanted, too, as the greatest of the lay prophets of the railroad, to report on possible routes for the inevitable locaters and graders. Was the South Pass the great gateway or would it be across Kansas and the Colorado plains through some hitherto undiscovered defile in the Shining Mountains above Denver City?

Greeley's diary of this safari read in part:

May 12. Chicago. Chocolate and morning journals last seen on the hotel breakfast table.

May 23. Leavenworth (Kansas). Room bells and bathtubs make their last appearance.

May 24. Topeka (Kansas). Beefsteaks and washbowls (other than tin) last visible. Barber ditto.

May 26. Manhattan (Kansas). Potatoes and eggs last recognized as "blessings that brighten as they take their flight." Chairs ditto.

May 27. Junction City (Kansas). Last visitation of the bootblack and dissolving views of a board bedroom. Beds bid us goodbye.

May 28. Pipe Creek (Kansas). Benches for seats at meals disappearing, giving place to bags and boxes.

In the Old West the Stagecoach Driver Was King

Until the coming of the brave engineer in his locomotive cab no figure of the frontier threatened the supremacy of the lordly stage driver, the hell-for-leather king of hurry, along the dusty highroads of Nevada and California. As remote from ordinary mortals as earls, most of them were also the glass of fashion. Jim Miller, shown here with his coach dog and whip of office, was a celebrated jehu in the employ of Wells Fargo and the watch shown above and visible in the photograph of its owner was presented to him in gratitude for saving the treasure box in an attempted holdup near Hamilton, Nevada. Another famous Wells Fargo whip was Pilsbury Hodgkins, known as "Chips," (*below*), who held the reins on the dangerous Sonora-Sacramento run with fortunes in gold dust in the boot of his stage. Wells Fargo gave him a miniature treasure chest in Comstock silver in appreciation of his long and honorable service.

(ALL PICTURES) WELLS FARGO BANK

The private coach, shown above, of bearded old Ben Holladay, the stagecoach king, was the forerunner of the private cars of the railroad moguls. It was fitted with an icebox, portable bar and a specially shaded lamp for night reading and in it he once broke all previous records by driving from St. Louis to California in twelve days. Most celebrated of all drivers was Hank Monk (*left*) who achieved immortality driving Horace Greeley over the Sierra to Hangtown in a manner to terrify the timid editor. This rare photograph from the archives of the Nevada Historical Society shows Monk with long hair in his youth at Virginia City. Below, Jared Crandall, "Prince of Stagers," drives his Concord on the San Francisco-San Jose run before the coming of the first railroad in California connected those terminals.

CULVER SERVICE

In 1862 while the menfolk were away at war, a Sioux uprising in northern Minnesota took the lives of 700 settlers in massacres such as that at New Ulm shown above. Troops were speedily recalled from the front, broke up the bands of braves (*center*) and thirty-eight ringleaders were promptly hanged at Mankato (*below*) in the best-attended hanging Minnesota had ever known.

CULVER SERVICE

LIBRARY OF CONGRESS

UNIVERSITY OF DENVER: WESTERN COLLECTION

ROAD TO RED RUIN

The fur trade of the thirties and forties in the West was floated on whisky brought in from St. Louis by the fur companies and bartered at a fantastic markup with the Indians (*above*) for otter and beaver plews, for their services as guides and for their women, who came cheap. The white man's fire water and the white man's diseases had started the tribes on their way to virtual extinction long before the graders started building the Union Pacific west from Omaha. "Ten thousand tracklayers will bring in with them enough whisky to kill every Indian within a hundred miles," said the practical William T. Sherman, who took a dim view of the redskin menace, as the tracklayers started across Wyoming. He was substantially right. Five years later tourists on the Overland route to California found the Sioux, Shoeshones and Piutes along the way reduced to pauperism and mendicancy. At Carlin, Nevada, (*below*) ragged beggars including the once proud chief Winnemucca cadged small change from fastidious Eastern tourists as the train paused to wood up before heading on toward Battle Mountain, the next stop of consequence.

Pike's

Peak

Or

Bust

Lured

Thousands

To

A

National

Anabasis

(ALL PICTURES) WESTERN COLLECTIO

Gold in the Shining Mountains Turned All Faces West

For half a century after the discovery of the Shining Mountains, as they were first known, by Lieutenant Zebulon Pike, the Colorado Rockies were the hunting ground of the Mountain Men. Then, in 1858, gold was found in substantial quantities in the region of which Pike's Peak was the symbol and the rush was on. Countless thousands gave up the security of farms and business in the East and converged on the Cherry Creek diggings at what later became Denver City. "Pike's Peak or Bust" became a national battle cry and the Great Plains was populous with emigrants afoot, in covered wagons and dragging their possessions in hand barrows as shown on the page opposite. A watermelon pushed from Lawrence, Kansas, in a wheelbarrow such as the one shown here sold for enough in the diggings to found the fortune of one of Denver's first families. One May morning in 1860 the sentry at the main gate of Fort Kearny, Nebraska, called in terror for his sergeant when the apparition shown below skimmed toward him across the prairie at twenty miles an hour. Its occupants civilly saluted the flag and sped onward to the West, their "Pike's Peak" banner flapping in the wind. A number of such wind wagons were built for prairie travel. This one carried a carriage lamp for night driving when the wind was fair.

The Pony Express Once Set the Nation by the Ears

E. S. HAMMACK

THE EXPRESS MAIL IS OFF, PONY BOB UP!

The Pony Express, an overland mail service between the Missouri River and California organized by the express firm of Russell, Majors & Waddell and later acquired by Wells Fargo, lasted but a few brief months in 1860–61 before the completion of the Overland Telegraph put an end to its usefulness. Yet until Admiral Dewey took his fleet around Cape Horn in a war four decades later, nothing so captured the public imagination of America as the idea of the mails reaching San Francisco from St. Joseph in the incredible time of ten days. Mails from the East reached the riverbank town of Elwood, Kansas, aboard the cars of the Hannibal & St. Joseph Railroad as shown here, the first railroad in the nation to maintain a Railway Post Office aboard a moving train. Thence they were carried westward by relays of swift coursers, night and day, storm or shine to the mining camps of the Comstock, across the Sierra to the Mother Lode and finally to San Francisco ten days from the most western railhead of the continent.

WESTERN COLLECTION

West of the Missouri the Pony mail was carried only at great peril and expense. Most hostile Indians were the Piutes in Nevada who frequently raided express stations, burned stables and butchered the stock tenders as shown above. The risk of procuring these artist's sketches on the frontier was comparable to that of war photographers generations later. During the Red Cloud War, Ridgeway Glover, an artist for *Leslie's* sketching the uprising, wandered outside Fort Kearny and was found next day tomahawked and scalped. As a result of such raids mail riders like Pony Bob Haslam sometimes rode 100 miles without relief or change of horses. Such was the hold of Pony Express on the public fancy, that forty years after its discontinuance it was still a subject for Beadle's nickle (not dime) novels. In the High Sierra, winter mails at the time of the Pony Express were for years delivered by a Nevada hero of legend known as Snowshoe Thompson (*below*) who threaded the winter passes, sometimes in dead of night with blizzards raging, a lamp strapped to his chest, to deliver mail between the last mail depot in Nevada at Mormon Station and the Mother Lode camps of California.

N. Y. PUBLIC LIBRARY
WELLS FARGO BANK

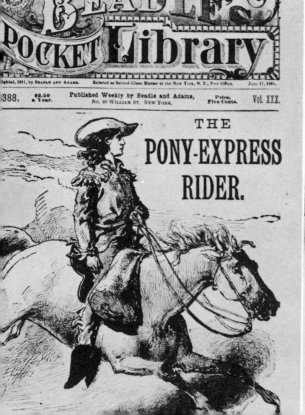

Montana Territory Had Its Gold Rush Too

The rich gold deposits available to placer mining at Alder Gulch, Montana Territory (*above*), were discovered in Civil War years by a group of prospectors of Southern sympathies. They wished the new township which came into overnight being to be called Varina after the wife of Jefferson Davis, but a Unionist clerk wrote "Virginia" in the datelines of the first state papers and Virginia City it remained to confuse several generations with Virginia City on Nevada's Comstock Lode. Montana's Virginia City in its roaring days (*center*) was the stronghold of the notorious Sheriff Henry Plummer whom vigilantes unmasked and promptly hanged as one of the boldest highway robbers of the old West. For a time Virginia City was capital of the by then State of Montana but in 1875 the boom town of Last Chance Gulch (*below*) later known as Helena wrested the seat of government for itself and the Virginia City *Madisonian* pettishly reported that the state government departed hauled "by a mongrel outfit of poor mules and lank cayuses." Helena's once rich deposits of precious metals declined with time but its recovery of copper ore soared to make it a citadel of copper. The photograph, taken in gold rush days of 1870, shows a ten-mule hitch guided by a jerkline or single rein held by the muleskinner.

(ALL PICTURES) WESTERN COLLECTION

The Latter-day Saints Went West the Hard Way

UNION PACIFIC RR.

Of all the well-defined groups which emigrated to the American West in the years before the railroad, the Mormons had incomparably the worst time of it. Driven from their holy city of Nauvoo on the Mississippi in dead of winter for a variety of causes secular and religious, some understandable and others preposterous, they made the long journada halfway across the American continent to Salt Lake in the face of the hostility not only of the land and elements but also of what population there was in the West of 1846. Once established, their kingdom extended from the Wasatch Mountains to San Bernardino and west to the foothills of the Sierra. No photographs of the original exodus exist, but this one, taken of a group of Mormon emigrants newly arrived at Coalville, Utah, twenty years later, is typical of their transport. In the below drawings Brigham Young, the Mormon's eminently respectable businessman-president is shown attending religious services in the Mormon Tabernacle at Salt Lake and at the bottom, the section specially reserved for his wives. Tourists after the completion of the Pacific Railroad who stopped off in Salt Lake for a study at first hand of polygamy invariably found it the best ordered, most prosperous and least exciting city of the West, qualities it has retained to this day.

N. Y. PUBLIC LIBRARY

That so large a portion of the life of the West should have been passed in saloons is an aspect of frontier times that has always fascinated the connoisseur of human misconduct and the amateur of robust and gaudy doings.

"In my time," remarked Wyatt Earp when once rebuked by some do-gooder for spending most of his waking hours behind swinging doors and practicing all his profession there, "there were no Y.M.C.A.'s." And that is as good an explanation as there is of the saloon life of the nation as it was conducted from the Mississippi to Market Street in the years before the railroad. But that is by no means the end of the story. The saloon and strong waters continued to be the most important social and in some ways economic aspect of the West long after respectable women and the clergy arrived on the scene and domestic existence became at least tolerable. Exclusive of the blacked-out barrel houses which are today known as "cocktail lounges," a slimy euphuism for the forthright "saloon" or more refined "buffet," a ponderable part of the life of the West is still conducted in premises presided over by men in shirt sleeves whose principal stock in trade makes the customers feel better than they did. The skeptical might resolve disbelief any time by a short stay in such communities as Carson City, Virginia or Las Vegas in Nevada, a commonwealth where the mortmain of the past is strong and whose inhabitants know that, as no less a notable than Lord Byron put it, "Man, being reasonable, must get drunk."

In the cow and mining towns which represented the concentration of population in the mid-nineteenth century in the open spaces, the staging companies and banks had their agencies in saloons just as later the bonanza railroads and telegraph stations were in barrooms and as, in more modern times, the automobile stage stations are associated with restaurants everywhere. The prostitutes of the town solicited trade in the music halls which were the annex of the saloons, and the arts as represented by music, plays and variety, were domiciled in a theater that was also an adjunct of a saloon. In the barrooms, in thousands of frontier towns, were the only touches of urbanity the community boasted: rich upholsteries, fine glassware, noble plate-glass mirrors, crystal lighting fixtures, carpets and comfortable furniture. The best food was served at their buffets and lunch counters and the hands were encouraged to keep their feet off the marquetry tables and be more accurate in the matter of cuspidors. The saloon, in contrast to the contrived nastiness of today's dismal emporiums of underproof spirits decorated in spurious *moderne* and orchestrated to the sentimental sewage of juke boxes, were resorts of cultivation, sophistication, comfort and comparative good manners. Shooting out the lights was a custom honored far more in the breach and beating up the girls was frowned on, a pastime viewed today as the merest commonplace in the Hollywood scheme of things.

Unlike the saloon, firearms, once universal in the days before the iron horse, tended gradually to decline in the railroad age and, eventually, practically to disappear from the once heavily heeled West save on the persons of constituted guards and peace officers. This is not to say that the modern rancher may not maintain a fully stocked gun room in his home and a loaded revolver in the glove compartment of his car, but the universality of sidearms began to decline as their need abated and this was accomplished in most localities when gamblers ceased to be gunmen and when law and the jurisdiction of courts became tolerably established.

In the earliest times of the railroad, not only was every plainsman, townsman of

118

the prairies, banker, roulette dealer, tradesman and city marshal of the West distinguished for the weight of armament he displayed, but a businessman or tourist from the East almost invariably boarded the cars of the Pacific Railroad at Chicago or Omaha with a Smith & Wesson revolver at the very least in the side pocket of his Gladstone or carpet bag. The father of one of the authors of this book, a Boston banker in the seventies, invariably went abroad in the West armed with a copy of Young's *Night Thoughts,* a square-faced bottle of Lawrence's Medford rum and a Starr's navy revolver in his valise.

It is notable that in the earliest gold camps of the Mother Lode weapons other than sporting arms were unknown for several years and currency and bullion were commonly left unprotected until an influx of Spanish gunmen, Mexican bandits, ticket-of-leave men from the British penal colonies of the Pacific and plain home-grown thieves and murderers made armor a protective necessity. The Texas cowhands who, along with the frontier marshals, were later to become the archetypal gun wielders and saloon fighters of the Southwest, had little use for revolvers away from the Mexican border save to shoot rattlesnakes until they came in contact with the chuck-a-luck hells and birdcage dives of the Kansas trail towns. "The long treks to markets and railheads," wrote Robert J. Casey, "brought the sheltered cowboy off his lone pray-ree to strange, ruthless communities where there were only two sorts of citizens—the quick and the dead. All of which considerations made it apparent to the waddie that he had better freshen himself up on the manners and crafts of the people into whose company a changing world had thrust him."

Next to the Texas border and the cow towns frequented largely by Texans in Kansas such as Abilene, Dodge and Hays Cities, probably the most gun-conscious communities of the early days were to be found in Arizona and along the Nevada-California boundary. Tombstone was forever immortalized by the Battle of the O.K. Corral involving the Earp Brothers and Doc Holliday and the followers of Ike Clanton, but even more famous for its gunfire and violent ways was Bodie, a mining town which flourished for three bloody decades in California's Mono County near Bridgeport. Bodie had no Bat Masterson or Wild Bill Hickok to lend it evil fame, but the record of its uninhibited ways gave origin to Mark Twain's "Bad Man from Bodie" and John Hays Hammond later deposed that when he once spent a week in Bodie in the late sixties there was a fatal shooting or stabbing every night with time off for the Sabbath.

The generality that the coming of the railroads abated gunfighting found a notable exception in Wyatt Earp's Southwest for it was from the vestibule of a Southern Pacific passenger train in Tucson that Earp ventilated Frank Stillwell, his brother's murderer, with a 10-gage-sawed-off shotgun. And no railroad ever entered Bodie from the outer world to diminish the gunfire that nightly resounded in the bars of the Bodie House, Stewart's or the Arlington Hotel.

SWIFT & CO.

VII

Longhorns

The Railheads Advancing Across Kansas Evoked the Great Texas Trail Herds, the Roaring Towns, the Cow Pokes and the Gaudiest Chapter in the Gunfire Epic of the Southwest

As a generality, the coming of the railroads brought a degree of law and order to the communities of the West. Determined ranchers, homesteaders and merchants rode in on the cars, often accompanied by families and other abatements of uproar, and the pioneers, the grizzled prospectors and riffraff fringe either departed for more remote havens of individuality or conformed, in a rough and ready way, to the more obvious conventions. Statutory courts, of a sort, succeeded the vigilantes. Substantial structures rose in the towns. The girls moved

120

across the tracks for greater privacy and, for the same reason, started hanging curtains in their windows. A degree of decorum, not too much, perhaps, but enough to outrage old-timers, came in on the cars.

The great and flaming exception to all this was when the railroads started building into Kansas and brought in their wake a civilization of unabashed license and tumult that overnight made the Kansas cow towns the most consistently violent chapter in the whole gaudy Western epic.

The pioneer Kansas railroads, the Kansas Pacific, the Santa Fe and the Union Pacific, did, to be sure, bring with them an almost unbelievable prosperity, both for still distant Texas and for the railroad towns themselves. Robert J. Casey in his *The Texas Border* has estimated that during the two decades when the great trail herds wound out of Texas bound for the Kansas railheads and loading pens, 10,000,000 longhorns were driven to the shipping points and brought $200,000,000 in minted gold into the pockets of Texas and Kansas, an almost stupefying sum in the purchasing power of the time. And, in a part of the world that was still essentially frontier, such wealth was followed by a wild and wonderful way of life that was never paralleled by the gold camps of the Mother Lode or even suggested by the silver-spangled Comstock.

It made the cow towns of Kansas an outpost of Texas away from home. They were for the thirsty cowhands what Paris was to become for Americans during the twenties, only with spurs and handguns. It evolved a gorgeous generation of peace officers whose notables included Frank, Virgil and Wyatt Earp, Bat Masterson, Tom Smith, Wild Bill Hickock, Charlie Bassett, Neal Brown and Bill Tilghman. It made death in the afternoon or any other time of day or night a commonplace and justified the seeming extravagances of a subsequent three-quarters of a century of fiction, newspaper features and the ultimate celuloid triumph of art, the cinema Western. Neither Abilene nor Dodge City in written or acted form has ever even approached its great original.

Kansas was the one place where the railroads brought in full tonnage of trouble and solid trainloads of it. Less than carload lots didn't count.

The first railroad to serve and exploit the longhorn cattle trade which was to become the hallmark and major preoccupation of Texas until the coming of oil was the Kansas Pacific which, in 1867, was reaching westward from Kansas City through Topeka toward Denver. Notwithstanding its right of way was more than 800 miles distant from Corpus Christi where the cattle drives had their origin, the Kansas Pacific and its connection, the Hannibal & St. Joseph, and its close follower, the Santa Fe, were destined to be fully as important in the social and economic history of Texas as were the railroads which later crossed the Red River and actually operated within the bounds of the Lone Star State. And they were to provide a pageant unmatched in the annals of the frontier.

Milepost forty of the westering Kansas Pacific Railroad was set out in 1867 at a hitherto unremarkable town in the Kansas prairie named Abilene, and thereafter for five roaring years Abilene was, by geographic paradox, the most important city in Texas. It also established itself imperishably in the legend of the American West. Abilene was for that period the closest railhead to the great cattle-grazing grounds of East Texas and over the famed Chisholm Trail, named for the half-breed Cherokee Indian who laid it out, there came the first of the fabulous cattle drives which in themselves are an epic in the conquest of the American continent.

LIBRARY OF CONGRESS

OUT WHERE THE WEST WAS BEGINNING

The building of the Kansas Pacific Railroad immediately after the Civil War was a comparatively simple task as the level Kansas plains obviated engineering difficulties and ties and tracks were often laid with no grading whatever. Fort Riley, Kansas, milepost 136 west of Kansas City, now a township of 3,500 persons, might not recognize this pastoral moment in 1868, but the railroad was even then heading for the roaring towns of Abilene and Hays City. Past this cottonwood grove more than a million longhorns were to pass in the next five years bound for the packing houses of Kansas City, St. Louis and Chicago.

KANSAS HISTORICAL SOCIETY

SADDLE & SIRLOIN CLUB

THE CHISHOLM TRAIL

Most famous of the traces followed by the long-horns to the northern railheads was the Chisholm Trail running from Corpus Christi, Texas, to Abilene, Kansas. Named for the Cherokee half-breed cattle king, durable old Jesse Chisholm, it abounded in perils, outlaw rustlers, Indians, drought and panic, brought on by storms at night. The portrait of Chisholm is a putative one, no original likeness being known, from the collection of Chicago's Saddle & Sirloin Club.

WESTERN COLLECTION

CULVER SERVICE

ACROSS THE RED RIVER WHEN THE MOON RIDES HIGH

Getting the longhorn herds across the rivers of Texas on the way to the railhead towns of Kansas was one of the calculated operational risks of the cattle trail. Some trail riders like hard-riding Jesse Chisholm liked a night crossing as shown in the contemporary drawing above. The film version of a river crossing, in this case the name river of the story (*below*), is from Howard Hawkes' Monterey production of *Red River*, a screen story based in its characterization at least, on the person of Chisholm himself.

"RED RIVER"

WESTERN COLLECTION

FOR CATTLE RUSTLERS: A NECKTIE PARTY

During the free-wheeling years between 1867 and 1871 more than a million longhorns were driven over the Chisholm Trail and its variants from East Texas to Abilene. Often they were attacked *(above)* by rustlers and border cattle thieves whom the Texans invariably identified as Mexicans. Herd riders defended themselves with Sam Colt's patent revolving pistols which had been introduced to the Texas Rangers a few years previous by Captain Samuel Walker. In the complete absence of statutory courts, rustlers when caught faced short shrift at the end of a rope. As the railroads advanced, their telegraph poles were found *(below)* to possess advantages in this function over cottonwoods. Frontier justice was one of the most fascinating aspects, to contemporaries, of the old West.

WESTERN COLLECTION

SANTA FE RR.

CULVER SERVICE

SHOOTIN' NEWTON

When the ambitious Santa Fe Railroad reached Newton, Kansas (*above*), wildest of the cow towns, in
1871, it was recorded by Joseph McCoy in *Historic
Sketches of the Cattle Trails* that "as many as
eleven persons were shot down in Newton in a single evening." It was in the cow towns of Kansas that
the words Texas and gunfighter became synonymous. Railroading, too, was wild and free and railroaders rolled their teapot locomotives with a jug of
Old Reprehensible on the cab deck. Below are frontier gamblers in Newton and a daytime, and therefore more placid view, of the town's main street of
the period. Newton's spacious and wicked ways became only a memory a few years later when the railroad forged westward to Dodge City.

KANSAS HISTORICAL SOCIETY

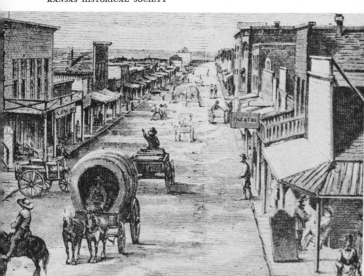

In its first months the Kansas Pacific's traffic was almost entirely carload lots of whisky, coaches full of gamblers, mopsies and madness, gambling apparatus and firearms, all the personnel and artifacts necessary to the establishment of a progressive frontier town. After that for five years its traffic was almost solely in the legendary longhorn steers which antedated the current shorthorn breed. In 1867 it carried 35,000 longhorns to the processing plants of Chicago and St. Louis. Next year the total was 300,000 and in 1871, its last year as a major industry, the K.P.'s teapot locomotives hauled 600,000 steers from the loading pens. Elsewhere, however, the trail herds were to be big business for another decade and a half.

The Texas cowboys who drove the herds north turned Abilene after their arrival to the wildest, most riotous town in the entire frontier record. They regarded Abilene as part of Texas and exercised to the full their established right to murder, mayhem, whisky by the gallon and uninhibited chaos. In six months its principal thoroughfare, Texas Street boasted twenty saloons, twenty gambling establishments, ten dancehalls and an unrecorded number of bagnios. There was also a lunch room and a general store.

PRELUDE TO PAY DAY

Abilene's principal junction, Main Street and Douglas Avenue, saw heavy traffic (*right*) when a trail herd hit town and the hands with gold in their pockets headed for the cow town's saloons, bagnios and fandango houses. The more prosaic business of loading the stock cars of the Kansas & Pacific Railroad (*below*) suggested material for a sketch in *Leslie's* by their western artist.

CULVER SERVICE

CULVER SERVICE

LIBRARY OF CONGRESS

WHERE THE BUFFALO ROAMED UNTIL THE RAILROAD CAME

Hunting buffalo from the steamcars was considered a prime sport in Kansas frontier days. "In the dark of the evening the great mass of animals could scarcely be distinguished from the prairie itself save for the flash of gunfire," wrote a correspondent for *Leslie's*. "A little in advance of the engine they closed with the track and ran into the fire of 200 guns. It was a race for life." The rich buffalo meat was left to rot on the plains but a considerable source of railroad revenue *(below)* was the tanning of buffalo hides and their shipment East for sleigh robes.

KANSAS HISTORICAL SOCIETY

SWIFT & CO.   N. Y. PUBLIC LIBRARY

FRANK LESLIE'S ILLUSTRATED NEWSPAPER

NEW YORK, JANUARY 29, 1881.   PRICE 10 CENTS.

ON THE LONE PRAY-REE

The most notable single contribution to the body of American folklore, the cowboy, was created or at least his character conditioned and modified by the advent of the cars. Partly fact and partly picturesque fiction, the cow hand of the Texas plains and the Kansas-bound trail herd, together with his guns, his pony and his inexhaustible capacity for uproar became a symbol of the romantic West of the nineteenth century. Above is shown an old-time cow hand practicing the *expertise* of his calling. At the right, and of sufficient public interest to occupy the entire front page of an issue of *Leslie's,* the then equivalent of the front page of *Life,* is the archetypal hand on the way to town, shooting out the telegraph insulators as he goes, while below he takes over a Kansas cow town for an evening of innocent mayhem and manslaughter.

CULVER SERVICE

The Alamo Saloon—all place names in Abilene showed it to be a mere output of Texas—maintained a staff of twenty-five bartenders on each of three eight-hour shifts seven days a week and its three orchestras played deafeningly right around the clock. The railroad brought in municipal riffraff from as far away as New Orleans and Boston, and Kansas shook at the impact of their gunfire and continual uproar and violence. Wyatt Earp, most celebrated of all frontier peace officers, was instructed to abate murder when possible but under no circumstances to interfere with the general merriment which was absorbing fantastic sums in gold eagles from the cowhand pay rolls. In Dodge City the pearl-gray derby and gold-mounted cane of Bat Masterson became a deceptive legend of elegance.

Presently it was found more convenient to load the longhorns at neighboring Hays City and then at Dodge, on the Santa Fe Railroad, where Earp again was marshal. Throughout the seventies the Kansas Pacific and the Santa Fe divided the cattle trade between them as it shifted to meet various conditions to Hays, to Newton, to Wichita, and Ellsworth. By 1879 when the Jay Gould interests merged the Kansas Pacific with the Union Pacific system the great days of the cattle drives were over, although they continued in diminishing numbers for another decade, but Abilene remained in the memory of the West as the wildest and most rambunctious of all the many outposts of Texas.

IN ABILENE'S TENDERLOIN

The rough-and-ready manners and morals of the Texas trail hands didn't altogether commend themselves to Abilene's respectable element and the now standard phrase "the other side of the tracks" came into the language when, at the command of Wyatt Earp, the town's love stores were moved to the south side of the Kansas Pacific tracks, an arrangement which for many years thereafter prevailed in frontier communities. "Hacks ran day and night to this addition," wrote a contemporary Kansas historian. "Money and whisky flowed like water downhill and youth and beauty were wrecked in that Valley of Perdition." The glad hurrah here depicted filled readers of the *New York Illustrated News* for 1869 with misgivings.

N. Y. PUBLIC LIBRARY

LIBRARY OF CONGRESS

CONTRIBUTING TO THE WESTERN LEGEND

To a certain extent the American cowboy of the nineteenth century was the creation of correspondents and pictorial artists for Eastern newspapers and magazines. Waddies in Texas learned that they invariably entered saloons on horseback, that gunfire accompanied their every waking moment and that tenderfeet

LIBRARY OF CONGRESS

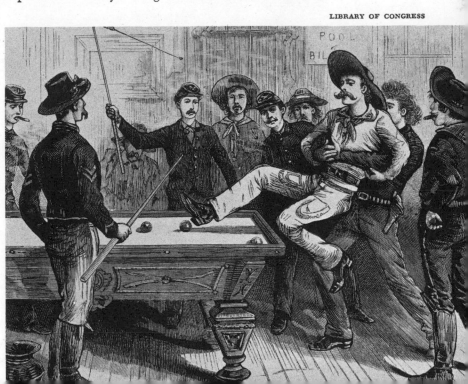

from the effete East were welcomed with ceremonies combining the best features of hell week on the campus and crossing the equator on shipboard. Being obliging, the cow pokes were ready to live up to their billing. Horses, hitherto tethered at hitch-racks, began appearing in saloons. Gunfire increased notably and at Elko, Nevada, the cooperative natives and a group of tame Utes staged an Indian uprising every time the train pulled in from the East. Tourists carried grim tales of bloodshed and violence back to drawing rooms in Beacon Street and on Murray Hill. In these drawings from a contemporary issue of the *Police Gazette*, trail hands from Texas are shown cutting capers in the pleasure domes of Ellsworth, Kansas, at the end of the drive.

LIBRARY OF CONGRESS

WESTERN COLLECTION

COW TOWN VIGNETTES OF THE SIXTIES

Frontier justice on the long trail from Texas to the Kansas railheads (*above*) was inclined to informality and a quick hanging of rustlers was felt to be salutary. In towns like Abilene where Wyatt Earp (*above*) was the most durable and long-lived of all city marshals the formality of justice wasn't overpowering. " 'The marshal will preserve strict order,' " said the judge in a contemporary news account. " 'Any person caught throwing turnips, cigar stumps, beets or old tobacco quids at this court will be immediately arraigned before the bar of justice. Trot out the wicked and unfortunate and let the cotillion commence.' The judge looked severely at the crowd and hitched his revolver a little to the left. He then surrendered the throne of justice to the Rev. John Walsh of Las Animas and stepped across to Hoover's for a drink of old rye." The longhorns in whose name justice was so frequently invoked, once safely in the pens at Abilene (*below*), boarded the stock cars of the Kansas Pacific for the long ride to St. Louis or Chicago.

CHICAGO HISTORICAL SOCIETY

ARMOUR & CO.

THE PACKING INDUSTRY ALSO RODE THE CARS

During the seventies the Missouri-Kansas-Texas Railroad evolved a "palace stock car" (*above left*) for hauling prize cattle to market and about the same time "Tiffany's Summer & Winter Car" (*upper right*) was the first refrigerator or reefer car built for G. F. Swift, the Chicago packer. Below are shown Philip D. Armour, founder of another great packing dynasty, and the Hough House, celebrated temple of beefsteaks in Chicago's first Stockyards. At the bottom of the page is a contemporary sketch of Armour's first packing plant in Kansas City in 1874.

CHICAGO HISTORICAL SOCIETY

BURLINGTON LINES

N. Y. PUBLIC LIBRARY

THE STOCKYARD LEGEND

The legends of the Chicago Stockyards in the nineteenth century (*above*) and the cattle auctions which took place there (*right*) are as earthy as the primitive methods of slaughter and meat packing. "Did you actually once work in one of those places where the roast beef comes from?" a dowager in a Gold Coast drawing room asked the great and gusty J. Ogden Armour. "My sweet lady," replied the T-bone tycoon, "I am busily re-writing the stately biography compiled about me by my family to tell how I once pushed a wheelbarrow full of entrails in a slaughter house with the guts forever trailing out and getting caught in my hobnail boots."

CULVER SERVICE

Now forgotten railroads which flourished wealthily during the days of the trail herds were the St. Louis, Kansas City & Northern, the Leavenworth, Lawrence & Galveston and the Missouri, Fort Scott & Gulf. When the Missouri-Kansas-Texas reached Denison it connected with the Houston & Texas Central and did a roaring business in the longhorned beef critters so long as the steers were shipped alive to Kansas City, St. Louis and Chicago. Today, with the packing industry in process of decentralization and small packing plants maintained nearer the grazing lands, the stock extra is largely disappearing and its place being taken by refrigerator cars. But once along the single tracks of the pioneer railroads into Kansas the teapot locomotives rambled westward ahead of ornate coaches loaded to the platforms with dangerous gunmen and blowsy madames and headed back toward the East with the wealth of Texas in T-bones in their long lines of hand-braked stock cars, where the drovers aroused the tired longhorns to their feet at tank stops with long poles thrust through the car sides and hence gained the immortal name of cow poke.

UP TO DATE

The first trail herds to wind dustily out of Texas in 1867 saw 35,000 longhorns headed for the loading pens of Abilene in a single year. Today, Kansas City's stockyards (*right*) can handle 175,000 head a day, each of them the equivalent in meat of nearly two of the original longhorns. Instead of the teapot engines of the Kansas Pacific, stock extras are largely handled now by Diesel units such as that of the far-flung Union Pacific shown below.

KANSAS HISTORICAL SOCIETY

UNION PACIFIC RR.

WESTERN COLLECTION

With the completion of the Pacific Railroad the United States came of age and achieved its continental dimension. An era of fabulous prosperity rode the steamcars as the West became available to all.

VIII

Toward Promontory

When the Gold Spike Was Driven at Promontory Point Manifest Destiny Was Realized, the Continent United, the Once Impervious West Open to All Seekers and Finders

THE ACHIEVEMENT of almost any transport facility in the nineteenth century was of necessity hailed with triumphant superlatives and crowned with the ornaments of oratory. The Erie Canal, in its time truly a wonderful undertaking, was universally known as "The Work of the Age." Somewhat later the completion of the Ohio & Mississippi Railroad evoked such mutual congratulations among all concerned that the beholder might have been excused for associating it with one of the better established wonders of the world. In 1832, somewhere in between these two earth-shaking events, the first horse-drawn rail omnibus was run through the streets of New York and at a monster municipal banquet that evening Mayor Walter Browne proclaimed: "This event will go down in the history of our country as the greatest achievement of man," while the *Courier & Enquirer,* greatly daring next day forecast that "the completion of this road will make Harlem a suburb of New York."

Obviously these breath-taking monuments to progress left very little in the way of rhetoric available when the most momentous achievement of them all actually came along, but the speakers at Promontory Point in May of 1869 and the nation's press the next day did what they could with the adjectives still at their disposal, which was considerable. The completion of the Pacific Railroad, one was informed at every hand, was the keystone of the Union, the final ornament in Columbia's already gem-studded crown, the bridge between the hemispheres and the through-bolt that would conjoin East and West in indissoluable alliance. Largely it was indeed all these things, although a more temperate generation where oratory is concerned, inclines to smile at the rotund similes evoked.

The Pacific Railroad, as the joint trackage of the Union and Central Pacific Railroads was generally known, was also a great many things that have been smeared, defamed and discredited by rancid little men in a later generation who were unable to abide the notion that anyone should make a profit out of their labor, resolution and risk of their material resources. It remained for moralists in an age of government boodling of hundreds of billions to the benefit of nobody to remark unfavorably on the sometimes questionable business ethics of a generation which netted an occasional dubious million while enlarging the national wealth a thousand-fold.

The Pacific Railroad, incidentally to forming "the keystone of the Union," created a number of amiable and upholstered millionaires whose florid tastes and uninhibited hospitality have always raised the blood pressure of little men born too late to get in on a good thing. A more realistic and humorous enemy of the Big Four of the Central Pacific during their lifetime was Ambrose Bierce who once, upon seeing the portly figure of Governor Leland Stanford disappearing behind the swinging doors of a San Francisco saloon, remarked to a companion: "Within those gilded portals the plunderers and pillagers of the people are taking their ease among rich surroundings and every appointment of luxury. The loot of a nation is being spent to fill their glasses with rare vintages and their plates with costly viands. I would that I were one of them."

The story of the building of the Pacific Railroad has already been retold so frequently and in such authoritative detail that its repetition would be redundant even if space permitted in this picture chronicle, but there are aspects of it which, even at this late remove, cannot fail to engage the interest of students of railroading and the West. Unlike the Erie Canal, which was undertaken in a surge of excitement, and the Baltimore & Ohio which broke ground with ceremonial hurrah, the Pacific Railroad got under way in something resembling obscurity and only achieved national fame and attracted world attention when well on its way toward completion. The first rail at the Union Pacific end of construction was laid and the first spike driven with a minimum of display at Omaha, the starting point of the line, on July 10, 1865. Ground had been broken at Sacramento for the start of the Central Pacific's track, a year and a half previously when Governor Leland Stanford, who was also the railroad's president, turned the first shovel of dirt at the junction of K Street and the Levee.

Actually the Central Pacific began to pay off long before its completion as a link in the transcontinental line. Agricultural products from the Sierra foothills, mine products from the diggings of the Mother Lode and, eventually, from the Comstock Lode in western Nevada became profitable carrying while the railroad was only a stub line probing into mountains and the desert regions of the West. The Big Four who built it were in the blue chips before they ever encountered their own monopolistic big bonanza.

At the western end of the route, the Central Pacific, at the beginning, received only adverse publicity from opponents of the road who christened it the "Dutch Flat swindle" in the belief that its backers while pretending to continental aspirations, actually intended to tap only the Nevada bonanzas and build a stub line no further than the foothills of the High Sierra. Aside from in Washington and the road's own offices and among its officials in New York and Boston, the Union Pacific was hardly reported at all in its formative stages.

In mid-August of 1865, however, nearly two years after its beginnings in Sacramento, the Central Pacific got a break. Speaker of the House, Schuyler Colfax, journeyed to the West to see and report to Congress the progress being made and was able to visit the end of track at the point named Colfax in his honor. With him were two astute newspapermen from the East, Samuel Bowles, editor of the influential *Springfield Republican*, and A. D. Richardson, a reporter on the staff of Horace Greeley's *New York Tribune*. Immediately impressed by the magnitude of the work already accomplished and assured of its continuance by the witness of grading operations far in advance of track and supplies on hand sufficient to refute the Dutch Flat rumors, both men filed extensive dispatches to their home offices. Grading crews, reported the *Tribune* on the right breakfast tables a morning or so later, were working a full twenty-five miles ahead of construction. A gang of 4,000 Chinese at the grading end were hard put to keep ahead of the bridge gangs and rail layers which followed in their wake. The rails would be into Salt Lake, the then envisioned goal, within three years.

Bowles, a Yankee and impressed with figures and solvent balance sheets, pointed out that the Central as of that date, had $6,000,000 in Government bonds in its vaults in Sacramento with which to finance its future activities and had already netted half a million on its operations between California tidewater and the ever extending end of track. State Street back in Boston was gratified and interested.

From that time until the completion of the project nearly four years later, the transcontinental railroad never lacked publicity, all of it good.

Most of the implications of the meeting of the rails have by this time been embedded in the national legend and, indeed, all but a few of them were obvious enough at the time. To be sure most of the contracting parties thought of the transcontinental railroad more as a link with the Orient than as an agency of intracontinental commerce, and many among those present that wet and windy day in Utah were fully persuaded that the expense of construction would effectively prevent the building of any other rail connection with the Pacific and that the Overland route would remain the unique highway between East and West for generations to come.

138

he Far-Reaching Southern Pacific Had Modest Beginnings

When Collis P. Huntington (*below*) and his Sacramento partners in the hardware business started to build the Central Pacific into the foothills of the Sierra their enemies in California politics called the venture "the Dutch Flat Swindle," intimating that it was planned as no more than a stub line to tap the traffic of the Mother Lode and connect with the wagon freight lines to the Comstock in Nevada. They declared the end of the line would be at Dixie Cut near Gold Run (*left*) and that only the gullible believed the "Big Four" intended to build across the High Sierra.

(ALL PICTURES) SOUTHERN PACIFIC RR.

The First Central Pacific timetable (*below*) listed service for mail, freight and passengers only as far as Newcastle, thirty miles out of Sacramento, while the first structure erected by the company that was destined to create millionaires by the score was a shack at Sacramento which served as tool shed and ticket office combined. The railroad began making handsome profits before it reached the summit of the Sierra.

CENTRAL PACIFIC RAILROAD.
NO. 1, TIME CARD NO. 1.
To take effect Monday June 6th, 1864, at 5 A. M.

TRAINS EASTWARD.			STATIONS.		TRAINS WESTWARD.		
t and Pass No 3	Frt and Pass No 2	Pass & Mail No 1.			Frt and Pass No 1	Pass & Mail No 2.	Frt and Pass No 3
P M leave	1 P M leave	6.15 A M, L	Sacramento.........		8.45 A M arr	12 M arr......	6.40 P M ar.
50 } mt frt 55	2.15	6.55........	Junction.........	18	3..........	11.20.......	5.55 } mt. Ft 5.50
09.	2.38	7.05........	Rocklin.	4	7.40	11.07........	5.37
22	2.55	7.15 meet F.	Pino...........	3	7.15 mt pass	10.56	5.25....
40	3.30 P M arr	7.30 A M arr	Newcastle.........	6	3.45 A M, L	10.30 A M, L	5 P M, L

Trains No. 2 and 3 east, and 1 and 3 west, daily, except Sunday.
Trains No. 1 east and 2 west, daily.

LELAND STANFORD, President.

Into the High Sierra the Engines Smoked and Pounded

SOUTHERN PACIFIC RR.

Much of the atmosphere of railroading in the sixties is caught by this yard picture of the Central Pacific at Colfax. The bearded train crew, the wood fuel, link-and-pin couplings supplemented by cables for emergencies and the spidery handcar, all are typical of the operations and properties of the period. Visible, too, is the corner of a passenger coach ornately decorated in the Eastlake style. In an age innocent of earth-moving machinery the vast fills essential to mountain railroading were built by Chinese laborers with hand barrows and mule-drawn tipcarts as shown at the lower left. As soon as passenger service reached that far, all trains paused briefly at Cape Horn high in the Sierra Nevada (*below right*) so that travelers might enjoy the awesome view of the American River thousands of feet below.

SOUTHERN PACIFIC RR.

Above Cisco They Rolled Through Lengthy Snowsheds

WESTERN COLLECTION

Snowsheds (*upper left*) solved some of the problems of the wintery Sierra and above Donner Lake at Cisco. The one in the foreground is in process of construction, still lacking its final timbers. In stretches where snowsheds were not practicable, ponderous rotary plows (*upper right*) powered by as many as four of the wood-burning locomotives of the era (*below*) cleared the track after each storm. No grades encountered by the Union Pacific building west from Omaha were comparable to those in the High Sierra and the storms which raged around them in winter months. As late as the winter of 1952 the high passes above Norden were closed for days on end and the de luxe *City of Sanfrancisco* spectacularly stalled in the drifts.

The Rails Followed the Truckee River Into Nevada

N. Y. PUBLIC LIBRARY

In constructing its line through the Sierra the Central Pacific's timber crews sent their completed ties down log shutes to the tracks where Chinese tracklayers (*above*) rushed them to the railhead. Below a Chinese road gang hitch a ride to the nearest town for Saturday night. At the bottom is the lumber town of Truckee, last stop on today's passenger trains before crossing into Nevada.

SOUTHERN PACIFIC RR.

COLLECTION OF DUNCAN EMRICH

As its rail advanced eastward across the Nevada desert the Central Pacific encountered Indian trouble, mostly in the form of braves stealing rides on freight cars. Here a party of Pah-Utes are having a rough time at the hands of a husky C.P. brakeman while the conductor and rear shack look on apprehensively from a sort of primitive caboose. Later the railroad gave passes to all chiefs and allowed lesser tribesmen to ride the rods unmolested. Many perished in the freight wrecks which were common occurrences in early times.

Few visitors to "The Biggest Little City in the World" today would recognize Reno's North Virginia Street (*below*) the year the Southern Pacific's first trains began rolling through for the East. Company engineers had originally located the townsite in 1868 as a division point on the railroad. Over the bridge in the foreground raced Wells Fargo's ponies with mails for the Comstock and over it, too, were dragged the first locomotives for the Virginia & Truckee Railroad built the year this picture was taken.

SOUTHERN PACIFIC RR.

Westward From Omaha Reached the Union Pacific

N. Y. PUBLIC LIBRARY

From its depot at Omaha (*above*) the rails of the Union Pacific commenced their westward march across the Nebraska plains. The station platform itself fascinated artists of the period who never tired of depicting its ever-changing crowds of frontiersmen, trappers, Eastern capitalists, Jewish pack peddlers, holidayers and the military. In the center of this busy scene, gold stock salesmen press their prospectuses on a well-dressed traveler from the East while a monocled Army captain with his pretty wife pauses en route to Fort Laramie. The desolation of the prairie where the rough ties were laid (*below*) was viewed by Samuel B. Reed, the U.P.'s construction engineer. At the lower right Irish track gangs push the railhead forward.

UNION PACIFIC RR.

(ALL PICTURES) UNION PACIFIC RR.

This re-creation of a frontier community in railroad construction times was erected in the Utah desert for the filming of the documentary epic *Union Pacific* directed by Cecil B. DeMille. Its every detail was painstakingly correct down to the last spike maul and brands of whisky in its bars. Rolling stock was authentic U.P. passenger coaches of the period secured from Omaha; locomotives were Virginia & Truckee old timers faithfully converted to the style of the sixties. In 1867 the end of track was passed by this wagon train at Archer, Wyoming (*below*) while at the lower right a deep cut is shoveled out by hand at Bitter Creek.

The U.P. Iron Stretched Across the Great Plains

UNION PACIFIC RR.

Travelers on the Overland Route recognize Green River, Wyoming, from the car windows by Cathedral Rock reaching skyward from behind the town. When the Union Pacific engineers were building their bridge across the Green River itself (*above*) it looked the same. The stonemasonry of Green River bridge was laid with hand cranes (*below left*) and construction crews lived in the rough hotels and shacks (*below right*) that lined the town's main and only street.

(TWO PICTURES) CULVER SERVICE

Eastern readers liked to hear about the perils of the West, particularly the menacing redskins, and magazine editors aimed to gratify the taste. Here a Union Pacific construction gang is standing off a Sioux war party somewhere west of Laramie, Wyoming, and making a dash for safety aboard a handcar. In the actual record massed and organized attacks on railroad workers were rare, and General William T. Sherman was of the opinion that whisky was a deadlier weapon against Indians than the rifle. At Laramie on the plains travelers of the seventies were familiar with the giant windmill which supplied the U.P.'s locomotives with water (*below*) but which has long since vanished.

But for all the obvious symbolism of the Golden Spike which President Leland Stanford was to drive and at the last moment missed, and despite the minor contretemps of a ceremony hastily arranged at a desolate upland infinitely further removed from the resources of civilization than the same spot would be today, the episode of Promontory Point * remains a vignette pleasantly etched in the national consciousness, an episode of the ever diminishing frontier forever recorded in the silver bromide of Colonel Charles Savage's collodion photographic plate. Probably, indeed, the familiar print, its participants and properties happily concentrating upon what is indisputably a bottle of champagne, is the most important single photographic record of the United States in the nineteenth century. In it were all the elements of greatness, resolution and rough humor that made the sixties what they were: the untidy regimentals of the Twenty-First Infantry; the polished Eastern manners and poise of Vice President Thomas Durant of the Union Pacific, the mahogany private Pullmans of the important executives, the newspaper reporters and photographers, the patient Chinese, the dishwashers from the local eating houses and the delegation of strumpets from Promontory's Virgin Street. Edwin Sabin, official chronicler of the event, describes them as "a quota of furbelows."

The circumstance that nothing went altogether right at Promontory—the ceremony itself was a day delayed, the weather atrocious, several of the dignitaries who should have been there such as Oakes and Oliver Ames, Charles Crocker and Brigham Young were absent, the telegraphic arrangements less than perfection— but reflected the difficulties and inconveniences of the time and place. From then on and through the agency of the steamcars the difficulties and inconveniences of the West would be in decline. If the telegraphic relays were snarled at Omaha and soggy track delayed the Union Pacific's special party for a full day along the way, these were but faint echoes of the days, not more than a decade before, when the Overland Mail required a full thirty days for its transport from Sacramento to Salt Lake and when the Pony Express messenger often arrived at the next station with Pah-Ute arrows lodged in his person and harness.

The old West was passing and the symbols of transition were Dr. Durant's and President Stanford's mahogany fitted business cars, the toasts drunk in vintage French wines from silver coolers at the conclusion of the ceremonies and the presence of news reporters and photographers with facilities for the instant transmission of intelligence to the farthest reaches of the continental empire. The pattern of Western life as it was to obtain until the coming of the first Pope-Appersons was shaping up.

The echoes and repercussions of Promontory had begun at least to the west of Utah some hours before the actual event they celebrated. San Francisco had gone on the assumption that the work was to be completed on the ninth and acted in this belief. Every shop, office and commercial establishment in the city hung up its shutters not to reopen for three full days. The reverse was true of the saloons in Montgomery, Sutter and Market Streets which arranged hastily for extra shifts of barkeeps, waiters, swampers and other functionaries to accommodate a press of business which immediately reached tidal proportions. A monster parade of celebrants progressed intermittently through the lower city for two days, pausing when the marchers needed refreshment and reforming after suitable rites had been ob-

---

* Historic Promontory Point near the northern end of Great Salt Lake is not to be confused with Promontory Point, a siding on the Southern Pacific eighteen miles west of Ogden and visible today from main-line trains.

served. From the dreary wastelands of Northern Utah Leland Stanford, apprised by telegraph of the premature demonstration, tried vainly to abate it with wires telling newspaper editors that it was all a mistake. Tomorrow was the day. San Francisco celebrated tomorrow and the next day, too.

At Sacramento, a hundred miles or so nearer to the source of news, cooler heads prevailed until the proper time when scores of extra trains brought in ranchers, miners and other countryfolk from miles around as guests of the railroad and to celebrate its completion with urban tumult. At Omaha a hundred field pieces spoke from Capitol Hill and a parade was formed whose like was never again seen in the Nebraska capital until nearly seventy years later when the film spectacle *Union Pacific* was first presented with three days of jollification which set an all-time high in a decade when such promotional extravagances were frequent and sometimes approached the cost of *Union Pacific's* launching: three quarters of a million dollars.

New York also exploded a hundred cannon but added piety to noise by singing a *Te Deum* at Trinity which was followed by a thunderous rendering of *Old Hundred* on the chimes in the steeple. Liberty Bell was tolled in Philadelphia; in Salt Lake Mormons and Gentiles joined in a service of thanksgiving at the great Tabernacle; in Chicago Vice President Schuyler Colfax headed a mile long procession which wound for hours in and out of saloons and restaurants, and in Washington a gold ball suspended from a pole high above the dome of the Capitol was released by magnetic impulse from Promontory Point itself and fell while a thousand silk hats waved and the people cheered outside the East Portico.

Filled as is the West with ghost communities, none is more ghostly than Promontory Point, upon which once and briefly the eyes of the world were turned. For a time, until through cars from Chicago to San Francisco were standard practice on the Overland run, passengers stopped over to change from the cars of the Union Pacific to the Central. The length of the stop was determined by a number of variables and often the travelers had ample time to patronize its saloons and blazing red-light district. Trains arrived and departed at all hours and the bars and love stores obligingly operated on a twenty-four-hour basis for the accommodation of visitors. Promontory Point gamblers were notable for their rapacity and the dispatch with which they cleaned the unwary, sometimes allowing an otherwise penniless and shorn lamb to retain five dollars to keep him in victuals until he reached the other end of the line.

Promontory's economic decline—it had long since, according to universal report, reached a moral nadir—began with the inclusion of through Pullmans in the consist of the *Overland Express*, predecessor of today's *Overland Limited*, so that only the most venturesome and resolute descended from the cars to investigate the town's possibilities. Helper engines and freight crews operated out of Promontory for a time but in a few years Ogden was made the junction of the two railroads and Promontory's fortunes declined even further.

In 1905 the Lucin Cutoff bridging Salt Lake was built and all important traffic routed over it at great saving of time and money; only occasional freights passed where once the engine pilots had touched head to head. During the Second World War the rails were torn up and the town itself disappeared completely.

Today Promontory appears on only the most inclusive maps. The cement obelisk marking the site of the Golden Spike stands alone in one of the most desolate imaginable landscapes.

Fatefully the Rails Converged on Promontory Point

Drawn by the locomotive *Jupiter*, the Central Pacific's special train from Sacramento spent the night before the ceremony on a siding at Monument Point overlooking Great Salt Lake. The steward went hunting and Leland Stanford's party had sage-fed quail for dinner. Tank car is an auxiliary for the engine's tender.

May 10th dawned wet and windy and Leland Stanford's private car and a baggage car filled with refreshments were pulled to Promontory Point by the *Jupiter* in the rain. Several dignitaries had taken cold and precautions, in bottled form, were taken against the elements by everyone.

The band of the Twenty-first Infantry from Fort Douglas under Major Milton Cogswell serenaded the *Jupiter* damply as it arrived at the scene of the ceremony.

(ALL PICTURES) SOUTHERN PACIFIC RR.

From the East, the U.P., From the West the Central

The Union Pacific's official cameraman mounted his box and exposed a collodion wet plate from the cab roof of No. 119 to get this view of the participants in the ceremony a few moments before the last spike completed the railroad. Town of Promontory Point was to the right and behind the photographer's back.

Cattlemen and ranchers from Utah's Box Elder County rode in in force to take part in the big doings and milled about as a railroad official hoisted an American flag to a nearby telegraph pole.

The Union Pacific's official photographic car, complete with darkroom for loading plates and developing them, and with Photographer J. B. Silvers aboard sported a pair of stag's antlers on the roof above its forward platform.

The Rendezvous at Promontory as the Camera Saw It

LIBRARY OF CONGRESS

The most important single documentary photograph in the annals of the old West was taken by Colonel Charles Savage, a Salt Lake photographer, as the engine pilots met after the driving of the Gold Spike at Promontory Point, Utah, May 10, 1869. Three weeks later, with remarkable fidelity of detail and spirit, it appeared fresh from the copyist's bristol board in *Leslie's*. Not for another generation was the half-tone process to become a commonplace in the reproduction of photographic prints.

N. Y. PUBLIC LIBRARY

And as Respectability Later Skirmished with Fact

CALIFORNIA HISTORICAL SOCIETY

Although Colonel Savage's wet plate is the standard record of Promontory and one of the world's most celebrated news pictures of all time, it never quite pleased Leland Stanford, President of the Central Pacific. For one thing, he wasn't in it. For another the picture seemed raffish, uncouth, and to a man in politics, a trifle boozy. At least three bottles showed in the photograph and the presence of others was strongly suggested. Stanford therefore commissioned Thomas Hill, an understanding artist to re-create the scene in a cleaned-up version which should plainly depict Stanford, always a candidate for public office, in association with the Rev. Todd who spoke the invocation. Stanford's commission also stipulated the inclusion of a good many people who had conspicuously not been at Promontory: the long dead Theodore Judah, first engineer of the railroad, Collis Huntington who was in New York at the time, Charlie Crocker and Mark Hopkins, who had been in San Francisco, and Brigham Young, who had emphatically refused an invitation when the railroad avoided passing through Salt Lake City. Upon its completion the massive scene included seventy likenesses painted from life, making it one of the greatest portrait studies in the history of art. Stanford refused to accept it. Several persons he thought might be useful to him politically were placed behind people of less importance. It hangs today in the State Capitol at Sacramento, a bogus re-creation of one of the epic carouses of American history.

Emergence of a Boom Town in the Utah Desert

N. Y. PUBLIC LIBRARY

COLLECTION OF DUNCAN EMRICH

By the time the trains were rolling through Promontory Point on regular schedules, pausing often for several hours to transfer mail and baggage from the cars of one railroad to the other, the shack and tent town had taken on lurid overtones of hurrah. Passengers descending from the cars were warned by train crews against the three card monte experts (*above left*), the prostitutes and the wild ways, generally, of the citizenry. Yokels wandering into cowboy resorts provoked tumult and indignity. This one (*above right*) thoughtlessly carried an umbrella in parts unaccustomed to such city ways and the waddies had sport with him.

The unwary dude who wandered into the Switch Key Saloon in a top hat could confidently rely on an enthusiastic reception at the hands of the committee on arrangements.

COLLECTION OF DUNCAN EMRICH

Promontory's main street, shown here in photograph and artist's impression, was practically all "on the wrong side of the tracks." It boasted the Echo Bakery & Restaurant and the Pacific and Sunny Side hotels, the latter a tent, while only moderately screened from view were the abodes of "the girls" who had moved in from Corinne down the line when that once roaring town was relegated to a flag stop.

Eighty-five years after its great day, only the decaying ruin of its post-office and general store remain of Promontory. Gone are the tracks. Gone are the shell-game artists and the girls who met all trains. If the shades of Leland Stanford and the Rev. Todd of Springfield haunt the spot they have cold and windy haunting to do. And if ghost trains roll across the Utah uplands at midnight, their spectral crews must still be warning passengers against the birdcage game in the Palace Saloon. "The dice are crooked," they admonish, "and the whisky is watered, and as for the girls; well, sir, you'd do better to stay aboard the cars."

SOUTHERN PACIFIC RR.
LUCIUS BEEBE

CULVER SERVICE

Travel aboard the Zulu cars possessed a community of interest not shared on the luxury cars. A New World lay ahead and the Old World behind the Westward-rolling trains.

IX

Zulu No Jug

To the Immigrants From the Old World the Zulu Cars Were a Passage to Illimitable Futures in Iowa and Oklahoma, Nebraska and Dakota, Wherever the Rich Land Called

BETWEEN the years 1870 and 1895 the population of the United States increased by more than 31,000,000 persons. Of this enormous advance a total of 10,339,000, or almost exactly one-third was represented by immigration from foreign countries, the vast preponderance of which was from the countries of Europe and less than a tenth from the rest of the known world. Over this same period Germans constituted precisely double the number of immigrants arriving from the country of next importance which was Ireland while the English and Italians followed in that order. Sweden was by no means negligible with a total of 660,000 expatriates and Hungary sent a quarter million. The Irish had already arrived in uncounted numbers before the beginning of the Civil War, driven from the Old Country by the great potato famine of 1845 and the years following.

By the year 1870 when this census count began, the railroads of the United States had opened all of what is generally known as the Middle West and were rapidly making available the Far Western states to colonization, farming and homesteading. No precise figures are available as to the exact distribution of these more than 10,000,000 new citizens or of the additional hundreds of thousands who were deserting New England, Pennsylvania and Ohio for lands adjoining to or west of the Mississippi, but the United States was during this entire period overwhelmingly an agricultural country and in 1890 it was estimated that there were 3,000,000 persons of foreign birth living in rural communities in states served by the Burlington Railroad, mainly Iowa and Nebraska, alone.

The railroads had brought the continental United States as it is known today into being and now they undertook to populate them. The record of that accomplishment is the record of the greatest mass movement of peoples in known history.

The primary objective of the granger railroads serving the agricultural states west of the Mississippi was the sale or other disposal of the lands acquired from the government in the form of land grants during their construction. Secondarily, but eventually of far greater importance, was the colonization of these lands with industries and thrifty people the products of whose toil should in years to come furnish the revenue freight which was to be the railroads' lifeblood. It was a long-range project of heroic proportions for which the railroads never received the full credit that was their due.

The technique of colonizing vast regions by private agencies and without the persuasion of the government or the force of the military was entirely new. It had to be evolved from scratch and depended altogether on the imagination and resolution of its entrepreneurs.

Certain factors favored the railroads in their efforts to settle the government grants in the West. Immigration into the United States was free and unrestricted by law or national quotas. All a native of Germany or Ireland had to do was secure the price of passage in steerage aboard a North German Lloyd liner or a Cunarder and, in a few cases, avoid creditors or the police, to step ashore a few weeks later at Ellis Island or Boston, a free man to choose freely from the variety of lives open to him. It was sometimes more difficult to emigrate from Russia or Poland, but easy ingress at this side of the Atlantic was available to all.

The problem which confronted the granger railroads was to persuade newcomers of the superior advantages of western colonization in opposition to the inducements offered to remain in the industrial East. The steel mills and mines of Pennsylvania and Ohio were booming and incessant in their demands for raw labor from Italy, Bohemia or Russia. The Irish were in requisition all the way from Boston to Chicago in capacities ranging from hod carriers to policemen. The French were wanted as lumberjacks in Maine and weavers in Rhode Island and the demand for Swedish domestics and German carpenters and artisans was universal. Getting emigrants past the eastern seaboard was a problem.

In the end the railroads solved it by a vast and highly successful campaign of education carried on in their home countries long before the new arrivals ever saw the American sky line.

The pioneer railroad in the technique of colonizing farmlands was undoubtedly the Illinois Central which, as early as the middle fifties, had undertaken a campaign to advertise Illinois, which spread from Maine to Florida. Seductive posters detailing the agrarian enchantments of Illinois were mailed to a list of 100,000 selected farmers, and others were fixed to the walls of post offices and country groceries. Advertising space was bought in papers with wide rural circulations throughout New England, New York and New Jersey, and news stories, in a manner that would have done credit to a professional promotion man of 1952, were placed with friendly editors of magazines and farm journals. Car cards were inserted aboard the horsecars of New York City and artful superlatives were evoked in free literature of amazing variety.

The results were stupendous. There was an exodus from New England which terrified and amazed the home guard in Vermont, Maine and Massachusetts. The value of rural real estate declined in some localities as much as 40 per cent and credit for the disaster was given solely to Illinois and the Illinois Central, although the opening of the California gold fields may have had something to do with it. New Englanders who remained at home may have found it more satisfactory to ascribe the apostasy of friends and relatives to the comparatively conservative agricultural allurements of Illinois than to the wholly abandoned and probably chimerical follies of Hangtown and Angel's Camp.

Heartened by these successes, the Illinois Central then turned to Europe itself with a corps of professional spellbinders who hymned the lyric glories of the Illinois soil and seduced the peasantry with tales of crops and fertility that suggested they had stopped at Blarney Castle en route. These campaigns were somewhat successful before they were interrupted by the Civil War, but they showed the way to new vistas of potentiality which were quickly to be exploited by other railroads once the shooting had stopped.

The Illinois Central showed the way in other aspects of colonization, too. It demonstrated that it was to the profit of colonizers to be generous in the matter of land for schools and churches and to be lenient with foreclosures when lean years came upon the farmers. These lessons also were taken to heart when the railroads of the postbellum years came to populate the seemingly unlimited farmlands west of the Mississippi.

After the completion of the Pacific Railroad in 1869 and the opening to settlement of the last frontiers of the continent, competition for the favor of emigrants from the Old World became cutthroat. The principle railroads engaged in this internecine strife were the Northern Pacific, the Union Pacific, the Burlington and the Santa Fe and to a slightly lesser extent the Missouri-Kansas-Texas.

Most enterprising of these in many ways was the Santa Fe (then the Atchison & Topeka Railroad) whose land agents and missionaries abroad carried the promotion and publication of western farmlands to heights never before essayed. One of its greatest triumphs was the securing as customers for its Kansas land grants of a group of 2,000 Menonites who arrived at Ellis Island in 1874 and, contrary to the custom of most such arrivals, brought with them $2,000,000 in gold drafts from Russia. The Santa Fe, as further inducement to these thrifty folk, chartered an Atlantic liner to hasten to Russia and bring over their personal goods and any other Menonites who might have heard the good news. It promised to haul building material for the colonists free for a year and it got the Governor of Kansas to promise them, since they were of a pacifist persuasion, immunity from military service. The Santa Fe got the Menonites.

Europe at one time was showered liberally with Santa Fe literature and books printed in a number of languages; French, German, Danish, Russian and Swedish were rushed into print containing graphic accounts of nature's positively spendthrift endowment of the Kansas and Nebraska countryside. It was delicately suggested that corn grew a great deal taller under the benevolent democracy of the New World than under the tyranny of various kings, dukes, czars, sultans and prime ministers. An exception to these innuendos was always made, however, in the matter of Queen Victoria who had invested heavily in Kansas real estate and was obviously as good as any other Chase County taxpayer.

Upon one occasion somebody in the Santa Fe promotion department erred gaudily when he had published an elaborate brochure entitled *The San Juan Guide.* Since the nearest the Santa Fe ran to Colorado's remote San Juan country was Pueblo, the Denver & Rio Grande's narrow gage fairly coined money taking immigrants and their possessions from Pueblo west to Alamosa, Durango and Silverton. Barlow & Sanderson's stages got the rest who wanted to get to Santa Fe town when the railroad of the same name stopped temporarily at Trinidad.

Other roads than the Santa Fe were offered inducements to get settlers along their rights-of-way. The Northern Pacific was abysmally land poor and at one time engaged the services of an English clergyman to recruit farmers from among the stalwart yeomanry of the Tight Little Isle. A group of Englishmen arrived and settled themselves in Minnesota in what they were pleased to name the Yeovil Colony, whereupon an anonymous pamphlet was circulated in the community under the title "Advice from an Old Yeovilian." It assured them in positive terms that the whole thing was a mistake. Minnesota, according to the pamphlet, was a harsh and inhospitable climate wholly unsuited to agriculture of even the crudest sort, and was possessed of inclement weathers that were fit for neither man nor beast, and the Yeovilians would be well advised if they removed forthwith to some more auspicious region, say Kansas, Nebraska or even Missouri. Northern Pacific detectives traced this scoundrelly tract to the colonization departments of the Union Pacific, Burlington and M-K-T and were able to expose the villainy just in time to prevent the Yeovilians, naive bumpkins that they were, from heading out of Minnesota forever.

The Burlington & Missouri River Railroad Company, most important antecedent of the Chicago, Burlington & Quincy, kept whole corps of promoters, lecturers and spielers touring the continent of Europe in the interest of inducing settlers to locate along its line in Iowa and Nebraska and such up-to-the-minute devices as stereopticon slides stampeded the peasants of Bohemia, Germany and the Scandinavian countries aboard the steamers and crowded the Zulu cars for years. Like other rival railroads, the Burlington encouraged the immigration of entire townships and communities or whole religious congregations in the assurance that these homogeneous groups would be more contented in their new surroundings. They were seldom mistaken.

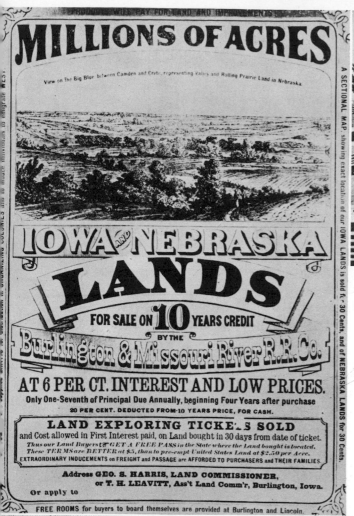

Such railroads as the Burlington and the Illinois Central flooded the old countries of Europe with the pictured likenesses of American farms such as the one shown above, each an abode of prosperity and plenty with the life-giving railroad running handy to serve all needs. For home consumption in the United States posters (*left*) painted in glowing terms the resources of the seemingly illimitable West and promised easy terms of credit to homesteaders who wished to settle on the railroad's land. The settlers came in millions.

BURLINGTON RR.

CULVER SERVICE

As potent as any factor in the decision of ambitious European peasants and farmers to try their fortunes in the New World were the to them substantial sums sent back to their families by emigrants already established in America. Here an artist shows Irish citizens of New York withdrawing sums from the Emigrant Savings Bank to send less fortunate relatives in the Old Country.

A LONG FAREWELL TO THE OLD COUNTRY

Lured by the promise of American plenty and persuaded by the propaganda of the railroads, Irish emigrants at Cahirciveen, County Kerry, board the stage which will take them to the dockside at Queenstown for the voyage across the Atlantic.

N. Y. PUBLIC LIBRARY

Beyond compare the most influential of the prophets of Western homesteading was Horace Greeley whose exhortation to youth to set its face Westward is classic. Uncle Horace's immortal line is popularly supposed to have been uttered when he was charged five dollars for a shave in Central City, Colorado, by the town's stylish barber, the Count Murat. The possibilities of the frontier had never been so forcefully illustrated to the *Tribune's* editor. Greeley knew the West at first hand and founded an agricultural community named for himself elsewhere in Colorado. Once when his train over the Monon Route broke down in Indiana he helped propel a handcar forty miles to keep a lecture engagement extolling the wonders of California. A folksy and homey editor with acute political ambitions, Greeley is here shown receiving a delegation at his home at Chappaqua, New York. Such rustic interludes contributed notably to the Greeley legend but failed to elevate him to political office.

Castle Garden Was the Gateway to the Western World

THE ROUTINE OF IMMIGRATION

Throughout the last three decades of the nineteenth century an unending river of emigrants attracted by the railroads' promise of land on easy terms and abundance and security as a matter of course poured into Castle Garden (*above*) in New York harbor, and to a lesser extent at Boston and Philadelphia. A bewildering variety of nationalities was screened by agents for the granger railroads of the West and passed through the formalities of immigration in a day which knew nothing of quotas. Now and then there were misunderstandings about such matters as smallpox vaccination (*center*) but soon racial characteristics and national garb such as that of the Sicilians at the bottom of the page began to blend into the American scene and much of the color of individualism was shed with the steeple hats of County Mayo and the pantaloons of the Hollander. On the page opposite an artist for *Leslie's* follows the newly arrived peasants from Greece and Bohemia through the routine of immigration until at last they board the cars of the Erie Railroad bound for the promised wonders of the Western land.

N. Y. PUBLIC LIBRARY
SANTA FE RR.

ring EMIGRANTS FROM AN INMAN STEAMER TO THE CASTLE GARDEN BARGE.

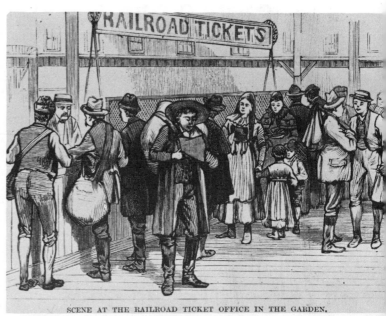

SCENE AT THE RAILROAD TICKET OFFICE IN THE GARDEN.

EXAMINING EMIGRANTS AT CASTLE GARDEN.

REGISTERING EMIGRANTS AT CASTLE GARDEN.

EMIGRANTS EMBARKING AT THE RAILROAD STATION IN NEW YORK FOR THEIR NEW HOMES IN THE WEST.

Day and Night the Zulu Cars Rolled Slowly West

LIBRARY OF CONGRESS

The Zulu cars which rolled Westward in the immigrant years had sleeping arrangements of a sort and were better upholstered than the regular coaches of eastern trains. Families and unmarried women were assigned one car, single men to a second and Chinese to a third. Trains stopped regularly at eating places and basic supplies such as tinned beef, coffee, towels and soap were peddled through the cars by news butchers. There were long halts and delays while scheduled trains ran around them, but homeseekers of a given nationality tended to band together and with the aid of musical instruments, bright expectations and mutual encouragement the trip was not too rigorous. Robert Louis Stevenson recalled that aboard the Zulu car in which he first went West was a misguided cornet player who repeated the depressing strains of "Home, Sweet Home" by the hour until a hard-looking traveler roared, "Stop that damned thing. I've heard enough of that. Give us something about the good country we're going to."

CULVER SERVICE

WESTERN COLLECTION

Bunting, oratory and the music of brass bands accompanied the departure (*above*) of a trainload of immigrants bound from Chicago to Horace Greeley's agricultural community in Colorado. In the picture below, silk top hats, peasant headdresses and working men's rough attire are represented in a group of homesteaders beside a Central Pacific train stopped at Mill City, Nevada, en route to California in 1880. The railroad was active in colonizing the fertile San Joaquin and Sacramento Valleys.

SOUTHERN PACIFIC RR.

All Nationalities Came to Build the Railroads

WESTERN COLLECTION

Large numbers of emigrants from Europe were employed in the railroad construction boom of the seventies and eighties, some of them on the very railroads whose promotion had brought them to America. Aboard the triple-decker bunk cars of the Great Northern (*above*) numbers of Irish and Germans went to build the line west from Minot, N.D. When the rails reached the mountains the cars were sawed off to fit the tunnels. When their enduring qualities and docility were discovered, large numbers of Chinese coolies were imported to help build the Central Pacific. They boarded the cars at Oakland pier (*below*) and in a few hours were grading and filling at the end of track in the High Sierra.

SOUTHERN PACIFIC RR.

N. Y. PUBLIC LIBRARY

YOUTHFUL BRANDS FROM THE BURNING

A novel experiment in colonization saw this group of wayward youths from the Earl of Shaftsbury's reform school in England traveling over the Erie for resettlement at College Farm, Wakefield, Kansas.

Occasionally the railroads ran into bad luck in their schemes for colonization and such catastrophes of nature as dust storms, grasshoppers or prolonged droughts made a seemingly promising region impervious to agriculture or industry. On such melancholy occasions the carriers packed up their charges and their belongings and relocated them in some more favorable portion of the still roomy West.

The origin of the name is lost in the mists of antiquity, but immigrants were traditionally carried by the railroads in Zulu cars. At first the Zulus were the oldest day coaches the line possessed with a common cookstove installed at one end and primitive plumbing at the other. In the eighties, however, there came into vogue a specially designed sleeper with double berths in each section but devoid of any mattress or bed linen. At the end of the run the car cleaners simply turned the hose on and washed the interior down. Nobody had any delusions about the sanitary habits of foreigners.

Zulus brought all their worldly possessions with them and the railroads carried it all free. If there were livestock a boxcar was supplied and Grampa or his Nevvy rode with the cow in approximately as much comfort as the folk in the sleeper. Forwarding agents for the immigrants liked to get their cars as far ahead in the train as possible so as to ride with less motion and jerking. In a day before tight-locking draft gear, the end car was no bargain. The agents made a practice of putting out a jug of Old Reprehensible for the train crew, and brakemen chalked the good or bad news on the side of the car: "Zulu Jug," or "Zulu No Jug" as the case might be for the guidance of switchmen. Rule G hadn't come to stay in those days.*

* Rule G is the universal rule governing the use of intoxicants by railroad employees on duty.

One railroad which contributed substantially to the population of the Far West without plan or premeditation was the Central Pacific. As is detailed elsewhere in this volume, Charles Crocker, in charge of the Central's construction gangs in the wintry Sierra, hit upon the idea of coolie labor and so successful was the scheme that before Promontory was achieved the railroad had imported several steamerloads of "Crocker's pets" from the large Chinese colonies which came into being on the Pacific Coast. In Nevada, Chinese track-laying gangs were still grading and spiking twelve years after Promontory when Darius Mills built the Carson & Colorado and considerable trouble was experienced with native American labor when the management employed large numbers of Celestials from Carson and Virginia Cities when the Virginia & Truckee was building. When the era of large-scale railroad construction drew to a close the Chinese gradually retired to the more domestic capacities today associated with them. In Sodaville, Nevada, after the completion of the C. & C., a community of Chinese for many years fiercely resisted all attempts to reconstruct their morals or introduce them to even comparative respectability. The town was widely celebrated for its opium dens, and venturesome travelers and prospectors weekending at Belleville or Candelaria often formed slumming parties to venture into wicked Sodaville for a skirmish with the pipe and poppy.

Most determined of all the colonizers of the West was James Jerome Hill who, acting through the agency primarily of his Great Northern and incidentally through the Northern Pacific and Burlington, set about settling Minnesota, the Dakotas, Montana and all the remaining Northwest with such energy that he failed to consider any of the agricultural and industrial limitations of his empire and brought ruin and grief to thousands whom he hoped to establish.

The legend of Jim Hill is a legend of irresistible resolution to evolve civilization from a wilderness, to populate it to his own and the general profit and to make a million blades of wheat grow where none had grown before and where, unhappily, none would for many years bloom again. Stewart Holbrook believes Hill actually considered himself as much of an empire builder as Genghis Khan or Napoleon without taking the trouble to see what became of their empires. Certainly his personal and business way of life was imperial and he handed on somewhat milder delusions of grandeur, so that for three full generations the Hills were national legends and a local saga in St. Paul where they lived.

A more modest empire builder, General Palmer of the Rio Grande had dreamed of a railroad that should unite Colorado, a single state, geographically and economically, connecting her mines and manufactures, creating these where none had before existed and bind the whole into a coherent usefulness whose character was to be determined by his own well-ordered and disciplined concept of society.

Hill was infinitely more ambitious. By sheer driving and unabated energy he created the Great Northern from small beginnings, drove it relentlessly across the continent to a Pacific terminal, acquired control of the Burlington and Northern Pacific and, linked in bonds of gilt-edged financial matrimony with the royal house of Morgan, set about populating and putting to use nearly a quarter of the American continent. Hill's dream of linking the Great Lakes with Puget Sound by a railroad uncontaminated by politics and the chicane of land grants was brilliantly achieved. His dream, too, of commerce with Japan through whose agency the Great Northern's cars should roll westward filled with wheat and manufactured goods

168

for the Orient while going east with lumber was eventually realized. It was his agricultural and colonial dream of populating the entire expanse of wasteland between the Twin Cities and the Pacific that came a cropper.

His colonization was conducted in a stupendous manner. To induce settlers on the lands along the railroad he dispatched literally hundreds of agents to Europe to persuade the yeomanry to emigrate to the United States. He imported the finest blooded cattle, gave away millions of bushels of grain for seed, instituted agricultural fairs, congresses and chatauquas where the most modern methods of dry farming and animal husbandry were circulated and free instruction given in every conceivable branch of agriculture. He gave prizes for the tallest corn, the fattest steers, the most productive acres, the richest milk and the biggest vegetables. He advertised his railroads as "The Route of the Big Red Apple" and "The Route of the Great Big Baked Potato." His experts toured Minnesota, Idaho and Montana preaching the gospel of bigger crops and more land under cultivation while Hill himself waged intermittent war with the Harriman forces over even more territory for his railroad empire.

Part of the Hill dream turned into nightmare after homesteaders, induced by Hill's promotion, had placed under cultivation a full million acres in Montana alone and proportionally almost as much in Montana and the Dakotas. Its weakness was an imperfect understanding of the effects of cultivation in a part of the world where the wind never stops blowing. An agricultural device known as "the summer fallow" came into favor by whose terms a given field or territory was harvested one year and allowed to be unproductive, that is, to lie fallow the next, on the theory that by this means the scant moisture that fell during a given season would be absorbed to make the soil doubly profitable on alternate seasons. This practice, of course, necessitated twice the acreage to produce a living for a given farmer, but land was the most easily available of all commodities and the unthrifty practice achieved a wide vogue. Better a crop on half their acres, said the farmers, than no crop on any of them at all.

The disaster inherent in all this lay in the fact that, during the fallow summer, when the surface soil was carefully broken up and freed of weed growths, it was ruinously sensitive to wind. The rich topsoil began blowing away in formidable dust clouds. The process accelerated to become a pestilence. Soil blowing, as Joseph Kinsey Howard has remarked, is factually a disease and it was one which wiped out millions of acres and hundreds of thousands of settlers in Jim Hill's empire of the Northwest. The settlers departed; the railroad's haul of agricultural products declined alarmingly, the good earth continued to blow away until an entire readjustment of agriculture, based on more mature science and knowledge of climatic habits, was accomplished throughout much of the stricken region.

Jim Hill's empire exists today but its feudal obligation to the railroads which brought it into being is largely abated. "Population without the prairie is a mob," was one of Hill's favorite axioms, "and the prairie without population is a desert." The population, in modified numbers, is still along the right of way of the Great Northern but it is not Hill's original emigrants from Norway and Sweden. And the prairie, too, is still there, right up to the tie ends, but it has changed materially since the first ties were laid. But, after all, what, in the economic profile of the United States in that period, has not?

Points of No Return Were Many in the Old West

WESTERN COLLECTION

THE JUMPING-OFF POINT FOR THE BLACK HILLS

In the Union Pacific depot at Omaha (*above*) emigrants bound for the Black Hills region were urged to do their last minute outfitting before leaving civilization for the wilds. Arrived at the nearest point on the railroad to their destination (*below*), they boarded the coaches of the frontier staging lines and headed cheerfully into the vast regions of the as yet untamed West.

WESTERN COLLECTION

Homeseekers Jammed All Trains for the Cherokee Strip

ROCK ISLAND RR.

The Cherokee Strip in Oklahoma was opened by the Federal Government for colonists to "enter and occupy" in 1889 and the move inaugurated one of the last great land rushes of the West. As the deadline approached trains of the Rock Island Railroad (*above*) were poised at Caldwell, Kansas, the roofs and interiors of their cattle cars jammed to bursting with eager homesteaders ready to pour across the line at the signal. Thousands were carried in a single train. Below is the Santa Fe's depot platform at Guthrie, Oklahoma, after the first trainload of immigrants had arrived. More than 40,000 settlers and expansionists fought desperately for homesites and business locations.

CULVER SERVICE

Jim Hill's Dream of Agricultural Empire Was Realized

Here an artist in somewhat lyric mood depicts "the settler's first home in the West" with the suggestion that, for all its satisfactions, better things are in store.

Where building materials were not available, the sod house was the rule. This Custer County, Nebraska, family of the eighties is far from badly off with a deep well and two spans of horses proudly included in the photograph to show their prosperity and the children neatly dressed. By virtue of the Burlington Railroad, Nebraska was a Hill feudal state.

In this moving photograph of a Nebraska pioneer family who have achieved the estate of a frame dwelling and windmill the patriarch has brought out the black-framed photograph of his dead wife so that she too may be in the record of success and happiness. He wears the ribboned badge of a pioneer society with his family grouped around while the hired hands remain respectfully in the background.

WESTERN COLLECTION
NEBRASKA STATE HISTORICAL SOCIETY
NEBRASKA STATE HISTORICAL SOCIETY

THE BIBLICAL HUNDREDFOLD WAS ABUNDANTLY RETURNED

The kind of landscape most admired by hard-bitten old Jim Hill was one like this: "The Dalrymple Farm in the valley of the Red River of the North—formerly a barren prairie." Hill's Great Northern Railway promoted products from its territory in window displays (*below left*) and an agricultural exhibition train (*bottom left*) toured the country to encourage homeseekers to migrate to the Northwest. When six-foot wheat was grown on Great Northern farmlands the greatest of the empire builders and his son Louis W. Hill, president of the road (*lower right*) were the first to be photographed with the visual testimony to the bounty they had brought into being.

(FOUR PICTURES) GREAT NORTHERN RR.

LIBRARY OF CONGRESS

The completion of the Pacific Railroad opened vistas of adventure and the free life of the plains and mountains to thousands to whom the West had before been but a dream. They came aboard the cars to seek gold, to exterminate the buffalo and build homes in the new land.

X

The Railroad West

Aboard the Cars Came the West of Fiction and the Colt's Equalizer, of Discovery by Eastern Editors and English Milords and an End to the Buffalo Grass and the Buffalo

THE PIONEER West whose character was to undergo such an over-all change with the coming of the railroads as to be almost unrecognizable as the same continental locale has left less of an impress upon the general imagination than it has upon scholars, students of historic matters and specialists in its various

174

related fields of information. The reason is at once obvious and valid. The railroad West was exploited, publicized, depicted and visited by an almost overwhelming number of professional reporters, artists, scientists, magazine writers and mere tourists who, to a large extent, created the West in the form already shaped in their own imagination, a sort of parody of caricature of the original West which came to be accepted as legal currency of folklore within a few years. The literature concerning the railroad West is limitless, easily available and written for vast popular circulation. The literature of the old West is limited in extent and availability, because the men who saw the actuality were few and their reports were not in any modern sense of the word devised for popular consumption.

The *Journals* of Lieutenant Zebulon Pike, Catlin's *Letters and Notes* on the Indians, Farnham's *Travels in the Great Western Prairies,* Parkman's *California and Oregon Trail* and a host of reports, surveys and journals by government agents, religious scouts, land company prospectors and even professional foreign explorers and scientists, all combine to form an impressive bibliography of the old West which was influential in its time and has been informative since. But compared to the railroad West created in the universal mind by the pen-and-ink artists of *Frank Leslie's Illustrated Newspaper* and the dispatches to the *New York Daily Tribune,* not to mention the columns of the *Official Police Gazette,* the *New York Illustrated News,* and the semifiction of Beadle and Adams forbidden and, therefore, universal dime novels (the English "penny dreadful" is more colorful) the West which made its way into government offices in Washington and onto library tables of gentlemen in Louisburg Square made a very poor running. It was, indeed, never in the money.

The entire profile of the Western American continent underwent a land change with the completion of the Pacific Railroad, and after Promontory, the West as it has ever since been established in universal fancy, the West of cattle and mineral wealth, of cowboys, peace officers, bonanza kings and the horseback life of the plainsman, was confirmed and given identity.

In actual fact the West of the pioneers, of Meriwether Lewis and Jim Bridger, of Peter Skene Ogden, Lucien Fontenelle, Peg-Leg Smith and Etienne Provost had disappeared almost three decades previously. The last great summer rendezvous of the fur traders, the Mountain Men and Long Hunters, the spacious years of the American Fur Company and the Hudson's Bay factors were already a legend.

Buffalo still roamed the plains in vast numbers to be slaughtered by passengers aboard the steamcars, and in the Dakotas, Montana and New Mexico, Indians still did the scalp dance when their hearts were bad, but the railroad brought a new order and what was more, it established the new order in the mind of the entire world.

The old points of no return and trading posts: Bent's Fort, Bayou Salade, the South Pass, Fort Union and Brown's Hole, disappeared from the maps to linger only in the memories of old men, and new vicinages crowded the news and the general imagination: Laramie, Cheyenne, Green River, Corinne and, briefly, Promontory itself. Independence was no longer the entrepot of the Western World; it was now Council Bluffs. The Long Hunter was supplanted by the frontier marshal, buckskin fringes gave way to broadcloth tail coats; Wells Fargo Company's route agent took over where once the bourgeois of the Astorians had reigned supreme; the Henry and the Sharp's were outmoded by the Winchester magazine rifle and Colt's patent equalizer.

All these changes either coincided with the railroad or were consequent upon it, and their establishment was certified by the surge of tourists, settlers, travelers, newspaper reporters and artists of illustrated periodicals which flowed Westward out of Omaha over the Union Pacific rails. Where once the Long Hunters had taken their beaver plews for the American Fur Company, the skinners now shipped buffalo hides to the East by way of St. Louis and the hand-braked boxcars of Kansas Pacific. Where Kit Carson and, mightiest of all the Mountain Men, and Jim Bridger, at mention of whose name a beardless generation may stand and uncover, had taken scalps from Blackfeet and Arapaho, English milords with ratcatcher suits and beautifully custom-built rifles went helling after antelope while their pony carts clattered behind laden with the best Stilton cheeses and tawny Port.

The West of Dick Wootton and Benjamin Eulalie de Bonneville had been depicted for a rigidly limited clientele by such artists as Alfred Jacob Miller and excitingly reported by Washington Irving in his *Astoria* published in Philadelphia in 1836, but now the photographic camera was frightening what was left of the Indians, and reporters for James Gordon Bennett's *New York Herald* were telling the customers all about the red-light district in Kansas City, which was considerable. Times were changing.

In addition to the reporters and the tourists, however, the railroads immediately began importing a degree of urban sophistication and the devisings of the ever crescent machine age to regions where morality had hitherto been almost exclusively Mosaic and the wooden butter churn the ultimate in domestic mechanization. Coal-oil lamps, whalebone corsets, wire bustles, mechanical harvesters, self-cocking revolvers, safety lamps for miners, Tom and Jerry machines, cookstoves from Malden, Massachusetts, and alarm clocks from Waterbury, Connecticut, baking pans, egg beaters and patent apple parers, derby hats, cam-set watches for men and chatelaines for women, Brewster wagons, Macassar hair oil and lightning rods and, only a few years later, gang plows, flush toilets, high-speed telegraph instruments and the Kock's patent barber chair, all contributed to altering the facade of the railroad West. The Chicago mail-order catalogue was discovered to have an infinity of uses denied the family Bible.

Cities of brick and stone, where the region afforded, began to appear here and there on the plains and prairies, although the false wooden front, wooden sidewalk and sheet-iron roof remain in many places to this day as testimonials to a simpler architectural urge. Everything was not only up to date in Kansas City, but also in Denver, Omaha, Salt Lake, Virginia City, and, of course, San Francisco.

By the early eighties, a scrutiny of the files will disclose the beginnings of a disturbing phenomenon in the reporting of the West by magazines and newspapers. Editors and correspondents were torn between the urge to proclaim the wonders of progress and a disinclination to abate the individualistic and often primitive aspects with which they had for more than a decade been assiduously investing Texas, Wyoming, Nevada and Arizona. Paved streets were coming to Fort Worth and Butte; evening attire for gentlemen was a commonplace in Leadville; a splendid hydraulic elevator had appeared in, of all places, the International Hotel in Virginia City, Nevada; French chefs were practicing their art in the most desolate mining camps in California and Oregon; the Windsor Hotel in Denver had mirrors worth $10,000 apiece whose plate glass was impregnated with diamond dust; Gatling guns promised to make mincemeat of the Indians; there were electric call bells in The Palace in San Francisco; the Amoskeag steam fire engine was supplanting the gooseneck hand pumpers in such cities as Bismark and Salt Lake; there was an all-night stockbroker's office in Hamilton, Nevada, and an electromagnetic device for detecting gunshot, first used on President Garfield, had been installed by a forward-looking medical practitioner of Bisbee, Arizona.

How to reconcile the advent of such up-to-the-minute boons and improvements with the rugged frontier so dear alike to publisher and public?

The solution of the problem was soon forthcoming in the form of an adroit editorial synthesis of progress and the picturesque. The adventures of New York millionaires among the mining towns began to be favored copy in popular periodicals. The hazing of eastern dudes by cowboys became institutional. Broadway chorus girls appeared unaccountably, but invariably in scanty attire, in private dining rooms and gentlemen's clubs in Leadville and Cheyenne. Cowhands dashed up and down the aisles of Pullmans on the *Overland Limited* terrifying the women and children with gunfire but meaning no real harm. And, invariably, the reverse of the medal depicted the rough diamond from Alder Gulch or Tombstone amazed and bewildered when first encountering such Eastern splendors as the barroom of the Astor House or polite company at Delmonico's.

The steamcars themselves, of course, figured heroically in the ever growing body of Western folklore. Train robbery became as much a property of the era as bootleggers were to be some decades later. Decorous romances flourished aboard the Palace cars. Celebrities were conveyed across the plains and foreign play actors and opera singers perforce traveled in private Pullmans. So urgent was this convention throughout the West that Mme Nellie Melba made a fine thing promotionally of the luxurious appointments and decor of her private car reticently named "Melba," and designed for her with a deal of press notice by the Mann Boudoir Car Company. Years later when the car was dismantled after the old lady's death it was found that its rare carved woodwork was plaster of paris and its sumptuous inlays mere painted canvas.

It was an age in which no silver senator from Nevada or Montana could afford to go across the continent except in his own private car. When a disgruntled eccentric lodged a slug in John Mackay, the bonanza king, Mrs. Mackay, fearing he was *in extremis,* was rushed from Europe and hastened to his San Francisco bedside aboard the Mackay car *Corsair,* but quite democratically. "Regular trains hauled our car," she told the press. "I do not like the jolting of a special engine pulling one car."

At the other end of the social scale from the railroad rajahs and bonanza barons in the Western legend was the intrepid cowgirl, for cheesecake is no twentieth century discovery, who saved the limited from disaster at the washed-out trestle, or the desert switchtender's daughter who flagged down the fast mail in the nick of time. In the news accounts she was given a gold watch and employment as telegrapher by the railroad. In popular fiction, she often met the son of the railroad's general manager, a handsome Harvard man.

The railroads gave the American West a substantial portion of its profile and character and in turn they gave the West to posterity and the world.

Frank Leslie Toured the West on Behalf of His Readers

N. Y. PUBLIC LIBRARY

From the time of the publication of Pike's diaries in the first decade of the century, Americans could never learn too much of the wonderful Western land where lay the nation's "manifest destiny." With the completion of the Pacific Railroad in 1869 their interest reached fever pitch and eight years later the West was still possessed of such a fascination that Frank Leslie, the most enterprising publisher of his generation, organized "a staff of artists, photographers and literary ladies and gentlemen" to tour its entirety. The party left New York aboard a specially built and sumptuously finished Wagner palace sleeping car (*above*) and the circulation of *Leslie's Illustrated Newspaper* boomed with each successive issue. The literary ladies and gentlemen discovered that their first stop, Chicago, was already a vast network of railroad yards (*below*) as seen from the Lake Michigan water front.

CHICAGO HISTORICAL SOCIETY

And Lusty Chicago Was First Stop on the Grand Tour

Even Chicagoans were impressed by the vast turreted depot of the Chicago, Rock Island & Pacific Railroad from which trains departed for Council Bluffs and the Pacific Railroad connection as well as the southwestern farming lands already served by the railroad.

CHICAGO HISTORICAL SOCIETY

Then as now, Chicago's railway depots were the quintessence of turmoil (*left*) and the Frank Leslie party were glad to retire to the comparative repose of the ornate Grand Pacific Hotel (*center*) which they had been assured compared favorably with the splendid new Palmer House recently built by wealthy Potter Palmer, and the highly respectable Sherman.

The Real West, Travelers Felt, Began at Omaha

FROM HERE ON GREW THE BUFFALO GRASS

By the middle seventies three railroads, the Rock Island, the Burlington, and the Chicago & Northwestern converged (*above*) upon Council Bluffs and crossed the long bridge (*center*) to Omaha to connect with the Union Pacific. At Fremont, Grand Island and North Platte (*below*) the Leslie party began to sense the extent of the West, to experience its distances and vastness.

WESTERN COLLECTION

Where the Great Plains Promised Adventure and Indians

WESTERN COLLECTION

Sometimes passengers on the Union Pacific encountered prairie fires (*above*) as they crossed Nebraska. Occasionally fires were set by Indians but more frequently by sparks from the wood-burning locomotives. On the plains, game was incredibly abundant (*below*) and riders from the East crowded the car windows to see herds of deer, antelope and sometimes the lordly buffalo along the right of way.

Plains Indians Came In Assorted Moods

N. Y. PUBLIC LIBRAR

Only a few years before the *Leslie* party explored the West, trains from Omaha on the Pacific Railroad had been attacked on the Great Plains by war parties of Sioux (*above*) usually with disastrous results to the embattled braves who consistently underestimated the powers of the iron horse and tried to ride it down. Engine crews, who went heavily armed, completed the rout where the implacable locomotive left off.

ASS'N OF AMERICAN RAILROAI

By the late seventies the Indians were more reasonable and staged pow-wows and ceremonial dances (*left above*) for tourists who descended from the cars to enjoy the novel spectacle. Sometimes hardy chiefs ventured aboard the trains to discover the palefaces at their own devotions (*right above*) grouped around an organ, standard equipment on luxury cars of the time.

Kansas City and Colorado Provided Picture Copy

Members of the Leslie party who made the side trip to Kansas City and rejoined the main entourage by way of Colorado had fine things to report. Everything *was* up-to-date in Kansas City, just as the song was to proclaim some decades later. In the barroom of the Coates House, a leading resort of Missouri stockmen, they encountered Senorita Guadalupe Suinago, daughter of a Mexican cattle millionaire, who caused a sensation by standing up to the bar and "taking her cocktail like a little man." Masculine privacy was no longer sacred in the American West.

In the foothills of the Colorado Rockies they were treated to the open-handed hospitality of fashionable hunting parties who outfitted their safaris at Denver City and lacked none of the amenities of table and cellar while camping out in the wilds. In more remote regions near the headwaters of the Arkansas they encountered a "party of English gentlemen catching trouts for breakfast" who courteously asked them to share their bag, as shown in the lower drawing.

CULVER SERVICE
WESTERN COLLECTION
WESTERN COLLECTION

Nobody Wanted to Miss Seeing the Latter-day Saints

LIBRARY OF CONGRESS

Riding the observation cars of President Brigham Young's Utah Central around the edge of Great Salt Lake (*above*) was a must for all visitors, but members of the Frank Leslie party observed no such scenes as that depicted in a contemporary (*below*) with the caption: "Arrival of a new batch of lambs for the Mormon fold—The deacons, elders, saints and prophets of the 'New Dispensation' selecting additions to their family."

COLLECTION OF STEWART HOLBROOK

Leslie's Train Had Every Convenience

On the Sabbath, as the cars rolled westward through Wyoming, Utah and Nevada, members of the party gathered around the Weber organ in the drawing room for an hour of devotional music. Upon other occasions the melodies were secular. "Here we find a cheerful party howling *Hold the Fort* around the organ," wrote a correspondent, "while three healthy children run races up and down the aisle scourging each other with their parents' valise straps."

Sometimes the members of the Leslie party visited the day-coach sections of the train (*below left*) and found the accommodations nothing to compare with their own luxurious palace cars. The train carried a printing shop for Leslie's "literary ladies and gentlemen," (*below right*) and at frequent points along the route local newspapermen were invited to come aboard and experience the novelty of setting up and printing a paper at twenty-five miles an hour.

(THREE PICTURES) CULVER SERVICE

All Trains

Paused

At

Promontory

WESTERN COLLECTION

Until the construction of the Lucin Cutoff across Great Salt Lake, the gamblers at Promontory where all trains made an operational stop were reputedly the most voracious and expert in the West. Mostly they had to fleece their victims in less than an hour and so developed a remarkable dexterity and expedition in chicane.

At Promontory the *Leslie's* reporters encountered one of the West's celebrities, Calamity Jane Canary, shown at the left in a photograph from the Western Collection in one of her more conventional moments with two equally famed scouts, C. S. Stobie and Jack Crawford. Near Promontory, too, in the desolate Utah upland, they passed the point where, back in 1869, the Central Pacific's Irish track gangs had laid ten miles of track in a day to win a $10,000 wager for their boss, Charlie Crocker.

UNION PACIFIC RR.

Nevada in the Seventies Was the Wildest of the West

COLLECTION OF DUNCAN EMRICH

Back in the effete East readers avid for Western glamor were enchanted to believe that, however physically improbable it might be, at Wells and Carlin in the Nevada desert cowboys on horseback enlivened travel by riding through the dining cars. Hotboxes (*lower left*) were commonplace on the long runs of the West and everyone descended from the cars to assist the train crew with helpful advice, while from the car windows the noble redman (*lower right*) was frequently visible in the depots engaged in the warrior's conventional occupation.

CULVER SERVICE

WESTERN COLLECTION

High point, both literally and metaphorically, in the trip across the continent was the passage of the High Sierra where a *Leslie's* artist sketched this view of the Canyon of the American River. The view of Donner Lake, the vast snowsheds above Cisco, the passage through Emigrant Gap, the breath-taking abyss below Cape Horn and the romantic associations of Gold Run and Blue Canyon excited the imagination of the traveler of the seventies as they do of the informed passenger today aboard the *Overland Limited* or *City of San Francisco*.

Cosmopolis of the Golden West Was San Francisco

WELLS FARGO HISTORY ROOM

Like all guests of distinction, Frank Leslie's staff put up in San Francisco at the recently completed Palace Hotel (*above*) the bedizened and eye-popping wonder of the western world where Russian Grand Dukes and English milords crowded bonanza kings from Nevada and the satraps of Wells Fargo and the Bank of California. They gaped at its world-famous Great Court (*lower left*) and learned that only the year before a spectacular dinner, its menu engrossed on solid plates of Comstock silver (*lower right*) had been tendered at the Palace to William Sharon, one of Nevada's high-rolling "silver senators" and Virginia City viceroy of all-powerful Darius Ogden Mills, California's master moneybags.

PALACE HOTEL

MENU.

Huîtres
Chablis.
Consommé Royale.
Sherry Isabella.
Saumon glacé au four à la Chambord
Sauterne.
Boudin blanc à la Richelieu
Château la Tour.
Filet de Bœuf à la Providence.
Champagne
Pâté de Fois Gras.
Château Yquem.
Timbale de Volaille Américaine au Sénateur.
Clos Vougeot.
Côtelettes d'Agneau sauté, aux pointes d'Asperges
Sorbet
Becassines au Cresson.
Château Margaux.
Salade à la Française.
DESSERT.

Dinner
to
Hon William Sharon,
by his
Old Friends
of the
Comstock Lode.
Palace Hotel.
Feb. 8th 1876.   San Francisco.
A. A. Selover.

Rails Came to Texas From the North

N. Y. PUBLIC LIBRARY

By the end of the seventies when Frank Leslie's special headed toward Texas (*above*) no railroad had penetrated the western marches of the Lone Star State beyond the Southern Pacific's railhead at El Paso. To achieve East Texas, therefore, the reporters' car was routed down through the Indian Territory of Oklahoma over the rails of the Missouri-Kansas-Texas into the wild and authentically woolly towns of Parsons, Denison and Witchita Falls. Wagon trains (*lower left*) were still heading westward across the as yet unfenced cattle ranges of Texas toward the new strike at Tombstone, Arizona, where Geronimo's Apaches were murdering prospectors from San Simon to the Huachucas. When J. Ross Browne (*lower right*) was sent by *Leslie's* rival, *Harper's Magazine*, to sketch the Apache country he "pursued the fine arts with a revolver strapped around his body and double-barreled shotgun across his knees." Geronimo was not finally subdued until a decade and a half after the railroads came to West Texas.

WESTERN COLLECTION

BROWN BROS.

CULVER SERVICE

"WILL YOU TAKE A HAND, SIR?"

Ever interested in human frailty as well as its virtues and achievements, *Leslie's* discovered that gambling was as prevalent in the Southwest as it had been in the frontier towns of Wyoming and Utah. The Katy's trains into Texas, despite the efforts of railroad detectives and Pinkerton's hired by the company, swarmed with plausible strangers with diamonds in their shirtfronts willing to engage country fellows in a friendly game of euchre.

Never a Dull Moment Along the Texas-Oklahoma Line

(TWO PICTURES) COLLECTION OF DUNCAN EMRICH

Denison, on the Texas-Oklahoma line, the reporters found to be full of *joie de vivre* which manifested itself at the expense of visitors in city clothes (*above*) and a flourishing bedlam of brothels and keno joints. "Red" Hall, a police officer who carried a Colt and Winchester, accompanied them on their sorties among Denison's riff-raff. At Witchita Falls a reporter whose silk top hat appears immune from molestation witnessed high jinks (*below*) in the hearty Texas tradition.

Morality In Texas Rode The Cars

At Waxahatchie a conductor's cord served for an impromptu lynching when the gentler sex objected to the attentions of a traveling masher, a commotion which amply demonstrated to the world that virtue and morality rode the steamcars.

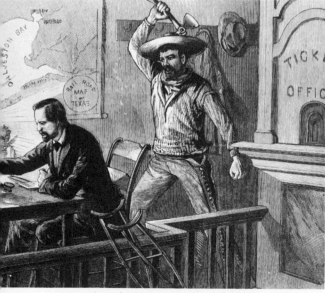

While the *Leslie's* party was investigating conditions in Texas a dastardly crime was committed at Webb Station where a one-legged telegraph operator employed by the Missouri Pacific Railroad was murdered at his desk. Mexicans were conventionally blamed for such departures from propriety.

But the proprieties and virtue were triumphant at Waco where the respectable element prevailed upon the engineer of a M-K-T switcher to put his locomotive to use on the side of the angels in removing a house of pretty girls which had set up for business complete with a bar beside the tracks.

XI

Folklore

For One Hundred Years Railroading Dominated the American Imagination, Conditioned the National Life and Thought and Established Itself in a Legend of Spacious Destines

THE ENGINES and the cars clattered smokily into the consciousness of the American people when the first train brigades commenced rolling through the meadows of New England and past the cotton fields of the South and they have remained there ever since, less poetic, perhaps, but fully as valid a symbol of national destinies as the American eagle and starry empyrean that figure in the Great Seal of the United States.

In this connection it may be noted that in the Great Seal of one of the states of the Union, Nevada, there is an entirely explicit reference to railroading. It is a train of the now vanished but immortal Virginia & Truckee Railroad crossing the high trestle at Gold Hill, and though the railroad now is gone, its memory is perpetual in heraldic emblem.

It is difficult at this remove to suggest the altogether compelling fascination which almost every aspect of railroading possessed for the national mind from its earliest inception. It became at once apparent, both to thoughtful and informed intelligence and to the common apprehension, that America was both literally and figuratively riding the cars to splendid destinies beyond dimly seen horizons. Almost overnight the steam locomotive became an instrument of continental implications. Only fifteen years after the coming of the trains the country was swept to a crescendo of emotional tensity by the phrase "manifest destiny." The United States was going places and, by tunket, it was going there in style aboard the railroad.

For three full generations the railroad was to be the essential tangible fact of American life. There were to be other agencies of change, progress and modification both abstract and concrete, but in some way or other almost all of them were to be conditioned by the existence of steam transportation over steel rails. With the exception of a very few mileposts of the years such as the Dred Scott decision, woman suffrage and the boll weevil, almost every fact of life in the American record has been in some way affected by the railroad.

With this background combined with the incomparably romantic appeal of railroading, its sights, smells and sounds, it is no wonder that there grew up around the cars and engines, the men who served and rode them, their depots, operations, achievements and catastrophes, a national folklore which expressed itself in song, story and ballad, in music, pictorial art and on the stage, in the national vocabulary and in artifacts and legend.

These manifestations are so various and so innumerable that their complete tally is obviously impossible in this space. Their existence is suggested by hundreds of geographic locales, "Railroad Gaps," "High Bridges" and the literally thousands of communities ranging from great cities to flag stops that were named after railroad builders, engineers, superintendents and mere track layers. The national vocabulary is the richer for such phrases as "across the tracks," "tank town," "highball" and "asleep at the switch." The legend of Casey Jones is as familiar to the youth of the land as the circus or the propriety of peanuts at ball games. In the field of fine arts the engines and cars have engaged the fancy of such various practitioners as Winslow Homer, Sheldon Pennoyer and Joseph Pennell, while in the realm of popular art one has but to consult the roster of Currier & Ives prints to discover its universal and overwhelming dominance in the mid-nineteenth century. In the annals of music the railroad theme runs from "I've Been Working on the Railroad," which is an American folk song of Stephen Foster dimensions, to Arthur Honneger's classic "Pacific 231." "The Wreck of Old 97," "The Chatsworth Wreck" and "In the Baggage Car Ahead" are securely rooted in the body of native American music, while "Union Pacific" is the title of a ballet not infrequently included in repertories of the dance. In letters, the bibliography of American railroading has engaged the attention of learned confreries and occupies a bulletin of some hundreds of pages of fine type references published by the Railway & Locomotive Historical Society, which has its headquarters at Harvard University.

A simple generation unaccustomed to the radio, streamlining or atomic fission was thrilled and delighted by the brave girl who threw the switch in time or flagged down the limited at the washed-out trestle. The roaring, smoky locomotive at the head end of a swaying string of varnish cars became a symbol of American resolution, one with the charge of the United States Calvary and the bold fireman mounting his precarious extension ladder amidst the flames.

Music-hall tenors assumed the vigilant pose of the locomotive engineer with his hand upon the throttle. The public consciousness was orientated to railroading. The first commercial motion-picture film ever released depicted *The Great Train Robbery*. Novels like *The U.P. Trail* had railroading as their setting. The first successful legitimate drama of railroading, *Under the Gaslamp* was followed by scores of plays such as *The Ninety and Nine, The Fast Mail* and *The Denver Express*. Only a few years ago Ben Hecht and Charles MacArthur confected a hilarious comedy-melodrama called *Twentieth Century* in which the entire action was realistically staged aboard the cars of the New York Central's most celebrated varnish flyer. A ponderable number of early film thrillers were railroad melodramas and such, mature semidocumentary films as *Union Pacific* have made fortunes for Hollywood. As a matter of fact this film, directed by the great Cecil B. DeMille, netted $5,000,000 for Paramount and proved to be fabulous publicity for the U.P. Railroad.

It is probable that the first aspects of railroading to become established in the national imagination and hence in its folklore were the visible attributes of the engines and cars themselves.

At a very early age of railroading, probably well before the year 1853 when William Mason of Taunton first undertook to design locomotives that should "look somewhat better than cook-stoves on wheels," the decoration and embellishment of railroad engines began to recommend itself both to professional and amateur artists. From the day when the first engineer left his terminal one fine morning with a pair of deer's antlers rakishly attached to his smokebox down to comparatively recent times, engines were possessed of personality and character, sometimes an individuality that verged on eccentricity. In a generation when locomotives carried names rather than numbers and were often assigned to service with a particular engineer and fireman and never operated by anyone else, it was not unnatural that the imagination and native artistry of the men who came to feel themselves the actual owners of engines should be represented in their appearance.

Most of the native American art that became incorporated in the design of clipper ships, fire engines and stagecoaches was the work of professionals assigned to their ornamentation by their builders. The figureheads of the clipper ships which toward the middle of the nineteenth century started sliding down the ways of shipyards at Bath, Newburyport and East Boston were the work of skilled Yankee woodcarvers who made a professional specialty of this type of art. The panels on the doors of the thorough-braced coaches built by Abbot, Downing & Co., of Concord, New Hampshire, were from first to last the work of John Burgum and his son Edwin.

Most locomotives of the mid-nineteenth century were characterized by varied and beautiful paint jobs. Driver spokes were painted fire red, drive rods were silvered, Russian iron on boilers was finished in steel blue and the trim and scroll-work on engine cabs, running boards and tenders as well as all lettering was characteristically engrossed in gold leaf and red varnish. Gleaming brasswork for handrails, bells, candlesticks and name plates was universal. The celebrated Taunton Locomotive works in Massachusetts thought so highly of the golf-leaf lettering used for the name plates on the black walnut cabs of a series of engines turned out for the Alabama & Chattanooga Railroad that it had them covered with plate glass for protection. Bell carriages or cradles were sometimes so elaborately floriated and so massively designed as to dominate the entire profile of the engine which carried them.

One of the early Baldwin locomotives delivered to the Pennsylvania Railroad in 1856, a 4-4-0, was named *Tiger* and an artist's graphic representation of a crouching Bengal man-eater in full color appeared on each side of the cab, but mostly such complicated scenes of landscape and natural life were reserved for enhancing the beauty of early coaches rather than engines.

Alongside of this native American folk art and complementary to it there grew up a variety of decorations and embellishments added to locomotives by railroad employees. In the Deep South on short lines and on the Southern Railway itself vestigial traces of these contributions to locomotive personality were occasionally visible into the forties of the twentieth century a full hundred years after their first appearance.

Regionally there seems to have been little difference in the tastes of the amateurs who sat about dressing up the iron horse. By far the greatest universal favorite was a set of deer's horns or stag antlers mounted either on the smokebox or atop the great storm lanterns of the period. It was visible on main lines and branches, great trunk railroads and short hauls alike from Maine to Florida and from Georgia to California.

Another favorite everywhere was an Indian profile cut from sheet metal by some mechanic in the railroad shops. Sometimes this was. varied by a mounted brave or a warrior with drawn bow and arrow.

Still a third was a brass spread eagle similar to those which long ago added a panache to the top of the high-pressure cylinder of every steamer to boast expansion engines. On locomotives the eagle usually rode the sand dome. Sometimes it gladdened the eye from a position on the smokebox.

The storm lanterns of the old wood burners are a subdivision of engine art by themselves. As long as engines were assigned by common usage and custom to a single engineer for their maintenance and operation the custom also obtained by whose terms the engineer supplied and owned his own headlight. Usually he removed it at the end of each run and often he took it home with him as a symbol of ownership and independence. The metal panels and glass sidelights of these lanterns offered illimitable possibilities for native artists, and the subject matter was only bounded by the imagination of their owners. Sometimes the engineer-owner tried his own hand with the paintbrushes, more often he commissioned a local decorator or other artisan to execute his wishes in lasting oils.

Few of all the thousands of these monstrous storm lanterns which once gleamed over the darkened rights of way have survived the years, almost none in their original condition. But once they were a common property of the American scene, one with the Gladstone bag, the Tom and Jerry machine in Railroad Street saloons and the hotel runner who met all the trains.

The death knell of decorative locomotives and their brass trim and scrollwork was probably sounded by old Commodore Cornelius Vanderbilt despite his own gaudy business car also named, appropriately enough, *The Vanderbilt*. When the story got around that parts of the Central's locomotive *Cephas Manning* were finished in plated gold, antirailroad agitators pointed to this as gratuitous voluptuousness and Vanderbilt gave the order to begin a regime of decorative austerity. Henceforth the Central's motive power was characterized by a general absence of the gingerbread and frosting which before that had been thought essential on any progressive railroad, and the other roads of the land followed its lead. The last great main-line road which kept alive the old tradition of bright color and brasswork was the Southern whose beautiful green locomotives, often embellished with "candlesticks" for their markers and ornate headlights, for many years gladdened beholders along the road's right of way in the Deep South.

Perhaps no other occupation ever fetched the American fancy as did that of the locomotive engineer. Not even the cowboy, the Indian scout, the godlike vision of Washington at Valley Forge or the swift facility of "Tinker to Evers to Chance" quite so effectively captivated the national imagination as the steam locomotive, its drive rods flashing obedient to the crossheads in their guides and the dynamic whole obedient to the visor-capped man at the throttle. His eagle eye pierced the impenetrable storm and saw to the farthest horizons; his controlling hand on the air-brake lever was the hand of Fate itself. The aviator of a later generation, a mere military mechanic cleaving his wide blue yonder, was never in the same league with the brave engineer.

And second only to the engine driver in mobile majesty was the train captain or, as he later came to be known, the conductor. His authority was and, indeed, still is absolute, comparable to that of a ship captain with the possible exception of solemnizing marriage and decreeing death. His insignia of office were his blue frock coat with brass buttons and heavy gold Albert watch chain festooning a liberal bay window. The conductor in the old days was the peer of senators, millionaires and, possibly, Buffalo Bill.

198

"Over The Splendor And Speed Of Thy Feet—"

Symbolic at once of the fleet-footed deer of the plains and of the engine's conquest of time and distance were the staghorns mounted on the storm lanterns and smokeboxes of old-time locomotives. These stag's antlers once rode proudly over the lonely right of way of the Rio Grande Southern above the high trestles of Ophir and into Telluride and Dolores, inaccessible mining communities in Southwestern Colorado.

LUCIUS BEEBE

Not only were bell cradles and headlights of ornamental design, as shown in the three photographs below, there were other decorative devices in the golden age of railroading. The Minneapolis & St. Louis's No. 7 mounted a cast-iron Negro post boy three feet high on its pilot beam above the cowcatcher, a fresh bouquet of flowers placed in his outstretched hand on every run by the engineer. No. 10 of the Iowa Central boasted a polished black walnut cab with red-plush cushions on both fireman's and engineer's seats and a gold-mounted Seth Thomas clock on the backhead while a gold eagle spread his wings over the sand dome. The drivers were trimmed with red and gold and the railroad's name on the tender sides was embellished with gold water lilies painted at the four corners.

UNION PACIFIC RR.   CHARLES CLEGG

Most Imperial of Railroad Dynasties, the Vanderbilts

N. Y. PUBLIC LIBRARY

"Stand there, familiar image of an honored man! Stand there to breast the storms or glitter in the sunshine of coming centuries!" Thus New York's elegant Mayor A. Oakley Hall apostrophized the statue of Commodore Cornelius Vanderbilt which graced the pediment of the great St. John's Park freight terminal (*above*) of the New York Central when it was dedicated with resounding municipal hurrah in 1869. James Gordon Bennett's argument that "so costly and splendid a monument should not be doomed to concealment where so few will see it" was many years later heeded when the statue was removed to its present position facing the Park Avenue ramp to Grand Central Station. The Commodore's freight and passenger stations were no more eye-compelling than his son's chateau (*below left*) in Fifth Avenue or the cozy décor of its library (*lower right*).

BROWN BROS.

BROWN BROS.

When he died at the age of eighty-two Commodore Vanderbilt left a triple legacy: the largest fortune yet to be accumulated by an American capitalist, the operations of the standard railroad of the world, and the family name which has ever since been synonymous with splendor and well-being. The Commodore, shown above from a photograph by Brady, together with his son William H. Vanderbilt (*left*) created in the New York Central Lines the model of railroad practice everywhere throughout the age of steam. As an investment it was for decades regarded as sounder than government bonds. When his granddaughter Consuelo became the bride of the Duke of Marlborough (*upper left*) a new social high was achieved by an American heiress. Not only did the inheritors of the Vanderbilt wealth and social distinction become part of the national folklore, a train of the Vanderbilt railroad, the *Twentieth Century Limited* became a household word and New York Central executives became the princes of the railroad world. Time has never diminished the Commodore as the superlative success story of the American chronicle.

NEW YORK CENTRAL RAILROAD

Loss of Life Was Commonplace on the Tracks

CULVER SERVICE

Death beneath the cars was a popular means of ending it all as is evidenced by the attempted suicide here shown of a "young woman betrayed in love near Leavenworth, Kansas." Natives of that prairie state may have been startled by the mountains in the background, but it was not too literal a generation and such lapses were accepted with equanimity.

N. Y. PUBLIC LIBRARY   ASS'N OF AMERICAN RAILROADS

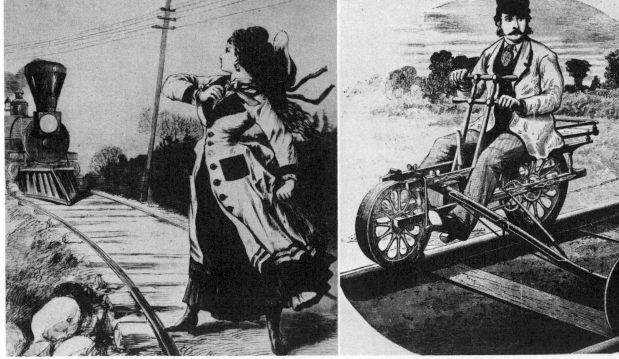

Still another candidate for *felo de se* in the seventies was a "young lady of New Rochelle, N.Y.," who in the absence of a friend presumably accomplished her dread design. Almost as potent an inducement to suicide was the privately owned rail velocipede sold to citizens in vast numbers in the model shown in this advertisement. To save walking the tracks, folk were urged to use the rails without the inconvenience of paying fare, and hundreds were killed before free riding was inhibited by law.

And so Was Its Saving in Heroic Circumstance

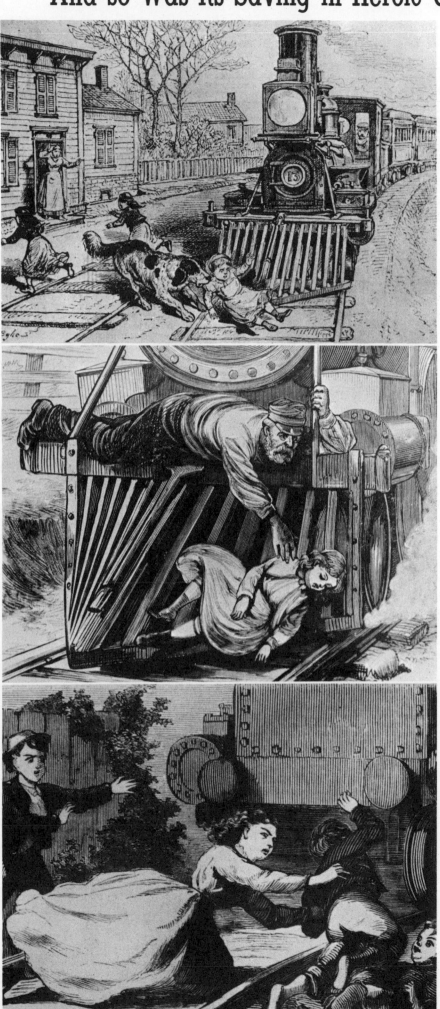

The rescue of tiny tots from certain death beneath the wheels of locomotives was an almost daily occurrence the length and breadth of the land and received widespread pictorial encouragement in periodicals whether accomplished by faithful Towser (*above*), the brave engineer (*center*) or little sister (*bottom*). In actual fact the slow rates of speed of moving trains did in many verified instances enable members of engine crews to climb out on the running board of their locomotive and snatch an infant from destruction. The same was doubly true of bystanders, and an age that delighted in sentiment and to applaud heroism however casual, gave humane endeavor its due.

(THREE PICTURES) N. Y. PUBLIC LIBRARY

N. Y. PUBLIC LIBRARY

ALL ART FORMS RODE THE RAILS

Even the field of ceramics felt the influence of railroads in the nineteenth century as is suggested by this coffee urn presented by friends to President Jefferson Davis of the Confederacy. Of the scores of dramas with railroad themes none was better known in its generation than Elmer Vance's *The Limited Mail* a poster for which (*upper right*) attracted thousands of playgoers to this lurid melodrama. The tally of railroads songs and ballads runs the gamut from "Working on the Railroad" and "Casey Jones" to more obscure compositions such as "Number Twenty-nine" (*lower right*) which was dedicated to Thatcher Perkins, Superintendent of Machinery of the Louisville & Nashville Railroad, by his fellow employees. Wit and oratory combined in the peculiar and universally recognized genius of Chauncey M. Depew (*below*) President of the New York Central Lines and the most famous after-dinner speaker of his time. Depew's reputation as a raconteur in the grand manner made him in demand for five generations of public ceremonies. His favorite maxim of health was "Walking downstairs for breakfast is exercise enough for any gentleman," and imitative wits sometimes addressed his mail "Chauncey M. Depot, Care the Grand Central Depew."

"NEW YORK HERALD TRIBUNE"

Incidents Along the Rails Were Very Definitely News

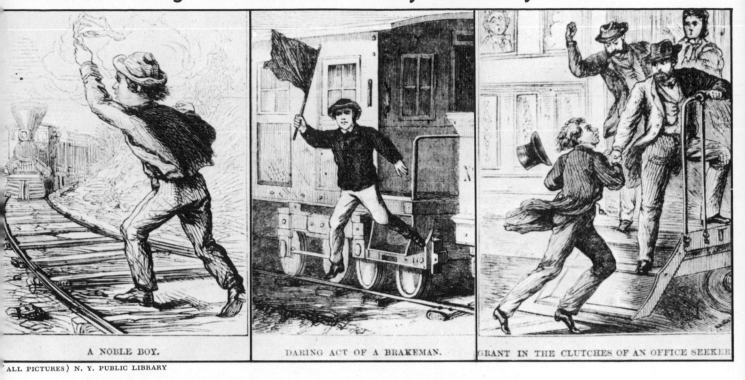

A NOBLE BOY.

DARING ACT OF A BRAKEMAN.

GRANT IN THE CLUTCHES OF AN OFFICE SEEKER

(ALL PICTURES) N. Y. PUBLIC LIBRARY

Narrow escapes, accidents of mischance, escapes of criminals from the cars, elopements, romantic interludes, tragedies and humorous situations on the railroads of the land were constantly brought to public awareness by the periodicals of the time.

"CLING CLOSE TO THE ROCK."

FATAL RESULT OF UNSAFE CAR COUPLING.

THE FATAL LEAP.

Some idea of the importance of railroads in the everyday life of the nation may be gleaned from the circumstance that the six vignettes reproduced on this page were culled from the pages of only two issues of *Leslie's* in the seventies while more important news stories of the railroads received far greater spreads.

Once, the Cars Were Used for Rolling Billboards

Barnum & Bailey's Circus missed no chance to advertise *(above)* nor did a hundred Tom shows *(below)* as they toured the country by rail.

A whole train was the vehicle *(above)* for advertising men's fashions, while *(below)* Sweet Caporals ("Ask Dad, he knows!") also took carside space.

Less exalted than the train captain or the brave engineer, but nonetheless fascinating to a generation of American youth to which pluck-and-luck and work-and-win were a fact rather than a humorous myth was the news butcher, a sophisticated gamin who was wise in the ways of the world and peddled tobacco, candy, cigars, joke books, tourist guides, sandwiches, soft drinks and periodicals in the aisles of the cars. From news butcher to railroad president was the theme of many of Horatio Alger's fictional exhortation to ambition, and Thomas A. Edison, who for a time worked the cars on the Grand Trunk, and William A. Brady, a gaudy theatrical impresario of the early twentieth century and father of Alice Brady, was another. Brady's route was over the lines of the Union Pacific and Central Pacific in the Far West in the early seventies when railroading was robust and the pickings for a smart lad not overburdened with professional ethics were often substantial. The cars in those days and places crawled with drunks and to these and gullible easterners Brady sold collections of fancy colored rocks labeled "Mineral Specimens," while aboard the immigrant cars he peddled bedding, soap, tinned foods and other such substantial matters. "Brady," says Stewart Holbrook, "was a general store on two legs."

Many of the American types who rode the cars in the years of the great riding were so well defined and established as to achieve for themselves an association with railroading almost as close as that of the train personnel itself. Drummers, professional gamblers, smoking-room raconteurs, newlyweds, bunco steerers and the genus *rusticus Americanus* became so identified with the coaches and Pullmans that, in varying degrees, they were translated to the estate of stock characters on the stage and in the repertory of national anecdote. Each had his identifying characteristic: the gamblers wore ratcatcher suits, smelled strongly of Macassar hair oil and possessed winning ways which covered devious designs; newlyweds were invariably on their wedding trip bound for Niagara Falls; the bunco steerers slyly exhibited gold bricks beneath the skirts of their traveling coats in the manner of Paris postcard vendors, the smoking-room raconteurs involved the drummers in their anecdotes which invariably began: "It seems there were three traveling salesmen . . . ," and the hick pulled the conductor's cord at the wrong time, had trouble with the toilet facilities and wore a duster coat and straw in his hat.

The homely types who rode the cars in the simple times of the dollar dinner in the diner and red-plush upholstery in the coaches may not have realized it, but they were riding on a one-way through ticket to national immortality.

At the other end of the scale from the homely annals of railroad workers and passengers and the world in which they moved were the exalted destinies of the railroad rajahs whose rise to greatness, whose fortunes, families and dynasties of authority have provided a gilded panache to an age of imperial aspirations. The rajahs were numerous, ranging from Jim Hill and Edward H. Harriman to Leland Stanford, General William Palmer, Cyrus Halliday and Henry Flagler.

The ballad lore of American railroading, while by no means as voluminous as its bibliography, is still both representative and extensive. True to established tradition, most songs and verses of the rails and railroaders are of a plaintive or downright melancholy order. A susceptible and highly sentimental generation was admonished that life was like a mountain railroad and that if it wanted to achieve its earthly terminal it should keep its hand upon the throttle and its eye upon the rail. The singer inquired if you heard the foreman calling: Dina, blow your horn? The terrified imagination knew that old 97 was going downhill at ninety miles an hour when its whistle broke into a scream. Americans rode vicariously on the little red caboose behind the train. A hundred lives were lost when the bridge was burned at Chatsworth and mother rode in a casket in the baggage car ahead.

But the words and music that have rocked Americans right down to their boots and probably will for generations to come were sold for a pint of gin by a round-house hostler and concerned an Illinois Central engineer named John Luther Jones.

Casey's name derived from the town of Cayse, Kentucky, where he had once lived and at the time of his death he was a well-known engine driver along the I.C.'s divisions in the Deep South. He was killed in 1900 in a rear-end collision when the fast passenger train, the *Cannonball* on the Chicago-New Orleans run, of which he was engineer crashed into a freight which had failed to draw completely into a passing track near Vaughan, Mississippi.

Jones' Negro fireman, Sim Webb, who lived for half a century after the accident, jumped before the crash and spent the rest of his days in the reflected glory of the event. His sentimental regard for the late Casey was shared by Wallace Saunders, a hostler at the Illinois Central roundhouse at Canton, Mississippi, where Jones' engine was regularly stabled. Saunders had a native talent for improvisation of plaintive melodies and his musical lament for his hero achieved a certain local vogue among the railroad men in the region. In the proper ballad tradition it was designed by its original author only to be sung or harmonized so that the imperfections of its metrical structure were inconsequential.

There is more legend than fact in the precise manner in which Saunder's round-house dirge became sublimated to a national institution, but one version has it that an itinerant music-hall performer, passing through town, gave the author a bottle of Saturday night gin in return for permission to write down the words. From there its progress toward sheet-music publication was a saga of popular success which ended in nearly fifty years of litigation, claims of proprietorship and suits over copyright infringements. Casey Jones was valuable property.

Casey's widow, who was known to both the authors of this book as a lively old lady living in Jackson, Mississippi, enjoyed much the same celebrity as Sim Webb. She visited conventions of railroaders, was regularly interviewed at suitable anniversaries and became a landmark of consequence in the countryside. Her greatest personal triumph was a trip to New York to appear on a national radio hour, an instrument of immortality of which Casey, in the Jackson cemetery these many years, never dreamed.

Gene Fowler has remarked that the story of Greece is to be found in its temples, that of America in its hotels. He might well have added that the cathedrals of America are its railroad depots.

No single structure or edifice, neither courthouse, church nor legislative hall has occupied as compelling a place in the American consciousness as the railway depot. The beat of the nation's heart for a century and a quarter has been most clearly discernible in the pulse of life as it flows through its stations whether they are such citadels of movement as the great Union Depot at St. Louis or venerable way stations in New England complete with telegrapher's bay window, hand-operated semaphore and leaky water tank.

The depot became important in the life of the community when the railroads were first building. At an early age, too, the railroad station became an object of abuse and public outrage for a variety of reasons: trains missed, unsatisfactory restaurants, lost baggage and boarding of the wrong cars. Depots, the public began complaining in the thirties, were poorly located and inaccessible, they were sooty and ill-ventilated, the depot functionaries were gruff or downright discourteous. The depot became a part of American folklore from the day of its birth.

As early as 1854 the newspapers were taking a dim view of station architecture which, they complained, "ran to wooden structures of Egyptian design," and when the Western Railroad station at Pittsfield was fired by sparks from a locomotive the local paper reported that "the flames presented a beautiful spectacle and the structure was never so much admired as during the last half hour of its life."

Of the New York & New England station at Woonsocket, R.I., it was said that during wet weather a Yankee made a good thing out of renting umbrellas to passengers in the waiting room, and a local antiquarian reported that, to the practiced archeological eye, there were marks of Indian warfare on its walls.

The Union Depot serving several railroads at New Haven was denounced by travelers with studious regularity. They claimed that the pickpockets were so thick, the cab drivers and orange vendors so strident and the engine bells and whistles so noisy that the premises might be considered an anteroom to hell. The elder Justice Oliver Wendell Holmes remarked that New Haven was "cursed with a detestable depot whose niggardly arrangement crowd the tracks so murderously close that *peine forte et dure* must be endured for an innocent walk on its platforms."

Alvin F. Harlow, an authority on New England yesterdays, chronicles that the frequent firing of wooden depot structures was an almost universal occasion for civic rejoicing and holiday expressions of satisfaction. At the time of the Great Fire of Salem in 1914 it was widely hoped that the fearful Gothic depot of the Boston and Maine, long an object of ridicule, might be burned, but it somehow survived.

Actually and despite the amount of abuse to which they were open and the dubious esthetic quality of Egyptian temples, French chateaux and Rhineland castles when adapted to station architecture, the depots of the nineteenth century were head and shoulders above their most modern counterparts in functional usefulness and the accessibility of trains. They were designed to facilitate movement to a maximum, provided direct access to the tracks and train shed and included vast loading sidewalks for passengers arriving by carriage or public conveyance. Modern depots, such as New York's Central Terminal with its interminable vistas of corridors and gangways which would baffle patrons of the Baths of Caracella, are designed to provide a maximum of show-window footage for the multitude of shops renting space from the railroad. Even such comparatively well-designed stations as the Union Depot at Kansas City are a good deal more of a shopping center than a functional railroad structure.

The Chester A. Arthur age in America, now widely patronized by a sophisticated generation, was more convenient in many of its appointments than the era of escalators, nickle pay toilets and electronically operated turnstiles.

This rehearsal of some of the indigenous folklore of the railroad is at best brief and cursory, omitting much detail which must occupy the attentions of the historian and meticulous scholar. For the engines and the cars have come a long way in the American *journada*. They have become integrated to the national record, economy, manners, speech and awareness.

Folkways and Folk Legend Gathered About the Railroad

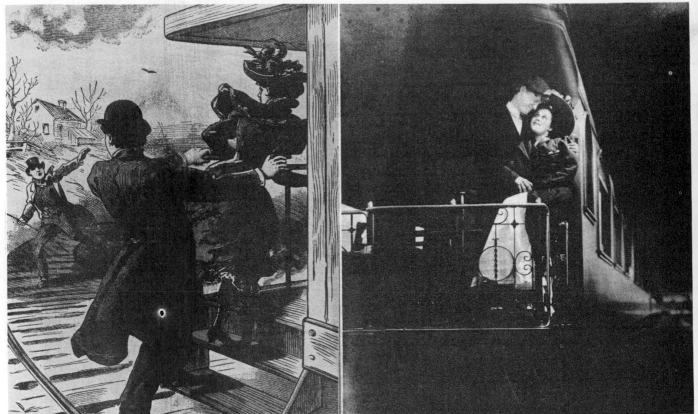

N. Y. PUBLIC LIBRARY

SOUTHERN PACIFIC RR.

Whether it was accomplished through the agency of elopement aboard the cars (*above left*) or more conventionally with departure on the brass-railed observation platform of tradition (*above right*) no venture upon the sea of matrimony for many years was to be undertaken without a honeymoon at Niagara Falls. Roebling's suspension bridge (*below*) was jointly owned by the New York Central and the Great Western, and all trains paused five minutes at Falls View or Inspiration Point for passengers to view the scenic wonder. For decades Niagara Falls was synonymous with romance just as, in later years, Reno was to be associated primarily with its dissolution.

NEW YORK CENTRAL RAILROAD

SANTA FE RR.

Headed aboard the Pullmans for sample rooms in the famous hotels of the land: the Planters at St. Louis, the Palmer House at Chicago or the St. Charles in New Orleans, the traveling salesman (*above*) became a character of American folklore early in the game. The prelude: "It appears there were two traveling salesmen" became a convention of national humor. The advent of the railroad also made it necessary for Americans to adapt themselves to an entire new pattern of public conduct. They had to learn not to shoot from car windows, hang their possessions from the conductor's signal cord (*lower left*) and, eventually, not to flush toilets while in stations. A classic of American humor, too, was the stranded ham actor (*lower right*) who, lacking carfare, trudged down the tracks from his most recent failure, a busted stovepipe hat on his head, a seedy Gladstone trailing shirts and collars on the right of way. These elegant but bankrupt mummers are playing golf on their way back to Broadway.

"RAILROAD MAGAZINE"   COLLECTION OF ARTHUR FOLWELL

N. Y. PUBLIC LIBRARY

Until construction began on the first Grand Central Terminal in 1879, New Yorkers had cause for complaint about the depot of the New York & Harlem Railroad (*above*) located at Forty-second Street and Park Avenue where Grand Central now stands. Pigs, ducks and other livestock belonging to neighboring squatters abounded in "Muddy Hollow" as it was known and the duckboards which served as platforms for mounting the cars sometimes disappeared under the weight of passengers into the malodorous ooze. From the railroad's downtown terminal at Twenty-sixth Street horses pulled the cars to Forty-second Street where steam engines took over. When it was completed under the eye of old Commodore Vanderbilt himself, Grand Central (*lower left*) became one of the outstanding sights of town and gave its location a centralized importance it has never lost. The station had its inconvenient features, but immediately became a New York institution and its monstrous train shed (*lower right*) occasioned pointing-with-pride as the biggest in the world.

CULVER SERVICE

ITS ASPECTS WERE HOMELY AND EXCITING, LOVED AND SOMETIMES REVILED

The gentleman with the valise descending the steps at the top of the page is not the object of mob violence, but a traveler whose patronage is being solicited by hackney coach drivers at New York's Grand Central Terminal in the seventies. Below him is a winter evening scene on a suburban depot platform near Chicago of the Illinois Central Railroad. The Pennsylvania Railroad's station àt Harrisburg (*third from top*) in the sixties was ornate and also served the Cumberland Valley and the Reading Railroad. A homely institution which has survived out of the past are the carpets and rocking chairs in the Baltimore & Ohio' station (*lower left*) at Baltimore. The old New York Central depot at Toledo was unpopular with the local citizens and when it burned to the ground in 1930 the conflagration met with warm approval, as is suggested by the newspaper clipping below.

N. Y. PUBLIC LIBRARY
CHICAGO HISTORICAL SOCIETY
BALTIMORE & OHIO RR.

CULVER SERVICE

Judge Roy Bean, "Law West of the Pecos," was celebrated in the Southwest in the nineties as a frontier magistrate who dispensed justice and Taos lightning impartially in a combination saloon and courthouse. His resort was called the Jersey Lilly Saloon in honor of the English-born friend of the Prince of Wales and stage favorite, Lily Langtry, whom he admired from afar. He also persuaded the Southern Pacific Railroad, when it built through, to name the water stop Langtry. Portraits of the stage beauty (*lower left*) and of Jay Gould (*lower right*), the rail tycoon whom he also admired from a distance, adorned the walls of the Jersey Lilly, which came by its spelling through a sign painter's error.

SOUTHERN PACIFIC RR.

E. S. HAMMACK

It was Roy Bean's dream, never, alas, realized, to persuade Lily Langtry to visit the town and saloon he had named for her. One day, however, he learned that the other object of his ardent if removed admiration, Jay Gould was due through Langtry on a west-bound special and, when the engineer slowed for orders, the Judge thoughtlessly waved a red bandanna handkerchief from the depot platform. The special ground to a stop and Gould appeared on the platform of his private car to see what was toward where Bean introduced himself and asked the financier to step across the street and meet the boys. Gould, like all the rest of the United States, had heard all about Bean and brought along a plate of ladyfingers to go with the case of champagne which was on ice in the Jersey Lilly against just such an emergency. As the afternoon wore on and traffic piled up across the division behind the stalled special, the chief dispatcher wired his Langtry agent in urgent terms demanding to know the whereabouts of Gould and the missing train. The agent, who by this time had joined the party, wired back: "Jay Gould, Roy Bean, Me spending afternoon drinking champagne, eating ladyfingers. Champagne and Gould special both gone." Bean's picnic hit front pages from coast to coast and became enshrined in the folklore of the Southwest.

The aspect of the Colorado narrow-gage era was captured by William H. Jackson, noted photographer of the West, when he caught this Denver, Leadville & Gunnison train in Platte Canyon in 1891.

XII

Narrow Gage

Colorado Rode the Little Trains Through the High Passes of the Rockies to a Dream of Riches, Dollar Princesses and the Outrageous Splendors of the Carbonate Kings

THE ESSENTIAL facts of Colorado's history in the nineteenth century, and, indeed, well into the twentieth although in diminishing proportions, were precious metals and the three-foot-gage railroad. These have in recent years been modified by the evolution of a less volatile economy and the more universal standard track span for railroads, but throughout its almost perpetual early excitements Colorado was predicated on gold, silver, the Rio Grande Railroad and a complex of other diminutive carriers. They were mountain railroads that delighted and enriched their generation and have ever since enchanted amateurs of the souvenirs of yesterday.

216

The original bonanzas of the region that David Lavender has called "The Big Divide" were the Rocky Mountain fur industry of the Long Hunters and the Mountain Men and the trade of Taos and Santa Fe. From the time of the publication of the diaries of Lieutenant Zebulon Pike, which was 1810, a vast national interest was aroused by the reported resources and wonderments of the mountain states. The great era of the fur trade drew to a close in the middle thirties and the names of the pioneers, Jim Bridger, Kit Carson, Louis Vasquez, Ceran St. Vrain and Jim Beckwourth, all indeed save that of Uncle Dick Wootton who was to live to see the Santa Fe's locomotives running through the Raton, had begun to take on the misty quality and exalted stature of legend.

But as the Santa Fe trade and the annual "ransoms" or fairs at Taos receded into history there were circulated rumors of far greater bonanzas, myths of mountains of shining metals, sly inuendos of diggings lost and forgotten but available to rediscovery, the merest whispered word of gold and silver in desolate creeks along the ramparts of the continental cordillera.

Suddenly, however, and against the best judgment of the remaining traders and trappers of the Rockies who had no wish to see their territory expropriated by irresponsible fortune hunters, the word was circulated in the East of fantastic recoveries of gold from the slimly populated diggings at Cherry Creek, a community which later was to become Denver City, and the Missouri River jumping-off towns began filling up with thousands upon thousands of wildly reckless prospectors. "Pike's Peak or Bust" became a universal slogan, not yet entirely vanished from American usage, to a generation in whose imagination that region represented all there was of Colorado. In mid-winter of 1857 six men arrived in Cherry Creek from Michigan pushing all they owned in the world in handcarts across the January prairies. In '59 more than 100,000 abandoned their homes in the East and headed for the Pike's Peak region.

The Cherry Creek diggings were largely a cruel hoax perpetrated by desperate outfitters along the Kansas and Missouri frontiers, but a few years later authentic strikes had been made, the most notable of which were in Leadville far inland from the Ramparts and south of Pike's Peak, in the Central City and Black Hawk diggings not fifty miles from Denver City and at Georgetown on the south fork of Clear Creek only a few miles removed from the tumults of opulent Central. Elsewhere, far to the west, precious metals were found in the San Juan Basin at Silverton, Rico, Ouray and up a dead-end canyon a few miles west of the Forks of Animas at Telluride.

One and all the Colorado diggings were inaccessible in the extreme. Pack and wagon masters, most notable of whom was diminutive, German Otto Mears, "Pathfinder of the San Juan," freighted in loads of blasting powder, Taos Lightning, Ames shovels, flannel shirts, cookstoves, picks and flour at exorbitant rates which in no way discouraged lonely prospectors and miners in established camps avid for artifacts of civilization.

Colorado was ripe for a railroad. It had been a bitter disappointment to Denver City when the Union Pacific had located and built through Cheyenne and Laramie a hundred miles to the north and merchants and once hopeful settlers had left the community in hundreds. The Kansas Pacific, two years after the close of the Civil War, was building toward Denver across the Great Plains, but the vast traffic from the cattle towns of Kansas slowed its westward progress and Denver citizens lost hope of ever hearing its locomotives whistle into their yard limits.

Even before the great silver stampedes of the seventies Colorado was in a fair way to have its own, home-financed, home-conceived railroad. General William Palmer Jackson, veteran of Union cavalry, had conceived the notion of a railroad running south out of Denver to skirt the Ramparts of the Rockies as far as the Raton Pass into New Mexico whence it should run to the Rio Grande at an unspecified point for eventual completion through to Mexico City. Along the line were to be established vast industrial enterprises based on the coal resources of the mines near Pueblo at Delagua and Trinidad, the whole linked to the agricultural potentialities of the Great Plains as they approached the mountain barrier.

There was nothing small about General Palmer's dream, and in point of fact, a great deal of it came true, but it was diverted from its original continental objective by two unforeseen circumstances. The first of these was the seizure and retention by the Santa Fe Railroad of the Raton Pass, only available gateway to the Southwest and the consequent exclusion of the Rio Grande. The other was the discovery of precious metals at Leadville. Together these unforeseeable contingencies combined with the happy fact that the Rio Grande had been planned and its early construction completed in three-foot gage instead of the conventional standard, to divert the course of the railroad from its progress southward and send it precipitously westward. General Palmer's first objective in the revised plan of empire was Leadville. Shortly thereafter the Rio Grande built its still operating narrow-gage division into Durango in the remote San Juan and only at a subsequent date did the management evolve the ambitious project of running the rails through to Salt Lake via Tennessee Pass and the canyon of the Colorado River. Eventually it was to build branches and stub lines reaching to Sapinero, Creede, Aspen, Ouray, Silverton, Crested Butte and Farmington across the New Mexican border.

Only the Rio Grande's three-foot gage with its consequent economy of construction costs and ability to thread narrow and tortuous passes impervious to the standard gage made possible this pattern of expansion. Even the most mature technique of railroad building in the twentieth century has been unable to devise the means to standard gage the road's last remaining narrow-gage operation of importance between Alamosa and Durango. Eventually its main line up the Canyon of the Arkansas to Salt Lake was standard gaged, but there are regions of Colorado which will never know the thunder of broad-gage traffic and which, until Judgment Day, will be pervious only to locomotives and cars of the narrow-gage line.

The success of the Rio Grande in achieving the most remote and improbable Colorado mining camps and extending its operations up grades and around curves that raised the hair on the heads of conventional railroad surveyors also raised the narrow gage to the estate of the inevitable railroad to serve a mountain terrain. For three decades thereafter engineers thought in terms of three-foot rails and even in the twentieth century when the Rio Grande's branch between Durango and Farmington had been imprudently laid to standard, it was eventually retracked to match the gage of the three other lines converging on Durango.

As new camps and mining regions joined the silver stampede other narrow gages snaked their way into the Colorado hills in picturesque profusion. Otto Mears, The Pathfinder, alone built four, three of them spreading like a fan and connecting with the narrow-gage Rio Grande at Silverton and his masterpiece, the Rio Grande Southern which wound circuitously over a whole series of mountain ranges and incredible grades from Durango to Ridgeway, 160 miles of railroad construction to gain a distance of twenty-five miles in an air line.

Perhaps the most romantic of all Colorado's narrow gages and certainly the one which still, long after its tracks disappeared from the high passes except for fourteen miles which still operate as standard gage between Climax and Leadville as the Colorado & Southern, was the Denver, South Park & Pacific. Begun in the early seventies to run between the Colorado capital and the South Park, a vast level agricultural and grazing region in the center of the state, it was caught up in the mining excitements of the seventies and pushed on to booming Leadville. Aboard its diminutive sleepers and parlor cars rode the carbonate kings—Haw Tabor; John Morrisey, who was a multimillionaire before he could tell the time of day from a watch dial; Sam Newhouse who became a friend of the Prince of Wales and built the Flatiron Building in New York; Charlie Boettcher who took a mine lease as security for a twenty-dollar cookstove and pocketed $150,000 because the owner never redeemed his household chattel; John Campion who for a few dollars bought a mine that nobody else wanted and turned up the Jenny Lind, one of the richest gold pockets in history; and, most fabulous of them all, Tom Walsh who was owner of the Grand, Leadville's finest hotel, when he bought an interest in the Camp Bird mine at Creede and took in as a partner King Leopold of Belgium. His daughter, Evalyn, already one of the richest women in the world, married more scores of millions in the person of Edward B. McLean, Washington publisher, and eventually became owner of the fabulous Hope Diamond and financial sponsor of President Harding.

All these picturesque characters rode the night cars, playing poker in their diminutive drawing rooms for fantastic stakes and downing the best bourbon with champagne chasers as the little trains pushed resolutely into midnight blizzards on the roof of the world and edged cautiously around hairpin curves above precipices which dropped sheer thousands of feet at the ties' ends.

The South Park exerted such a profound hold on the Colorado imagination and affections in 1950, years after it had become no more than a memory among the souvenirs of old-timers lounging in the lobby of the Vendome Hotel in Leadville, it became the subject of a published monograph more than 500,000 words long and somewhat larger in format than the New York telephone directory. Sections of the light South Park rail taken from Alpine Tunnel and designed as paperweights sell to this day on souvenir counters in Denver and Colorado Springs. The South Park was beyond doubt the best-loved and best-remembered narrow gage in the record.

Another celebrated Colorado railroad in the narrow-gage area was the Argentine Central running from Silver Plume to the summit of Mt. McClellan by way of the celebrated Georgetown Loop, for years one of the great tourist attractions of the West whose only rival as a wonderment of railroad engineering was the more spectacular but infinitely more remote Ophir Loop of the Rio Grande Southern. Until comparatively recent times the Colorado & Southern maintained its narrow-gage operations up the two forks of Clear Creek, one to Idaho Springs and Georgetown, and the other to Black Hawk and Central City, the celebrated ghost town of opera and restoration fame.

Still another notable narrow gage which came into being toward the end of the era of three-foot construction and after many of the narrow gages such as the

Colorado Was the Frontier in Narrow-gage Days

N. Y. PUBLIC LIBRARY

GENERAL PALMER'S CARS BROUGHT A MEASURE OF SAFETY

In the days before the narrow-gages came to the Colorado Rockies road agents roamed almost at will to hold up the stages of old Ben Holladay and Barlow & Sanderson (*above*) and molest the pack trains which connected the early mining camps with Denver City. When General William Jackson Palmer (*below*) undertook the building of the Rio Grande Railroad a degree of security came to travel even in the more remote regions and travelers no longer secreted their gold watches and Albert chains in the bottom of their Gladstones when on the highroad. Gold and silver shipments, too, from the ever descending mine shafts came intact to the vaults of banking houses such as Cook & Co. (*below*) for deposit.

RIO GRANDE RR.

WESTERN COLLECTION

BUT THE COLORADO FRONTIER STILL HAD EXCITEMENTS

WESTERN COLLECTION

From the ever advancing railheads an army of gold and silver prospectors fanned out into the as yet unexploited creeks and river bottoms, pausing only at frontier general stores to outfit (*above*) before setting forth into the wilderness in search of wealth and adventure. The narrow-gage cars of the Rio Grande (*lower left*) and later of half a score of three-foot carriers took the fortune hunters to the end of track in comparative luxury and safety and were a fabulous improvement over the pack trains that had once set out from Cherry Creek. Romance and excitement still rode the cars, however, and the night sleepers to Leadville, Gunnison and Durango (*lower right*) still carried dangerous gamblers and were the scene of high poker stakes and occasional gunplay in the boom years.

CULVER SERVICE

Idaho Springs and Georgetown Once Were Golden Names

CHARLES CLEGG

WESTERN COLLECTION

Every Western mining town that struck it rich had its own particular French Louis, Emile or François, whose classic cuisine was locally famous. Georgetown, fifty miles out of Denver, boasted its very special French Louis Dupuis whose Hotel de Paris (*upper left*) was noted everywhere for its recherché atmosphere and the temper of its proprietor and is still standing today, a souvenir of the glorious past. The Georgetown Loop (*upper right*) over which the narrow-gage rails spiraled into the Rockies was in itself one of the sights and wonders of Colorado's pioneering days.

GRAHAME HARDY

WESTERN COLLECTION

The little passenger trains of the Colorado Central, such as the one posed at the left for its portrait beside Clear Creek, ran until the thirties between Denver and the rich mining communities of Georgetown and Idaho Springs. Another branch of the narrow gage served the even more wildly booming Central City, passing above the roofs of Black Hawk (*right*) on a lofty trestle to reach its destination another mile up the canyon. Ores from the Boston Mine at Central made millionaires commonplace in the lobby of Denver's world-famous Windsor Hotel.

Central City Society Flourished Opulently Then and Now

WESTERN COLLECTION

GOOD TIMES IN EUREKA STREET

Fashions in gentlemen's evening dress have changed since the *Police Gazette* in the seventies depicted (*above*) "a gay party of youthful adventurers in the Colorado mines celebrating a rich strike with a banquet in Teller's Hotel at Central City." Seventy-five years after this stirring episode, however, the Teller House in Central City's steep Eureka Street handily adjacent to its classic gold-and-old-rose opera house is still the scene of dinner parties during the summer "season" when champagne in cloudbursts and dinner clothes are taken for granted where once Haw Tabor and Tom Walsh gloried and drank deep. Parties in the Teller's nobly proportioned dining room in the fifties (*below*) include the presence of ladies and names of such argentine effulgence as those of the Fred Mac-Farlanes, Ann Evans, Evalyn Walsh McLean, Spencer Penrose, Edith Carlton, Crawford Hill, Helen Bonfils and countless Chapelles, Boettchers and other pioneers and descendants of pioneers have appeared on the Teller's ancient register during recent opera years. The narrow-gage Colorado Central (*insert above*) is gone and its mahogany and red-plush coaches only a memory, but Central still lives in the vivid past and ceremonial present.

"ROCKY MOUNTAIN NEWS"

Colorado's San Juan Country Was and Is Rugged

WESTERN COLLECTION

The life of the early miners in the San Juan basin (*above*) was never anything but rugged and until Otto Mears built his sensational Rio Grande Southern such mining camps as Rico (*below*) were served altogether by ox team and pack train. To attract business over his four Colorado narrow gages, Mears distributed passes, like the silver card shown here, to important railroaders and shippers such as Jay Gould. Some were in flat silver and gold, others ornamented with filigree and a few were printed on white buckskin.

WESTERN COLLECTION

CHARLES CLEGG

LUCIUS BEEBE

THE FACE OF SUMMER

The three-foot rails of the D. & R. G. W.'s track from Durango to Silverton is the last narrow-gage railroad with regular scheduled passenger service in Colorado. In clement seasons its three times a week mixed train, shown here en route to Silverton (*below*), passes through hayfields and tall stands of pine, skirting the abyss of the Canyon of Lost Souls 800 feet above the river bottom.

PROFILE OF WINTER

When snow mantles the Uncompahgre Mountains the railroad fixes a snowplow to the pilot bar of engines on its Silverton trains and stokes up the cannonball stove in the wooden combination car and the caboose. From its northern terminus at Silverton three other narrow-gage short lines once radiated into the mountains which encircle Silverton to tap rich mines in their snowy depths.

WESTERN COLLECTION

main line of the Rio Grande had been standardized was the Florence & Cripple Creek which was built to the latter community after the great strikes at Cripple Creek and Victor made the region behind Pike's Peak one of the most spectacular of all bonanzas. Just as the early narrow-gage lines of the Rio Grande had engaged the particular attentions of William Henry Jackson, so another photographer of the old West, L. C. McClure, achieved fame for his pictures of the Florence & Cripple Creek and it will live forever in his silver bromide record of a notably picturesque narrow-gage mountain railroad.

Like the other bonanza railroads of Nevada and the Mother Lode, the narrow-gage railroads built in Colorado to advance the mining of precious metals and to exploit the resources of remote and desolate regions reflected the character of the times and the men who built and rode them. The division of the Rio Grande running between Alamosa and the uncommonly tumultuous mining center of Durango was noted for its violent and godless ways. A series of severe wrecks when it was under construction were a prelude to a mature age which was orchestrated to gunfire and peopled with hard characters. One day a notorious pistol packer rode into Durango on the overnight sleeper out of Denver. His first thought was to seek refreshment in immoderate quantities at Fitch's Nosepaint Saloon. His next was to attempt the holdup of Banker A. P. Camp's First National Bank. Less than six hours after his arrival a committee of vigilantes had hanged him from a convenient oak in the Rio Grande freight yards where any arriving gunmen could get a good view of him from the car windows. Durango was proud of the dispatch with which it handled such matters.

The cars of the Colorado Central, however, serving Central City were notable for the urbanity and good manners of passengers bound for the Teller House and other strongholds of wealth in the Rocky Mountain cosmopolis. Booth and Salvini the Younger rode the narrow gage to appear at Central's magnificent opera house, which stands to this day a functioning and annually revived testimonial to the workmanship of the Victorian era. Central was an established community of *ton* and well-groomed silk hats.

A mecca for gourmets and tourists generally aboard the cars of the other branch of the Colorado Central which followed Clear Creek was the Hotel de Paris at Georgetown maintained by French Louis du Puis, the restaurauteur who hated his customers. French Louis—scores of western mining communities from Angels' Camp to Tombstone each had their own particular French Louis—was famous throughout the Rocky Mountain region for his cuisine, and eastern bankers and visiting English milords boarded the cars at Denver, fifty miles distant, to experience his snails *Bourgignone* and souffles *au parmesan.* They dined expensively and in style, too, off Sevres china in a beautifully furnished library whose shelves contained many volumes of the French classics, Racine, Molière and Dumas, while the host, scowling, according to legend, and hating his guests, stood by ready to pour the Romanee Conti on command. One guest, however French Louis did not despise and that was the Bohemian actress, Mme Franziska de Janauschek, who made the trip up Clear Creek aboard the cars for the express purpose of visiting her fellow continental. Tradition holds that upon this momentous occasion the doors of the Hotel de Paris were barred to all customers and the shades drawn for a period of three days during which time the awe-struck natives could hear the vibrant tones of the actress raised to the emotional pitch of *Phaedra* or *Mary Stewart,* dramas in which she had appeared during her American tour. The cellars were nearly emptied of French Louis' choicest Burgundies and the last of his Comet Year Cognac was reported to have been consumed during an impassioned reading of *Medea*.

An episode in the narrow-gage saga of Colorado which still figures in the Sunday supplements of the *Rocky Mountain News* whenever the little trains are in the public eye was the advent of the circus train over the South Park rails to Leadville during the late seventies. A few miles from town the head of steam in the locomotive had been exhausted, the grade was 3 per cent and attendants feared the train would never make it in time to pitch tents and put on the scheduled show. In this emergency the head keeper remembered his elephants. Calling the mahout, he had the beasts led from their cars and stationed with their heads against the rearmost car ready to push when the engineer should whistle for additional motive power. The circus rolled grandly into town with the mahout aloft shouting encouragement to his charges, but several confirmed Leadville alcoholics who beheld the spectacle were reported to have taken the pledge forthwith.

Two narrow-gage railroads, the Rio Grande and the South Park, raced for Leadville when that carbonate citadel was at the height of its boom. The Rio Grande, which was already in operation up the Canyon of the Arkansas, got there first by the simple expedient of building a five-mile branch connecting with the main line at Malta. Aboard the first train to reach Leadville as guest of General Palmer in his private car *Nomad*, was ex-President Grant, then returning from a trip around the world. Twelve brass bands, each playing a different tune at the same time, were on the depot platform and chairman of the reception committee was the Lieutenant Governor of Colorado and architect of Leadville's florid destinies, Horace A. Tabor. Tabor, who had raced up from Denver by stagecoach to be on hand, smelled powerfully of strong waters and the neck of a whisky bottle protruded from under the skirts of his Prince Albert. The onlookers noted that his top hat was in need of a lure. When Tabor greeted Grant with a sort of windmill salute executed with both arms, the windows of nearly a score of bagnios, which were located in the same street as the Rio Grande depot, flew up and a hundred bedraggled harridans screeched a welcome. It was a very informal first train.

Eight decades after they first began to roll in the shadow of the Rockies, the last narrow-gage passenger services west of the Mississippi were maintained by the Rio Grande which ran a daily passenger train with a tiny parlor-lounge named the *San Juan* over the 200 miles between Alamosa and Durango and a twice a week mixed run from Durango up the Canyon of Animas to ghostly Silverton. The lonely Rio Grande Southern had given up all regular operations of any sort a few years previously, but its rails survived the scheduled trains and it was possible for groups of tourists to charter their gasoline powered rail buses locally known as Galloping Geese for special runs over the abyss of the Ophir Loop and up to another ghost community, the once roaring mining town of Telluride.

The narrow-gage trains for the most part had made their final run and were forever stabled in the roundhouse of memories but they were a part of the mighty past of the Great Divide, an integral portion of Colorado folklore, one with the diamond-dust mirrors of the Windsor Hotel in Larimer Street in Denver, Mme Modjeska starring in *Mazzeppa* in the opera house at Central and Uncle Dick Wootton selling Taos Lightning from the tailboard of a covered wagon in the streets of Trinidad when the world was young.

Once the Railroads Raced for Booming Leadville

WESTERN COLLECTION

At one stage of railroad construction as the Rio Grande and the South Park raced to see who should be first into the wildly booming carbonate citadel of Leadville, the South Park's railhead paused briefly at Webster Station (*above*) where prospectors, gamblers and freighters disembarked to complete the journey by pack and wagon train and stagecoach. Hardships of the road were mitigated by informal oases (*lower left*) along the way where the pilgrims paused and gave thanks while the ponderous mining machinery (*lower right*) breasted the high passes behind teams of twenty and forty sweating mules.

N. Y. PUBLIC LIBRARY

CULVER SERVICE

(ALL PICTURES) WESTERN COLLECTION

FLESHPOTS FLOURISHED AT LEADVILLE

Once arrived in Harrison Avenue, shown at the bottom of the page in a photograph taken before the railroads came, travelers found the solaces of the flesh even more readily available than they had been on the road. Hurdy-gurdy houses (*upper left*) flourished with dances at four bits with willing partners imported at great expense from Denver City, while the same amount secured a night's lodging (*upper right*) in what was known as "billiard saloon." Then, as later, closing hours in the town's night spots were held to be an infringement of the rights of honest miners and steps were taken to circumvent them. What must have been one of the first blind pigs in the Western record is shown at the left enjoying a liberal patronage. The honest miner inserted two bits in the upper slot and was rewarded by appearance at the service door below of a chalice of refreshment. Leadville wholeheartedly approved this testament to progress.

Leadville Provided Many Contrasts

CULVER SERVICE

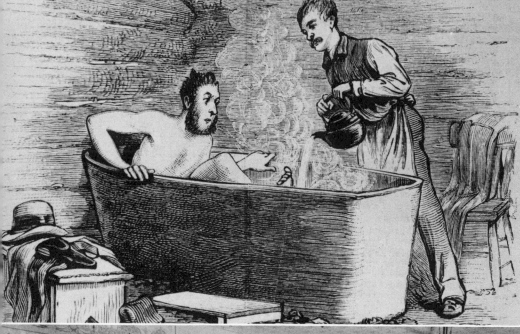

The Gaiety Music Hall in Leadville advertised "thirty lightning acts in succession, no long waits," and included in the bill "Messrs Homer & Holly, Emperors of Song and Dance," "A Sparkling Oleo," and "an overall top-notch performance concluded with Lew Spencer's great act: 'Who Stole Keyser's Dog?'" An evening at the Gaiety is shown above. Below: baths until the coming of the lordly Clarendon Hotel were at a premium and a contemporary artist took pleasure in showing a visiting English milord at his ablutions.

The hotel bars in Leadville such as this were second to none in substantial comforts of decor and cellars. The City Hotel, Grand, Tontine, St. Nicholas, Windsor and Vendome imported the best Kentucky spirits and expert bartenders for their management. Tabor's favorite bar, next to the Clarendon, was the Saddle Rock which boasted a chef in its restaurant lured from the precincts of Delmonico's in New York. In Tiger Alley and along Chestnut Street the resorts are patterned for the less fastidious. Leadville at the height of its fortunes had 120 saloons. The one in the picture stocks a beverage on its back bar labeled "Elk's Milk."

(TWO PICTURES) WESTERN COLLECTION

The miners who worked Leadville's deep diggings, the Winniemuck, Little Pittsburgh Consolidated, Crysolite and Matchless (*above*) lived a good deal less grandly than the carbonate kings of Harrison Avenue. A vista of their cheerless cottages is visible at the bottom of the page. Their entertainments were less opulent and Colorado still remembers the time the circus (*upper left*) came to Leadville and its train had to be helped over the grade at Climax by the performing elephants. In later years the Burlington came into possession of this section of the old South Park and the middle photograph shows the last train out of Climax for Leadville before the track was standard gaged. The new rail shows in the picture as does the train of workmen who placed it.

(ALL PICTURES) WESTERN COLLECTION

Haw Tabor's Leadville Was Rich and Rowdy

CULVER SERVICE

The portion of Leadville society which had no taste for grand opera provided patronage for a number of not-so-formal music halls such as that pictured above. But Haw Tabor (*below left*) with the wealth from his Matchless Mine (*below right*) and other happy ventures in finance patronized them all impartially and still had money left to throw at the birds.

WESTERN COLLECTION

BROWN BROS.

But Tabor's Opera House shown at the bottom of the page was the showplace of town in its golden age as was the similar edifice he built at Denver. Leadville boasted numerous hotels, the Clarendon favored by the carbonate kings, the Grand of which Tom Walsh, later multimillionaire father of Evalyn Walsh McLean was owner, and the conservative Vendome whose stage (*below*) met all trains.

WESTERN COLLECTION

WESTERN COLLECTION

E. S. HAMMACK

WHEN GRANT TOOK LEADVILLE

Guest of honor aboard the first train into Leadville over the rails of the Denver & Rio Grande Railroad was ex-President U. S. Grant who was welcomed by Lieutenant Governor Haw Tabor and a multiplicity of brass bands all playing different tunes simultaneously. As the special drew in at an early hour of morning, the reception committee was augmented by a large delegation of strumpets, madames, cafe entertainers and other representatives of the community's cheery night life who had not yet retired. An estimated thirty thousand citizens of the booming mining town roared a welcome as Tabor's carriage drawn by four black horses turned into Harrison Avenue en route to the Clarendon Hotel. It was Leadville's banner day and so great was Tabor's personal triumph that by evening he was uncommonly drunk, even by Leadville standards, which were liberal.

Fabulous Wealth Rode the Narrow Gage From Ouray

(THREE PICTURES) WESTERN COLLECTION

The great Camp Bird Mine at Ouray, deep in the Uncompahgre Mountains (*above*) assayed values as high as $3,000 a ton in tellurium gold and was one of the fabulous bonanzas of American mining history. It elevated the family (*lower left*) of rugged Tom Walsh, the modestly successful hotel owner of Leadville, to the most exalted social circles of Europe and the United States. In their Ouray days the Walshes had considered the Beaumont Hotel (*lower right*) quite grand, as indeed it was in the Colorado wilderness. Many was the friendly glass Tom Walsh hoisted with his partner in the mine's beginnings, Andy Richardson, in Thatcher Bros. Miners' & Merchants' Bar there as their fortunes prospered and the money rolled in in stupefying sums. Southwestern Colorado had never known anything like it.

To Create a Legend of Lavish Living in World Capitals

BROWN BROS.

JEROME ZERBE

When the Walsh millions were joined by the marriage of Evalyn to those of Edward B. McLean, a toweringly wealthy Cincinnati newspaper publisher, the combined fortunes allowed Evalyn Walsh McLean to purchase the Hope Diamond (*upper right*) and give dinner parties such as the one shown (*upper left*) for the exalted of the world in their Washington home. The little mixed trains of the Denver & Rio Grande narrow gage, like that shown below, carried out from Ouray the millions that so fascinated King Leopold of Belgium (*lower right*) that he bought into partnership with Tom Walsh. Ouray never saw its royal taxpayer.

WESTERN COLLECTION

CULVER SERVICE

Three Railroads Ran to Colorado's Last Bonanza

(FOUR PICTURES) WESTERN COLLECTION

In the best mining camp tradition, Cripple Creek in its early days was a shack town as is suggested by the adjacent pictures. Four years after the discovery of gold in the shadow of Pike's Peak, however, the first railroad's first train (*below*) arrived over the newly laid rails of the narrow-gage Florence & Cripple Creek Railroad whose style was "The Golden Circle Route." Two other railroads, the Colorado Springs & Cripple Creek District and the Midland Terminal, were built to standard gage and Cripple Creek became a three depot town. Despite its transport facilities, however, most of the town's shacks stayed on until the "great fire" of 1896 marked them for destruction.

N. Y. PUBLIC LIBRARY

THE COLORADO FRONTIER LASTED UNTIL CRIPPLE CREEK

Cripple Creek and its adjacent township of Victorville roared and swaggered in approved mining camp fashion. The meanest shacks such as those on the page opposite rented for $25 a month, water was five cents a bucket, wood four-fifty a cord. Wages were low and Cripple Creek and its neighbors, Goldfield, Independence, Gillett, Anaconda, Altman and Mound City were racked by labor violence. Still the rich gold ore which went racketing down the grade to the smelters at the Springs paid out, and many Colorado fortunes to this day had their origins there. Until the coming of the railroads Cripple Creek was strictly a shanty town with unpaved streets which turned out to be almost bottomless after heavy rain, as indicated above, and a lamentable lack of formal plumbing. When it was completed, the Colorado Springs & Cripple Creek District, as depicted in this photograph by the noted L. S. McClure, was one of the scenic railroads of the world, winding above dizzying abysses and over spidery trestles with Colorado Springs for miles visible below its car windows. Its right of way today is an equally scenic motor highway.

WESTERN COLLECTION

Life and Death of a Hotel in Cripple Creek

Cripple Creek's Palace Hotel, built in the staging days before the railroads reached the District, was the first structure in town to boast two floors and brick construction. Travelers drew up to its door in a Concord stage that has seen service back in the days when Denver was simply the Cherry Creek Diggings.

The Palace lobby, if one is to trust the drawing of a contemporary artist, wasn't altogether palatial, but it resounded to the ever-optimistic talk of prospectors, miners, speculators and stock promotors lured by the promise of Colorado gold.

Longevity was not the destiny of the Palace. Four years after it was completed Cripple Creek's "great fire" came almost to obliterate the town and the Palace was dynamited in an effort to check the flames in their progress down Chestnut Street. No more would its stages meet all trains at the depot of the Midland Terminal, the Florence & Cripple Creek.

(THREE PICTURES) WESTERN COLLECTION

FRANK H. SCHELL

And Life and Death of a Mountain Railroad

NO MORE TO VICTORVILLE

By reason of its many mountain grades and spectacular vistas, railroading in Colorado once possessed and still owns not only implications of industry and commerce, but attractions for tourists not encountered elsewhere. The route of the Colorado Springs & Cripple Creek District here shown with the Springs and the Great Plains in the distance was one of them. Today the Royal Gorge of the Arkansas through which the Rio Grande tracks wind excitingly is another; so is the breath-taking Moffat Tunnel with its steep ascent and distant view of Denver from the lounges of the *California Zephyr*. Last of the three railroads to serve the Cripple Creek District in the golden noontide of its prosperity was the Midland Terminal whose ore trains (*below*) continued to thunder up the steep grades at Woodland Park and Divide until the middle of the century to serve the reducing plants of the Golden Cycle Corporation at the Springs. No longer will the Terminal Railroad and its once flourishing connection, the Colorado Midland of fragrant memory run wildflower trains and picnic specials in the spring to Mountain Falls and Crystola. A huge cyanide plant has been built at Victorville and the gold goes down the hill in bullion bars in trucks.

WESTERN COLLECTION
CHARLES CLEGG

LIBRARY OF CONGRESS

Not all railroad strife was between owners and workers. This difference of
opinion, near Duanesberg, New York, in 1852, arose between rival factions of
stockholders for control of the Albany & Susquehanna Rail Way.

XIII

Sounds of Strife

Throughout the Nineteenth Century Railroad Warfare Flared Between Titans of Finance, Between Rival Empire Builders, Between Workers and Owners Everywhere

THE HISTORY of American railroading has been, among other things, the
history of many wars variously fought between forces variously allied. The
earliest feuds seem to have been strictly intramural between groups of
workers on the same railroad: Irish against Italians, Irish against Germans, and,
most frequently of all, Irish against Irish. Track gangs battled roundhouse workers
and train crews fought with section gangs. In construction days in the Far West

240

there were frequent wars between the Irish and the Chinese and when the Central and Union Pacific were building parallel to each other's right of way in Utah there were spirited battles with giant powder and blasting gelatin between the grading crews of the two rival railroads. In the building of the legendary Virginia & Truckee Railroad in Nevada, as well as other western carriers, the wars between Chinese and Irish laborers were on a truly Homeric scale.

There appeared, too, at an early stage the strikes of employees against their employers, many of them bloody and all of them costly, which came to a climax in the great strikes started on the Baltimore & Ohio of the late seventies. Blood was shed and vast destruction of property accomplished on the Michigan Central, the Pennsylvania, the Erie and the Burlington. In 1894 there was the great and bitter Pullman strike which was known as the Eugene Debs Rebellion.

But the grandest aspect of railroad warfare were the battles between railroad and railroad some of which such as the epic engagement between the Santa Fe and the Rio Grande for the Raton were fought on location, as it were, with gunmen, workers and hired plug-uglies, while others were fought between the titans of finance in the counting house and Stock Exchange of Wall Street.

No episode in the record of American finance with the exception of the market decline and subsequent panic of 1929, can compare in overtones of the spectacular with the uproar over the Erie of the decade following the Civil War. At this period the New York & Erie Railroad was a carrier of far greater national economic consequence than it has ever been since and its stock, as a result, was available to considerable speculative manipulation. Into the affairs of Erie, which from its earliest years had always been hard up for working capital, came three altogether unwholesome characters, Uncle Dan'l Drew, an excattle drover and the most unscrupulous scoundrel of an era studded with rascals, Jay Gould who was later to become one of the great if unscrupulous geniuses of American railroading, and Jim Fisk, a Vermont peddler of notions and kitchen utensils.

For $3,000,000 cash on the barrel-head Drew bought himself into the directorate of Erie and shortly brought along his friends Gould and Fisk. The trio then set about baiting the aged Commodore Cornelius Vanderbilt with the suggestion, adroitly circulated in financial circles, that he might by purchase, gain control of Erie and hence eliminate an important competitor to his own New York Central System. Vanderbilt rose to the lure, commenced buying heavily into Erie while Fisk, Gould and Drew kept the presses busy printing thousands upon thousands of shares of Erie stock without any legal authorization whatsoever. The rise of Erie stock on the New York Exchange under this cutthroat manipulation inaugurated a dreadful excitement in the money markets of the world. The stock exchanges in London, Amsterdam, Paris and Brussels were affected by a wild wave of buying of Erie. Bears who had sold short and moderate investors who had sold at a low price suffered in countless thousands.

The daily scenes in Wall Street were almost beyond description. As Erie rose and rose under Vanderbilt's implacable buying the excitement mounted to a national hysteria. Outside the New York Exchange, according to a contemporary newspaper account, "gray-haired gentlemen rushed from their offices in common with clerks and messenger boys. Omnibuses, drays and hacks were disregarded. People ran under the horses and narrowly escaped. Cable telegrams from Europe arrived with increasing frequency and excitement rose to fever heat."

Strife Was Everywhere

(ALL PICTURES) CULVER SERVICE

Nothing could be further from the truth than the idea that railroad warfare in the nineteenth century was all between management and labor. Battles between bondholders (*upper left*) were commonplace. In this scene the minority shareholders of the Lafayette, Muncie & Bloomingdale Railroad in Indiana defy the opposition by chaining an engine to a trestle and stopping all traffic. Warfare between nationals (*upper right*) was commonplace and anti-Chinese riots were instigated, mostly by the Irish, in California, Nevada and Colorado. And the Irish fought the Irish (*below*). In this instance a group of Tipperary men are shown in 1850 attacking a train on the Erie near Hornellsville, New York, manned by sons of Cork.

Usually hailed by the labor press as "the dastardly Pinkertons," operatives of this detective agency were frequently retained to protect railroad property in troubled times of the nineteenth century. Here they are shown firing from the cars on a mob in which the artist has thoughtfully included women and children, but since the occasion is not specified it may be assumed to be mythical. In the scene below a trainload of Republicans bound for Baltimore to vote for Grant and Colfax is fired upon in the suburbs by unknown miscreants during the election of 1868.

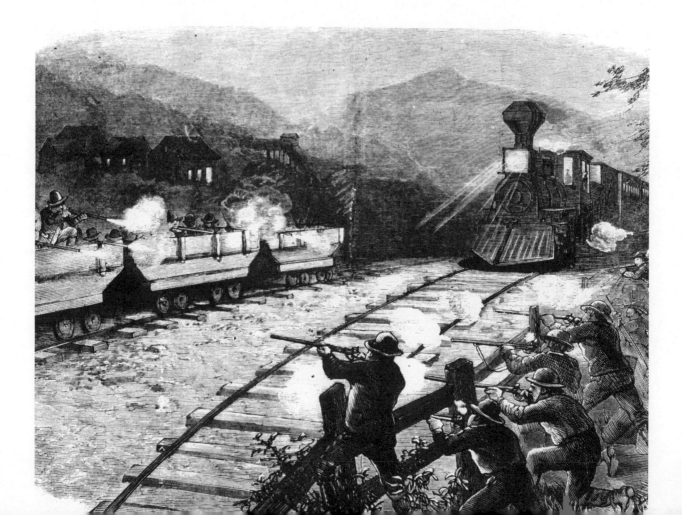

In the end Vanderbilt sought through court action in the State of New York to halt the flow of worthless Erie stock from the presses. The boodlers of Erie, Drew, Fisk and Gould, fled to New Jersey aboard a New York harbor ferryboat in dead of night taking $6,000,000 in cash with them, and prepared to resist a seige in a headquarters at Taylor's Hotel staffed with several hundred hired thugs, gunmen and plug-uglies. Before the Battle of Erie was over Vanderbilt had taken a terrific shellacking, thousands had been ruined by the irresponsible assaults of the Erie boodlers upon respected stocks and securities; and Jim Fisk had been murdered by Edward Stokes, a New York society figure, over the favors of Josie Mansfield, a witless and uneducated vaudeville performer whom Fisk had tried to promote as a great actress. Erie was ruined as an investment for the next seventy years and the New York Stock Exchange had acquired a reputation as a financial shambles from which it was never entirely to recover.

DUN & BRADSTREET

From a Vermont peddler's wagon such as this, Jim Fisk rose to affluence as the buffoon of the war between Commodore Vanderbilt and Jay Gould and Daniel Drew, the looters of the New York & Erie Railroad. For a time Fisk flourished ostentatiously and maintained Josie Mansfield (below) as his mistress while giving lavish supper parties for half-world characters in New York lobster palaces.

N. Y. PUBLIC LIBRARY

THE VANDERBILT SWEEPSTAKES

The greatest of all railroad feuds, the battle for Erie, was recognized as an epic struggle early in the campaign (1870) when this cartoon showed Vanderbilt and Fisk squaring away as on a racetrack. Fisk was murdered two years later in shabby circumstances but Vanderbilt's home life (*below*) was the quintessence of Victorian propriety.

BROWN BROS.

Death Comes

For

"Admiral" Fisk

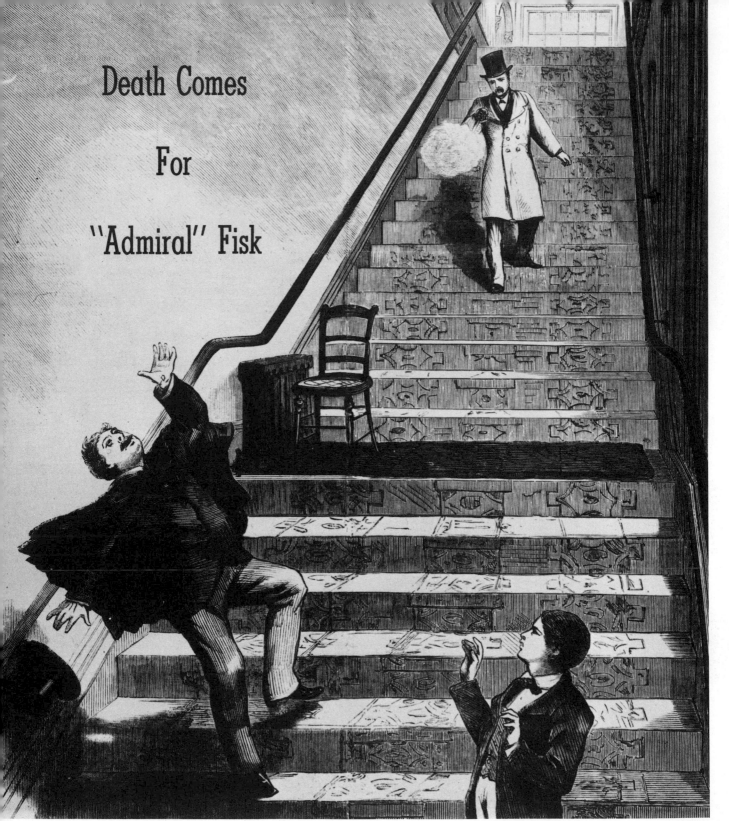

(ALL PICTURES) N. Y. PUBLIC LIBRARY

JIM FISK COMES TO NO GOOD END

What Harry Thaw's killing of Stanford White was to a later generation of newspaper readers, florid Jim Fisk's death at the hands of socially prominent Edward Stokes on the grand staircase of the Broadway Central Hotel was to New York of the seventies. The cause was Josie Mansfield, a music hall figure of mediocre talents, but the sensational press played it as a story of romantic love and death in the grand manner while other directors of Erie shuddered and averted the gaze from the public prints.

Long before Hearsts's *American* and Pulitzer's *New York World* established "yellow journalism," the New York press of the seventies knew what to do with the details of the murder of Jim Fisk, once flamboyant "Prince of Erie." *Leslie's* devoted its entire front page to "The Vacant Desk," an artist's concept of Fisk's tenantless office at the Erie's headquarters in the Grand Opera House, a foretaste of the mawkish sentimentality of tabloid journalism in the 1920s. Fisk was given a monster funeral (*below*) at which dignitaries mourned and regimental bands played. No Chicago gangster in the yet undreamed age of prohibition had a more gaudy send-off.

Standing Room Only at the Big Erie Show

LIBRARY OF CONGRESS

At the height of the troubles which beset Erie the citizens of New York came to view the commotions which accompanied the maneuverings of Vanderbilt and Gould as a public spectacle with comic-opera overtones. Boards of directors came and went like substitutes on a football team and at one time the railroad was getting a new president every four months. Crowds stood all day in Wall Street (*above*) to hear the latest dispatches from the battle front, while on the Stock Exchange itself pandemonium reigned as Erie's fortunes ebbed and flowed at the will of the money kings, as shown in the scene below.

CULVER SERVICE

N. Y. PUBLIC LIBRARY

In the age before news photography the illustrated periodicals of the seventies, of which *Leslie's* was foremost, kept readers informed of the Erie excitements by complete coverage with sketch artists scattered on the various New York battle fronts. The scenes at the top of the page depict brokers and their customers at the Fifth Avenue Hotel, a leading rendezvous of finance of the era. In mid-page is a reporter for the Associated Press with a portable telegraph instrument with which he was able to follow stock fluctuations and other events on the floor of the Stock Exchange itself, while below are crowds besieging the doors of the Exchange and messenger boys clinging to a post on the Exchange floor while seeking out their employers in the tumult.

N. Y. PUBLIC LIBRARY

Dan'l Drew's Printing Presses Ran Overtime

(ALL PICTURES) CULVER SERVICE

Lunch hour at Delmonico's Restaurant in Broad Street (*above*) as it appeared to a news artist during the Erie war. The below picture shows Daniel Drew (*feet on mantle*), the evil genius of Erie, dispatching a broker's boy with orders to sell another 50,000 shares of Erie Common to Commodore Vanderbilt's brokers. "We'll give the old hog his belly-full, if the printing presses don't break down," said the inelegant Drew.

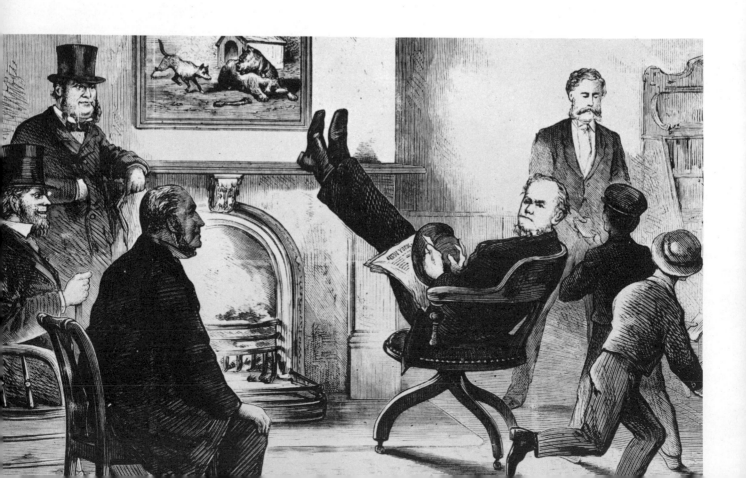

While the stock exchanges of the world seethed with rumors and counter-rumors of Erie (*above*) and repercussions of the struggle were heard in Paris, London and Brussels, the imperturbable Jay Gould maintained a standing army at the Erie offices in the Grand Opera House (*below*) to protect him from legal attachments or the service of papers by the Vanderbilt faction. Both sides employed armies of plug-uglies and bribed the New York police, city officials and state legislature with impartiality.

The Affairs of Erie Were Strenuous

Jay Gould and his cronies had stolen $10,000,000 and probably more outright from Erie, not to mention their huge profits on illegal stock sales, before they were ousted from office and partial retribution demanded. When a new directorate voted Gould out of the president's office, Gould avoided process servers by fleeing with his bodyguards from the Grand Opera House (*above, left*). A scuffle followed (*above, right*) before the new administration could lay hands on Gould's books and the new board of directors had to force an entrance to their premises before they could assume authority (*below*). New York had never witnessed such financial melodrama.

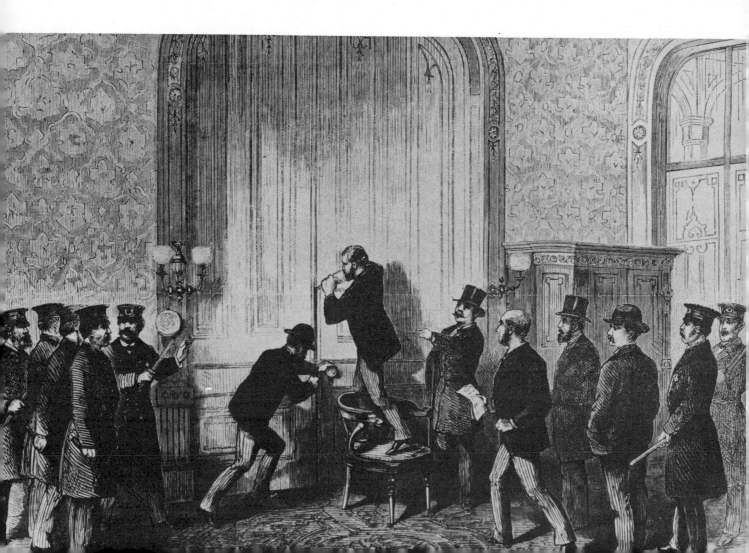

But Scarcely Conducive to Profit

Even with Gould and his associates out of the Erie directorate its financial troubles were by no means over. In 1875 the railroad was so far in the red that it was sold at auction (*above*) for a mere $6,000,000 to Edwin Morgan, former Governor of New York. A new directorate was organized (*below*) with Hugh L. Jewett as president but it was to be sixty-seven years before Erie again paid a dividend, so complete had been the looting of its resources.

The Baltimore & Ohio Is Beset With Violence

N. Y. PUBLIC LIBRARY

The great railroad strikes of 1877 had their inception at Martinsburg, West Virginia, where disaffected train crews (*above*) refused to let loyal employees operate cars and engines of the Baltimore & Ohio Railroad. The military were called out to protect passengers and company property and were immediately set upon by armed mobs of strikers and sympathizers (*below*) in a series of riots that soon spread to Baltimore.

N. Y. PUBLIC LIBRARY

Although the latter years of the nineteenth century were studded with labor disturbances among railroad workers, two major tumults were of such dimensions as to precipitate national crises, alarm government officials and require the military for their suppression. The Pullman strike of 1894 which led to a number of sympathy strikes among the uneffected railroad unions was principally notable for spotlighting the person of Eugene Debs, a union organizer, who seemed at the time the embodiment of anarchy, lawlessness and antisocial violence. Debs remained in the public eye for many years as a candidate for the Presidency of the United States. The Pullman strike was a dismal, but violent failure. It frightened the public and made the country aware of the increasing violence and irresponsibility of union leaders and caused unmitigated hardships for thousands of railroad workers who were never again able to find employment on any railroad because of their implication in the strike.

The earlier nation-wide railroad strikes of 1877 were far more dangerous and destructive both of property and human life and accomplished a country-wide dislocation of ordered affairs which, like the later Pullman strike, served to prejudice the unions in the minds of millions who might otherwise have been sympathetic to their cause. There was no doubt then or now that the railroad workers were being exploited to an intolerable degree by ruthless corporate overlords and that their provocation was great. But the reign of terror and murder which was occasioned by the strike wholly alienated public sympathy and did incalculable damage to the progress of orderly unionization and betterment of working conditions.

The strikes of 1877, which at times assumed the proportions of civil war, had their beginning on the Baltimore & Ohio where a wage cut was announced in July by the railroad management. Freight trainmen at Martinsburg, West Virginia, at Grafton and Wheeling refused to handle their trains, although passenger service was at first uninterrupted, and militia and the regular Army were called out to protect strikebreakers hired by the company.

The strike spread to the nearby Pennsylvania Railroad which had also announced a wage cut and it was here that mob violence reached its most chaotic stage, ending with the burning of the Union Station and Hotel at Pittsburgh, the destruction of the railroad's offices and roundhouse, the looting of thousands of freight cars and sabotage of more than one hundred costly locomotives and other expensive equipment. Inflamed to madness by stolen liquor and the incendiary oratory of union organizers, strikers and thugs then turned their attention to the city of Pittsburgh itself and pillaged and fired hundreds of private residences and homes of people in no way involved in the dispute. Fire hoses were cut and police assaulted while terrified women and children sought safety in churches and other religious premises.

In the end order was restored by the presence of 10,000 assorted troops and special police but not before the toll of dead had reached twenty-five or thirty and the list of injured run into thousands. Pennsylvania trains started running with troops on the car tops and machine guns mounted on the engine pilots.

Also affected by disorders were Chicago where a general strike briefly tied up all rail movement, St. Louis and San Francisco. The damage ran into millions and the dead were counted by scores. In the end very little was gained by any union except on the Vanderbilt road, the New York Central, where, although a strike was called, there was little or no violence.

Gore Flows Again In Baltimore

(ALL PICTURES) N. Y. PUBLIC LIBRARY

The railroad strikes of 1877, taken collectively, were the closest thing to social and economic revolution by force ever experienced in the United States. They embraced wholesale destruction of property and life, organized resistance to all forces of government and such pillage, terrorism and open warfare on the public welfare that organized labor was to suffer from their consequences for a generation to come. Among the earliest and bloodiest the clashes between armed strikers of the Baltimore & Ohio and the police and military in Baltimore's Eutaw Street, shown on this page, were so violent as to be reminiscent of Civil War times.

Incited to violence by leaders completely lacking in responsibility and inflamed with a lust for loot and pillage, the Baltimore mob gathered outside the Baltimore & Ohio's Camden Street depot *(above)* and were for a time restrained by Gatling rifles placed in the streets. Soon, however, and emboldened by the passive attitude of the military, a group *(top right)* attempted to fire the building while others *(below)* assaulted individual sentries on duty around the premises. Faced with no alternative if they were to survive the soldiers opened fire on the rioters *(right)* with decisive effect and in a few moments the assault on the station was over and the strikers *(bottom)* were bearing their dead and wounded from the scene. The pattern of insensate violence was followed by strikers elsewhere in the land for weeks to come.

Chaos and Murder Stalk the Streets of Pittsburgh

LIBRARY OF CONGRESS

As a consequence of the industrial character of the city, the worst outrages of the railroad strike of 1877 centered around Pittsburgh and the property of the Pennsylvania Railroad. A mob of thugs and strikers estimated at 20,000 laid seige to the Pennsylvania's roundhouse where a regiment of Philadelphia militia had taken refuge, setting fire to the structure so that the military had to shoot its way out (*above*). Twenty rioters were killed and the mob, now gone completely berserk, set out for the residential portion of the city where it burned and looted private homes while women and children sought sanctuary in neighboring churches. Barrels of whisky stolen from a burning warehouse were broached in the streets (*below*) and even Bishop Twig who mounted to an engine cab was unable to make himself heard. In the end 10,000 troops were required to quiet the city and open the Pennsylvania main line to Harrisburg.

(TWO PICTURES) LIBRARY OF CONGRESS

(ALL PICTURES) CULVER SERVICE

Pittsburgh thugs staged a riotous parody of the "Spirit of '76" (*above*) while others of the city's criminal element entered private homes and destroyed all they could not steal. The Coal & Iron Police, the governor of the state and the Philadelphia militia made their headquarters in a business car of the railroad (*below*) and some semblance of order was finally restored with Gatling guns mounted on flatcars.

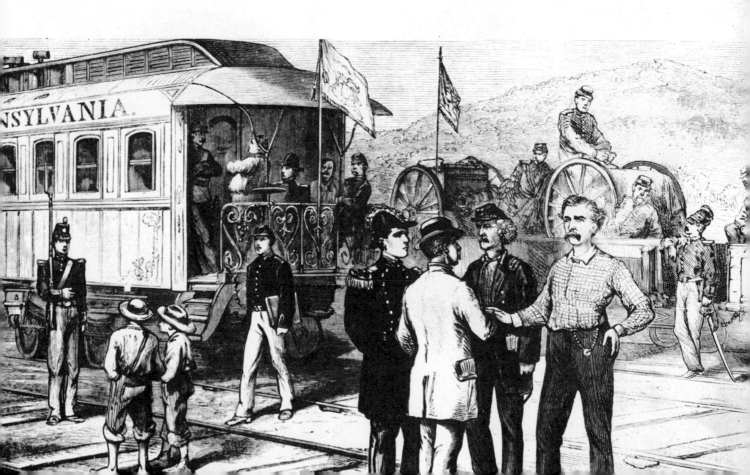

Trouble

Along

The Erie

LIBRARY OF CONGRESS

Already looted from within by Gould and Drew, the Erie whose fortunes were at perpetual low ebb, saw less bloodshed and destruction than other railroads during the strikes of 1877. Disaffected workers stopped trains (*above*) sometimes dragging loyal workers from engine cabs (*below*) and greased rails over which troop trains were to pass (*bottom*). At Hornellsville and elsewhere along the line citizens undertook to protect workers remaining on their jobs and took over the running of trains as in the below drawing which *Leslie's* captioned "The Nobby Fireman."

(THREE PICTURES) N. Y. PUBLIC LIBRARY

Accustomed from its earliest years to warfare of all sorts, strife between factions of workers, scuffles with the money barons of Wall Street and engagements with farmers along its right of way, the Erie was again mauled by the strike of 1877. Troop trains were derailed (*top*) strikers attacked the militia in upper New York State (*center*) and in some instances attacked passengers who were defended by the military (*bottom*). At the lower left is a scene vaguely reminiscent of Gilbert and Sullivan in which New York City police in Tompkins Square keep tabs on a group of strikers and thugs who had come to the city with the aim of fomenting sympathy strikes among other laborers.

(ALL PICTURES) CULVER SERVICE

The Mob

Attempts

To Loot

Chicago

The little local strike which had started on the Baltimore & Ohio in West Virginia finally spread to Chicago where a reign of terror was inaugurated by thugs and hoodlums who were told that the revolution was at hand by the hired rabble rousers of the unions. Mobs gathered to steal whatever might be encountered and boldly invaded the city's business district where they were met by mounted troops at the Halstead Street viaduct (*above*) and put to rout. In the best tradition of labor agitation, union organizers in person were conspicuously absent in the Chicago riots and perusal of the casualty lists at a later date failed to disclose that any single friend of the people had been injured. As the rioting abated clergymen ministered to the dying in the streets (*below*) and in a few weeks the better element among the rail workers, aware that they had been the dupes of professional trouble makers, returned to their posts.

LIBRARY OF CONGRESS

N. Y. PUBLIC LIBRARY

LIBRARY OF CONGRESS

Alarmed by the violence of underworld mobs who invaded Chicago's business area with the aim of looting shops, warehouses and private homes in the name of the railroad strikers of the Middle West (*above left*) vigilance committees of honest citizens were formed (*above right*) to protect loyal workers who remained at their posts so that the strike achieved little or no success in Chicago. After the bloody weeks of the summer of 1877 peace reigned in the railroad industry save for minor clashes between workers and the management until anarchists engineered the great Pullman strike nearly twenty years later when again Federal troops (*below*) were required to abate the violence of the Chicago mob.

BROWN BROS.

"NEW YORK HERALD TRIBUNE"

One of the more outrageous and costly railroad wars of the nineteenth century was that waged between the Pennsylvania and the New York Central and fought by the titans of Wall Street rather than the hired hands. Its focal point was the West Shore line, built by General Horace Porter who was in part financed by George M. Pullman to embarrass the Central when that road refused to operate his sleepers. Shortly after its completion the West Shore, which paralleled the Central's main line to Albany, was bankrupted and a quantity of its bonds fell into the hands of the Pennsylvania which began a murderous rate war against the Central by lowering the entire tariff schedule of the West Shore.

The fare from New York to Albany dropped to $1.42 and that to Chicago to $8 and operating revenue of the Central was cut in half. In retaliation the Vanderbilt road moved into the Pennsylvania territory and started construction on a road to be known as the Pennsylvania Central between Harrisburg and Pittsburgh and only twenty-five miles removed from the Pennsylvania's main line. So bitter and costly was this war between the two greatest railroad systems in the land that J. Pierpont Morgan, the country's most important banker, felt called on to interfere. He summoned aboard his palatial yacht, *Corsair*, the then president of the Central, Chauncey M. Depew, and representatives of the Pennsylvania, and while the yacht cruised in Long Island Sound he laid down what he felt were equitable terms of peace to the rival magnates.

Such was Morgan's authority that they were accepted almost without argument. Vanderbilt withdrew from his Pennsylvania adventure and the partly completed road was absorbed by the Pennsylvania and subsequently abandoned. The Pennsylvania in turn surrendered its West Shore bonds to Vanderbilt and that unfortunate road was taken over by the Central. Stockholders in both great railroad systems breathed easily again and Morgan emerged from the negotiations as the ranking figure in the American financial scene.

SCENES OF THE *PAX PIERPONTIS*

Summoned hastily from London where he is shown in this rare photograph by the threat of full-scale warfare between the Pennsylvania and the New York Central, J. Pierpont Morgan, the colossus of nineteenth-century finance summoned representatives of the two hostile roads aboard his yacht, *Corsair* (*page opposite*) and there dictated terms of peace. Such was the financier's prestige that a truce was declared on his terms and a major financial panic with widespread loss and ruin was averted. Morgan pocketed a fee reported at $3,000,000 in his capacity as arbiter and the year 1885 closed with the Stock Market so strong that its employees and members staged a New Year's Eve celebration on the floor of the Exchange (*below*) which dwarfed all previous jollifications.

CULVER SERVICE

BROWN BROS.

Tumult and Shouting in the Royal Gorge

WESTERN COLLECTION

In the all-out wars between the Sante Fe and the Denver & Rio Grande for possession of the Raton and Royal Gorge passes, Uncle Dick Wootton, the old Indian fighter, and Bat Masterson (*below*) the dude gunfighter of the Kansas cow towns, were allies of the Santa Fe. Uncle Dick's assistance gained the Raton Pass into New Mexico for the Santa Fe while Masterson captained the Sante Fe's hired private army in the later battle for control of the Royal Gorge leading to the rich Leadville mining district. Backed by court injunctions, however, such forts as this one erected near Canyon City by the Rio Grande's deputies turned the tide of battle in favor of the "baby railroad" and won for it all of Southwestern Colorado. The war was very noisy but almost bloodless.

WESTERN COLLECTION
BROWN BROS.

WESTERN COLLECTION

Construction gangs such as the one shown above pushed the iron of the triumphant Santa Fe over the stiff grade of Raton into the empire of the Southwest much to the chagrin of the rival Rio Grande. Where today the Super Chief thunders magnificently up from Trinidad on its west-bound run (*right*) in the railroad's early years it was necessary to conquer the grade up the Raton with switchbacks as depicted below. The grade was nearly 6 per cent and ran 8,000 feet into the New Mexican air. The first engine over was the *Uncle Dick* named for Uncle Dick Wootton, the railroad's old friend and ally in the Rio Grande war. A few years after the line was complete a tunnel was bored making the shoofly obsolete.

WESTERN COLLECTION   LUCIUS BEEBE

The Light of Battle Gleamed in Hill's One Eye

GREAT NORTHERN RR.

Crusty old J. J. Hill (*above*) greatest of the empire builders whom Stewart Holbrook describes as "the barbed-wire, shaggy-headed, one-eyed old sonofabitch of Western railroading" waged war with everything and everybody in the name of his Great Northern Railroad. He fought the elements to fling a line of rails across the continent and through the Cascades via a mighty tunnel. He fought E. H. Harriman for control of the wealthy Burlington and again for the Northern Pacific. Still again he sent construction crews (*below*) to forestall Harriman's entry into central Oregon. He waged perpetual warfare with communities that didn't see eye to eye with his line location, freight rates or passenger schedules. When a township offended Hill he simply ran his rails around it leaving passengers (*above*) stranded at a depot serving no railroad at all. There is no recorded instance of Hill's ever losing a battle.

GREAT NORTHERN RR.

E. S. HAMMACK

CATACLYSM AT WAYZATA

Terrible-tempered Jim Hill stood for no nonsense from anyone. When influential summer residents numbering the Pillsburys and Lorings of Wayzata, Minnesota, a resort on Lake Minnetonka, protested that the Great Northern's switch engines made night hideous near their villas, Hill ordered Wayzata eliminated as a passenger stop for his trains. Passengers and freight had to board the cars at a depot a mile down the tracks to the great inconvenience of everyone. The first train to pass through liquidated Wayzata thundered through so emphatically as to fire the water tank with sparks from its engine exhaust. It took nearly two decades for the village to make peace with Hill so that once again summer visitors might be set down at the proper station.

Most spectacular of all the railroad wars and the one most frequently chronicled in story and fiction and now depicted in the cinema, was the prolonged and noisy but not notably bloody battle between the Santa Fe and the Denver & Rio Grande, first for the right of way over the Raton Pass between Colorado and New Mexico, and later for the right to build up the Grand Canyon of the Arkansas. Pictorial interludes from both of these melodramatic engagements are embraced by this chapter.

At this remove, however, one of the more interesting aspects of all the deep breathing and swearing which made things lively in the Colorado seventies is the impression conveyed to later generations that the Santa Fe won everything it wanted hands down and that the outsmarted Rio Grande retired ignominiously amidst the sneezes and jeers of the beholders. The fact of the matter, of course, well known to all railroad historians and amateurs of the old West is that each won an important concession from the other, but for eighty years more or less the Santa Fe has said it won so loudly that a number of persons have been gulled into believing something that is patently not so.

It has been cynically remarked that throughout history the British have won every engagement in which they have had control of the cables and the legend of the triumphant Santa Fe has much the same basis. The Santa Fe has had many de-voted biographers. The tally of books hailing the Santa Fe's achievements, both well established and available to question, fills a generous shelf. The railroad has retained adroit press agents and masters of public credulity to proclaim that the Santa Fe has always been invincible.

Such, just for the record, is not the case. The Santa Fe very badly wanted the route up the Arkansas which was awarded to the Rio Grande. It has wanted a num-ber of other routes, privileges, concessions and assets which have long been with-held from it or only partly achieved but which are no concern of this brief essay. In the Colorado wars the Santa Fe got the better press but to this day the Rio Grande runs up the Grand Canyon of the Arkansas.

The last of the great railroad construction wars never engaged the public fancy as did the mighty swearing and nose punching between the Santa Fe and Rio Grande back in the Colorado seventies, but the epic battle for control of central Oregon involved swaggering captains of finance and ended an era of strife with some of the grandest battle music imaginable.

Edward H. Harriman, who owned and controlled the rich and powerful Union Pacific, had for years leered possessively at the Burlington, a property which, could he acquire it, would make his domination of the heartland of the West an accomplished fact. Aware of his intentions, the equally crafty and formidable team of Jim Hill and J. Pierpont Morgan bought a majority of Burlington shares from under the very nose of Harriman and added that line to the Northern Pacific-Great Northern empire already established by the shaggy, one-eyed old King of Get. Harriman was outraged and inaugurated a campaign of his own to buy great quantities of N.P. securities and the battle lines were drawn.

The field of battle turned out to be in Oregon, a territory which Harriman, by virtue of his Southern Pacific domination and proprietorship of the Union Pacific's Oregon Short Line considered his own private preserve. Into this hitherto unpoached domain came Hill breathing heavily and promising to build a railroad of his own right from the Columbia River to San Francisco, a proposal which set

Harriman's mustaches quivering with rage. So upset did Harriman become that he burst his appendix and was rushed to a hospital where, the moment he emerged from the anesthetic, he seized a bedside telephone and called Hill on long distance to tell him just what he meant to do to him and his insufferable Oregon Central. The looping catenaries of the Bell system were nearly melted and the railroading world watched from the sidelines with bated breath.

Hill had started construction of his Oregon Trunk down the east bank of the Deschutes River and almost in a matter of hours a vast grading gang of Harriman men appeared following location stakes along the west bank in the name of what their employer chose to call the Deschutes Railroad. Hill's chief engineer was John F. Stevens who had only a short time before completed an assignment for the United States government of building a canal across the Isthmus of Panama. George W. Boschke, who had erected the great sea wall around Galveston, Texas, was Harriman's field marshal.

The war was waged with all the devices and overtones of the Santa Fe-Rio Grande campaigns of a generation previous and much of the time in similar geographical circumstance. Just as the track gangs of the Colorado builders had battled in the narrow confines of the Royal Gorge, so did Hill's and Harriman's stalwarts engage each other in the narrow canyon of the Deschutes. Charges of dynamite showered the opposite river bank with debris and boulders. Whole sections of spiked-down track disappeared in nocturnal explosions. Workmen hurled all and any handy objects at each other across the water. Grading tools and costly equipment disappeared mysteriously. Magnificent Saturday night engagements were fought in the boom-town saloons where enemies foregathered and replacements of drinking equipment and mirrors were rushed in haste to such scenes of carnage as Bend and Metolius.

Chicanery on a grandiose scale also figured in the struggle. At a crucial moment in the progress of the Harriman line a telegram was received by Chief Engineer Boschke with the alarming intelligence that the Galveston sea wall had collapsed and demanding his presence, instanter, in Texas. Boschke, however, knew the worth of his own handiwork and disregarded the telegram for the canard that it was. The grading continued and the rival gangs also continued breaking up barrooms and tearing the ears off each other on Saturday nights.

The Deschutes River war was the last of the great railroad conflicts. It was also one of the noisiest.

Eventually a truce was made between the warring tycoons and Hill agreed to stop construction at Bend, a central Oregon crossroads which had never before figured in the news dispatches. But he continued to raise Harriman's blood pressure with such harassments as a steamship line between Portland and San Francisco and other inconveniences to the Southern Pacific until Harriman's death in 1909 put an end to hostilities. There were giants in the land in those days and nothing gave the giants more pleasure than to tangle with each other in mortal combat.

LUCIUS BEEBE

For eighty years the operations of the Virginia & Truckee Railroad in Nevada, its diamond-stacked engines and open platform cars, were a chapter of the old West.

XIV

Rails of Gold and Silver

Serving the Swaggering Boom Towns, Bonanza Railroads Added Color and Counterpoint to a Spacious Age and Played Golden Roles in the Melodrama of the Old West

IN A manner of speaking almost all the nineteenth-century railroads of Nevada, California and Colorado were bonanza railroads. The Central Pacific was first conceived as no more than a link between Sacramento and the Nevada mines and it was not until its progress beyond Dutch Flat that it was acknowledged to be a part of the continental dream. The Denver & Rio Grande Western, first planned to extend all the way to Old Mexico, was diverted into the passes of the

272

Rockies as was the Colorado & Southern, when rich strikes were made by the first prospectors in Leadville, Silverton, Ouray and Creede. Silver and gold were the most urgent matters in the Far West of the midnineteenth century and in one way or another all the railroads west of the Rockies were touched by precious metals.

But in general usage and convention the bonanza railroads were those which not only were inspired by treasure lodes but whose entire life span was involved in the recovery, transport and processing of ores. In nine cases out of ten the bonanza railroads disappeared from the map of the old West when the bonanzas themselves ran out. When the mine hoists ceased their clatter and the stamp mills fell silent, the doors of the roundhouses, too, were closed for the last time. And finally the word bonanza, itself, was never currency either in the Rockies or east of them. It was native to the regions where Spanish influence was strong, in Arizona, New Mexico, California and Nevada.

Therefore, while many of the early narrow-gage railroads of Colorado were primarily concerned with the exploitation of precious metals they shall be considered in the space devoted in this book to narrow-gage operations. Conversely, while several of the bonanza railroads of Nevada and California were also narrow gage, they have been assigned to this chapter dealing with railroads whose traffic and dominant concern was with silver and gold and people and enterprises associated with it.

Gone from the *Official Guide* these many years are the Pioche & Bullionville, the Nevada County Narrow Gage, the Carson & Colorado and the Nevada Central. In many cases the towns, camps and diggings, and sometimes "cities" they served, are as ghostly as the names of the railroads themselves. Rhyolite, on the margin of the great Amargosa Desert in southern Nevada, where at one time three railroads converged, is now inhabited by a single native who maintains a curio shop on a site where thousands lived. Candelaria in central Nevada, for several decades known as one of the shootingest communities in all the shooting West and served by Darius Mills' little Carson & Colorado, is now a heap of rubble and fallen electric power wires seven miles over a dubious trail from Sodaville, also a mere place name in the desert. Virginia City, most fabulous of all the bonanza towns and situated on top of the mighty Comstock Lode, years ago said farewell to the fantastically profitable Virginia & Truckee Railroad and now 500 artists, saloonkeepers and strip miners are permanent residents in a community that once boasted 30,000.

The Dollar Princess of the bonanza railroads of the old West was the celebrated and historic Virginia & Truckee. For eighty years Americans who had never been farther west than Albany knew about the V. & T. The nineteenth century knew it as the gilt-edged railroad which made possible "The Big Bonanza" in Virginia City on the Comstock Lode which created the Bonanza kings, Flood, Fair, Mackay and O'Brien, and about whose very trestles and switchstands was clustered such a wealth of legend as to rank its fifty miles of light iron on a par in the general imagination with the New York Central & Hudson River of the Vanderbilts or the New York & Erie. A later generation was to read entire books devoted to the V. & T., some were to come and ride its yellow wooden coaches in a wistful gesture of recapturing the wonderments of vanished times, and untold millions were to see the V. & T.'s equipment, locomotives and combination cars in cinema Westerns ranging from the classic *Union Pacific* to *The Return of Jesse James*. If ever a railroad were assured of immortality it was the V. & T.

The last flurry of railroad building to exploit bonanzas of precious metals was

From The

Beginning

The Comstock

Roared

A decade after the rush of 1849 for the goldfields of the Mother Lode in California, tremendous riches in silver ores were discovered in the Washoe Mountains in the Territory of Western Utah, later to be Nevada. On the side of Mt. Davidson, twenty-five miles south of today's Reno, a group of prospectors discovered traces of gold, unaware of the presence of much greater values in silver, but their claim was jumped (*above*) by a plausible ancient, Henry Comstock, whose name is preserved in the Comstock Lode. None of the first discoverers got rich, but a tent city sprang up overnight and another rush was on. Virginia City got its name when another boozy oldtimer named James Finney, locally known as "Old Virginny," one night dropped a bottle of whiskey and, unwilling to let it go to waste, turned the accident into a christening party (*below*) roaring that the new camp should be called Virginia. Ten years later the coming of the railroad to the Comstock was to turn its already vast mining operations into the greatest bonanza of riches in history.

MERVYN EIDENMULLER COLLECTION

COLLECTION OF DUNCAN EMRICH

Before the coming of the Virginia & Truckee Railroad to transform Virginia City into the most important and urbane community between Chicago and the Coast, its life followed the violent and gaudy pattern of the mining camps of the period. Saloons stayed open all night and miners brought their burros, locally known as "Washoe canaries," in to drink with them *(above)*. Street shootings *(below)* were a daily commonplace. "All men went armed and stabbings were beneath mention in the columns of the *Territorial Enterprise,* a pioneer institution of note and authority and one still being published on the Comstock.

NEVADA HISTORICAL SOCIETY

The Comstock Was a "National Wishing Well"

(ALL PICTURES) LIBRARY OF CONGRESS

SIGHTSEERS FROM EVERYWHERE CAME TO VIEW THE DEEP MINES

The deep shafts of the Comstock Lode were the wonder of the mining and financial worlds. Mining experts from Europe, Russian grand dukes, American millionaires, statesmen and stage celebrities, all came to Virginia City once the Virginia & Truckee Railroad was in operation to admire the huge hoisting works, the "square set timbers" (*above*) of winzes and stopes, the Cornish pumps and powerful air blowers serving the shafts. The two views below show miners working in the lower levels of Crown Point Mine.

Milling the silver ore from the Comstock depths was a vast operation as shown by the extent of the reducing works above the shafts of Consolidated Virginia Mine (*above*). Also big business was the freight traffic of the Virginia & Truckee Railroad which brought up timbers in fantastic quantities to shore up the ever lengthening underground shafts. In the below photograph V. & T. cars on the siding at the California hoisting works are delivering huge timbers for the "square sets" far below ground. Without the railroad the deep mines of Virginia City could not have operated.

The Comstock Noontide

N. Y. PUBLIC LIBRARY

In the days of 'The Big Bonanza' Virginia City's C Street (*above*) was as much in the world news as Wall Street or the rue de la Paix. The six-story International Hotel (*lower left*) boasted the first elevator west of the Mississippi and the mansions of mine superintendents (*lower right*) flowered in "Millionaire's Row" in wonderful and ornate profusion. The railroad made them all possible.

"TERRITORIAL ENTERPRISE"

LUCIUS BEEBE

E. S. HAMMACK

CELEBRITIES RODE IN AND GOLD WENT OUT ON THE V. & T.

"THIS WEEK"

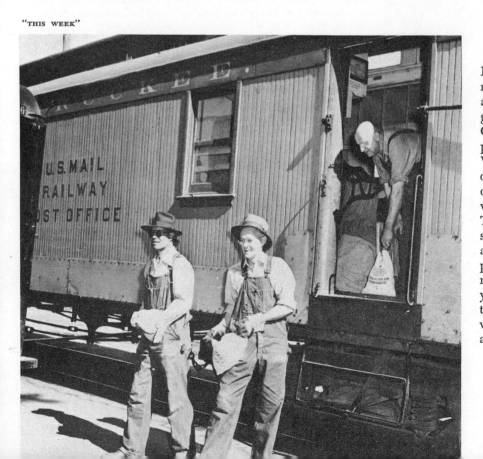

In the middle seventies when as many as forty-five train movements a day were scheduled on the Virginia & Truckee between Reno, Carson City and the Comstock, passengers were set down at the Virginia City terminal in the shadow of the Frederick House (*above*) one of the town's luxury hotels in whose basement was the Alhambra Theater, one of the Comstock's several playhouses. Bullion, ore and currency continued to be important freight on the bonanza railroad as late as 1949, the last year of its operations when (*below*) the last shipment of silver dollars was unloaded from its treasure car at Carson City.

LIBRARY OF CONGRESS

As Virginia City flowered into the swaggering cosmopolis of the American West *(above)* with a population of 25,000 persons and hotels, saloons, theaters and residences of wealth and substance, the artery of its life was the Virginia & Truckee Railroad which eliminated the teamster and his ore wagon *(left)* and hauled mine products cheaply to the mills on Carson Water. Three quarters of a century later Virginia City approximated a ghost town, its old houses *(below)* resting in sunlit mellow age. As a ghost town it is inhabited by lively recollections of its voluptuous youth. The *Territorial Enterprise*, most celebrated of all newspapers of the pioneer West, still appears weekly, and Virginia's twenty remaining saloons are tourist meccas of rococo proportions.

WESTERN COLLECTION GUS BUNDY

COMSTOCK MEMORIES

The bonanza kings, Flood, Fair, Mackay and O'Brien in partnership with Henry Yerington, general manager of the V. & T., owned vast resources of timber at Lake Tahoe which were essential to shore up the deep mine workings of the Comstock and feed the furnaces of the reducing works. To carry logs from the Sierra heights to Carson Valley where they were shipped aboard the cars to Virginia City, the world's longest flume, fifteen miles in extent, was built, and Flood and Fair, to win an impressive wager, once made the trip in a specially fashioned canoe. Drenched, contused and terrified, they won the bet but swore never again to essay such rashness. The afternoon departure from the depot at Virginia City of the V. & T.'s luxurious *Pacific Express* with through sleepers via the Central Pacific for San Francisco was an event still remembered as a high point in the daily life of the old Comstock. Shown at the head (*below*) was the beautiful engine *Reno*, beloved by a generation of Nevadans. In the background are the hoisting works of the Consolidated Virginia and California Mines.

CALIFORNIA HISTORICAL SOCIETY

Loneliest Little Railroad

CALIFORNIA HISTORICAL SOCIETY

The narrow-gage Carson & Colorado was largely built by Chinese labor. After its completion they settled in numerous colonies along its right of way, most famous of which was at Sodaville in the Nevada desert where its opium dens (*above*), were a great tourist attraction. Last vestigial trace of the lonely C. & C. seventy years later was the narrow-gage Owens Valley branch of the Southern Pacific whose trains (*center*) operated for freight only. But once its nearly 300 miles of slim-gage track serving Mina, Candelaria, Benton and Owenyo, boasted a daily train in each direction known as the *Slim Princess* which connected with the V. & T. at Mound House. Here the *Princess* and her entourage pose for a court portrait (*below*) at the Nevada-California boundary high on the slope of Mt. Montgomery.

CHARLES CLEGG

E. S. HAMMACK

DARIUS MILLS TOOK A DIM VIEW

Excited by the promise of the "Southern mines" of Nevada and California's Inyo County, Henry Yerington and banker William Sharon persuaded Darius Ogden Mills to extend the Virginia & Truckee south into California over a narrow-gage connection known as the Carson & Colorado. The C. & C. traversed Mt. Montgomery Pass and reached Keeler by Owens Lake. When the loneliest of all railroads was shown by Yerington to Mills the banker remarked sourly that "Either they had built it 300 miles too long or 300 years too soon."

San Francisco Glittered with Comstock Wealth

(ALL PICTURES) BANCROFT LIBRARY

San Francisco in the seventies was largely created and sustained by Comstock wealth which flowed into the counting houses of Montgomery Street and created a cosmopolis of archmillionaires. Most spacious manifestation of Virginia City's riches which rolled out aboard the Virginia & Truckee Railroad was the Palace Hotel whose great court (*above, lower right*) was world famous. Scores of other structures owed their being to the Comstock, the Flood and Sharon Buildings, Lucky Baldwin's Hotel, Senator Hearst's *Examiner* and the mansions of the nabobs themselves on Nob Hill. Nevada miners who could not afford the glories of the Palace favored the What Cheer House whose *ton* was indicated by a sign "Gentlemen Will Please Not Sleep on the Stairs." It was also celebrated for its three-course dinners for two bits.

part of the Tonopah boom in the southern mines of Nevada at the turn of the century. Darius Ogden Mills' and Henry Yerington's narrow-gage Carson & Colorado had been built in the eighties to serve the promising camps of Hawthorne, Luning, Belleville, Candelaria, Bodie and Aurora, but the nearest its rails came to Tonopah when that district started booming wildly in 1900 was at Tonopah Junction nearly seventy miles away and its narrow-gage equipment was entirely inadequate to the demands upon it which were created almost overnight.

To remedy this deficiency the narrow-gage Tonopah Railroad shortly was built to Tonopah, and broad-gaged and extended another thirty miles to Goldfield when that camp exploded into life a few years later. As the wealth of the Nevada desert continued to pour in floods from the hoists and mine shafts of the two towns, the Tonopah & Goldfield Railroad enjoyed a brief but hilarious life span. Solid trains of Pullmans rolled in from San Francisco, St. Louis and Denver. The private cars of such financial notables as Charles Schwab, Bernard Baruch and the acquisitive Senator William A. Clark of Montana arrived with their cargoes of champagne, geologists, stock operators, journalists and chorus girls. In 1906 Tex Rickard staged the Gans-Nelson fight in Goldfield and the world of sport arrived in bowler hats and ratcatcher suits for the gala event aboard the T. & G.

Before the bonanzas at Goldfield and Tonopah and their attendant excitements ran out a fresh series of strikes even further south in the Nevada desert set the mining world by the ears. Grizzled prospectors uncovered gold-bearing quartz in the so-called Bullfrog District adjacent to the eastern boundaries of Death Valley. A modern city with steel and cement construction, banks, granite office buildings and all the attendant razzle-dazzle of a mining boom sprang up in the plutonian reaches of the Amargosa Desert at Rhyolite. Soon three railroads converged on roaring Rhyolite: from the north the Tonopah & Bullfrog was built while from the south and west came the advancing iron of the Tonopah & Tidewater, connecting with the Santa Fe at Ludlow, and the Las Vegas & Tonopah. A union station was built, apparently for the ages since it is still intact today but no train will ever again roll up to its platforms, for Rhyolite, for all its plate-glass windows and four-story office buildings, became the ghostliest of all ghost towns within five years. The bottom fell out of its mining shares in 1909 and the desert began to reclaim its cement sidewalks and paved avenues.

Two of Nevada's older and even more spectacular bonanza railroads survived for a few years in the central portion of the state. The narrow-gage Eureka & Palisade had been built back in 1875 to connect the Reese River mining district with the main line of the Central Pacific and five years later the also three-foot-gage Nevada Central had begun running between Battle Mountain on the Central, and Austin, principal city of the White Pine district. Both railroads were richer in romance than in revenue, but somehow they continued in operation until the closing years of the nineteen thirties.

The Eureka & Palisade probably saw more gunfire than most small railroads even in the West of the late seventies, and a paragraph in the *Eureka Daily Sentinel* for April 9, 1878, gives a clue to this:

> G. W. Wright, President of the Bank of Nevada, had a rather ghastly experience on his recent trip to San Francisco. Just after getting started out from Oakland a tramp's legs were cut off, the result of an attempt to steal a ride. Between Lathrop and Sacramento a sick man yielded up the ghost. After leaving Sacra-

mento a son of William M. Evarts, Secretary of State, died a victim of consumption. Mr. Wright had just arrived in Eureka when the playful pistol announced another tragedy and he saw the body of Gus Botto, murdered at Bigelow's Music Hall, borne past to his residence. Fearing that his arrival at Pioche might be the signal for a general immolation, he tarried the night with us.

Even in an unsentimental century, the Eureka & Palisade enjoys a fragmentary immortality. Its right of way has long since returned to the elemental Nevada desert and the hundred-mile-an-hour traveler on the Southern Pacific passing through Palisade is at a loss to see where once its engines ran, but a complete E. & P. train with its two gayly painted cars and diminutive engine stands on a length of track at the Pony Express Museum at Santa Anita, California. A hurrying world pauses to admire it as a souvenir of heroic times.

A few miles removed to the west from the Eureka & Palisade was the three-foot Nevada Central Railroad built to connect the booming town of Austin in the Reese River diggings with the Central Pacific at Battle Mountain. Austin was famous for a number of institutions—among them the "Sazarac Lying Club"—and for being the home of Mme Emma Nevada, a nineteenth-century diva of local if not positively international fame. When the N.C. was chartered the terms of a subsidy of $200,000 from Lander County stipulated that construction should be completed by December 31, 1878, or the sum be forfeited. On the appointed night the end of track was still several miles from town and a frantic populace was building bonfires to thaw the ground so that ties could be laid in a raging Nevada blizzard. In an inspired eleventh-hour gesture, the city fathers met in a leading saloon and obligingly extended the town limits to meet the railroad. This device was used elsewhere in the land, notably upon the coming to Fort Worth of the Texas & Pacific, with commendable success.

Elsewhere in the western sagebrush there were bonanza railroads. Across the California line from Nevada in Mono County was located at Bodie the wildest mining town of them all, if contemporary accounts are to be credited. "The Bad Man from Bodie" became part of the American language along with the "Wild Man of Borneo," and even Mark Twain was impressed with the community's excessive wickedness and predilection for murder. A short-lived, three-foot-gage road, appropriately enough called the Bodie & Benton, was built to roll the ores from Bodie's opulent deep mines down to the Carson & Colorado's main line at Benton in the shadow of Mount Montgomery. It stopped short at Mono Mills, however, some miles from Benton, remaining for its brief life span a railroad from nowhere to nowhere, and today not even the informed historian can find a trace of its once strait but hopeful right of way.

It is probable that the bonanza railroads, like the narrow gages, have always occupied a position and magnitude in the public consciousness and in railroad literature out of all proportion to their importance. But their freight was more than the wealthy ore of the Ophir and Gould & Curry Mines; it was the stuff of fabulous romance and the legend of valiant achievements in an as yet untamed frontier. Their passengers were not mere bankers, financiers and mining experts; they were the custodians of the wishing wells of the world where everyone might become rich beyond the wealth of the Great Inca merely for the dreaming. Now all of them are gone, but they will never disappear completely from the most splendid and glamorous pages of the national history.

MACKAY SCHOOL OF MINES

High in the Sierra, the mining camp of Grass Valley was connected with the Central
Pacific main line at Colfax by the Nevada County Narrow Gage, a railroad of recognized personality. Its Bear River trestle (below) contained 300,000 feet of timber and
a Howe truss 300 feet above the water. Most famous of its regular passengers was Lola
Montez (center) a dancer whose love affairs were notorious in two continents and made
her the reigning celebrity in her home town of Grass Valley.

NEVADA HISTORICAL SOCIETY

The Wealth of Austin Rode the Narrow Gage

MOODY PHOTOS

Deep in the Nevada hills the boom town of Austin, connecting with the main line of the Central Pacific by the narrow gage daily mixed train of the Nevada Central (*above*) was renowned for its Austin Liar's Club, its skilled gamblers (*center*) and as the source of the famed Austin Flour Sack whose repeated sale at auction helped finance the Sanitary Commission, predecessor of the Red Cross during the Civil War. Wells Fargo's durable shotgun messengers brought out the wealth of Austin in treasure cars like that shown below at Battle Mountain.

As Did Rich Ores from the Mines of Eureka

Sixty miles distant from Austin, Eureka (*top*) was also joined to the outer world by a silver-financed narrow gage, the Eureka & Palisade, one of whose diminutive ore trains is shown at the left. Most notable of Eureka's citizens was Emma Wickson, known to the world of music as Mme Emma Nevada (*below*) who earned her first pennies singing outside the swinging doors of the Hurry Back Saloon. With the eventual decline of silver mining the little railroad was abandoned and only an occasional rotting tie in the desert marks its once prosperous path. Its yellow-and-green-trimmed coaches and combine are preserved, however, in a Las Vegas museum, souvenirs of the great days and aboard which was carried the wealth of Ruby Hill and Secret Canyon from a bonanza camp that boasted nine graveyards.

MOODY PHOTOS
CHARLES CLEGG

Last Of All
Roared
Tonopah
And
Goldfield

SOUTHERN PACIFIC RR.

The last of the great booms in precious metals took place at Tonopah and Goldfield in the deserts of Southern Nevada shortly after the turn of the century. Great freighting wains that had seen service in the rush to the Comstock, the Reese River and White Pine districts (*above*) brought in the first household goods and mining equipment. Twenty-four mules guided by a single jerkline hauled wagons with wheels eight feet high across the sagebrush. After the building of the Tonopah & Goldfield Railroad solid trains of Pullmans, diners and private railroad cars of such notables as Charles Schwab, Senator William A. Clark and Bernard Baruch rolled into town. The photograph below shows a train of sports and gamblers arriving at Goldfield in 1906 for the Gans-Nelson fight promoted by Tex Rickard.

"TONOPAH TIMES BONANZA"

"TERRITORIAL ENTERPRISE"

NEVADA PHOTO SERVICE

The Tonopah & Goldfield Railroad ferried strange cargo across the Nevada dessert. It carried out gold and silver-bearing ores (*upper right*) sometimes valued at $575,000 for a single forty-eight-ton carload. It also brought in adventurers such as the Count Constantin Podorsky (*upper left*) whose continental ways and costume cut a swathe in the mining camp. The Count broke up a Goldfield home and was promptly assassinated while dining in the Palm Grill, Goldfield's de luxe restaurant. It was the town's most aristocratic shooting. The T. & G. ran until the end of the Second World War (*below*) bringing in fuel to the flying field at Tonopah after which it was abandoned.

CHARLES CLEGG

CULVER SERVICE

"Was it the Rube Barrows gang?" exclaimed the *National Police Gazette* nervously after this holdup of a Louisville & Nashville train at Flomaton, Alabama, in 1890.

XV

Car Robbers and Bindle Stiffs

Jesse James and Other Violent Men Besieged the Carriers for Three Shooting Decades, but Hoboes Have Been an American Institution Since the First Drifter Rode the Blinds

For a period of approximately four decades beginning with the close of the Civil War and ending shortly after the turn of the twentieth century train robbery in its several forms was an American institution. In its early years when the memory of desperate times was fresh, when railroad magnates and

292

bankers were pilloried as face grinders of the poor and when the postwar crime wave was universal, train robbery enjoyed, if not a positive general approval, at least a certain tolerance. Cold-blooded assassins like the James brothers were romanticized in the public prints and in cheap literature. In the Middle West where the grangers sought to foment class war in the name of justice to the farmers and where, in some instances, the church of God was hostile to the carriers because they operated on the Sabbath, robbing the cars was occasionally hailed as a Christian agency and a gesture of defiance to monopoly. Ministers of the gospel applauded the Younger brothers, a posse of second-rate thugs and renegades, from their pulpits.

With better times and more enlightened public sentiment train robbery, during the eighties, fell into universal disfavor and newspapers and pulp novels began glorifying sheriffs, Pinkerton detectives, special officers and loyal railroad employees who thwarted and sometimes exterminated bandits individually and in gangs. By the nineties rail banditry was in decline and disappeared after the turn of the century except in a few isolated instances in Texas and the Northwest. The steel mail and express car, improved methods of communication and a general revision of the technique of crime detection and prevention eliminated one of the favorite characters of the Sunday supplement editor.

There is some debate among historians as to what constituted the first train robbery, but Alvin Harlow believes it took place on the tracks of the Ohio & Mississippi Railroad in May 1865, less than a month after Appomattox, when a St. Louis-bound train was held up fourteen miles north of Cincinnati and the baggage and express cars overturned and looted. In the light of the record this would seem to be a clear-cut first, although in the Deep South in the years following the war minor stoppages of the cars and more or less casual theft of watches and whisky at a drunken pistol point were counted as "train robbery," a term which would have surprised the dangerous bandits of Missouri and the Far West.

As robbing the cars became a more established form of activity among the gunmen who had previously devoted most of their attention to banks, so too did the prevention of train robbery and the eventual detection of holdup men become more scientific and better organized. By the early seventies the forces of detection and law enforcement had divided the United States very nearly in half. East of the Mississippi with only occasional forays into Kansas, Oklahoma and Minnesota was the province of the detective organization evolved and perfected by Alan Pinkerton; the Far West and Southwest were the stamping ground of the armed guards, detectives and special officers of Wells Fargo & Co., the treasure expressmen and bankers, and the Southern Pacific Railroad.

In both hemispheres the properly constituted forces of law and order were supplemented with more or less frequency by groups of cynical citizens who felt that one sure way to cure a thug with an itch for holding up the express cars was a stout length of rope thrown over the crosspiece of a handy telegraph pole.

The first well-organized group of train robbers, the Reno gang, who practiced their calling throughout Ohio and Indiana after the close of the Civil War, came to an end through this informal agency. Several suspect members of the confraternity were seized by the law after robbing an express car on the Ohio & Mississippi Valley Railroad, but neighbors along the road's right of way, who thought highly of its services, were impatient and took six hoodlums, some accounts say five, away from the sheriff and hanged them practically instanter. Shortly thereafter four more members of the Reno gang, three of them actual Reno brothers, were removed with a minimum of legal fuss from the jail house at New Albany, Indiana, and strung up from convenient fixtures, and that was the end of the first organized gang of train robbers.

Although it has been deplored as in bad taste by both nice-mannered citizens and hangmen cheated of a fee, lynching was one of the most salutary crime preventatives known in the lawless era which followed the Civil War. It precluded beyond all possibility the repetition of offense and served as a notable deterrent, both at an absolute minimum of expense and delay.

It is notable in this connection that the chapter that spelled the end of the greatest gang of train robbers of all, the James boys, was written at Northfield, Minnesota, a decade after the first robberies of the cars in Ohio and Indiana, not by organized agencies of law enforcement, but by a number of irritated private citizens who blew the tripes out of three of Jesse's ranking cutthroats and crippled four others with such a weight of lead they were never again good for much. Jesse James himself, a wanton murderer and cheap show-off of vast proportions, came to his end at the hand of an amateur. Some fool wrote a silly song about poor Jesse James being laid in his grave but most of the United States shouted "Hooray."

Still another gang of train and bank robbers who earned their first bad fame by making a nuisance of themselves to the Southern Pacific's mail and express cars in the San Joaquin Valley and in New Mexico and who, in turn, came to an exclamatory end at the hands of unofficial justice was the so-called Dalton gang.

For several years in the early nineties four brothers, Bill, Bob, Emmett and Grattan Dalton had made a practice of recruiting other thugs and gunmen in the cause of train, bank and stage robberies, holdups, assassinations and beatings. A troglodyte tribe of congenital degenerates, the Daltons contrived for years to evade the special police of the Southern Pacific but met their match when they undertook to hold up an entire community on the Kansas prairies named Coffeyville. The affair was a close parallel of the Northfield massacre of the James gorillas, in that the Daltons tried in force to hold up two banks at once and were substantially ventilated for their pains. Bill Dalton was in jail at the time of the Coffeyville affair, but his three brothers assisted by three ambitious but somewhat inexpert gunmen rode into Coffeyville one morning in 1892 and were surprised by an alert citizenry as they were engaged in pillaging the First National and Condon banks.

The populace of Coffeyville leaned from windows of their homes and places of employment, peered from under swinging doors and around back porches and had target practice with the Daltons. They killed Bob, Emmett and Grattan and two of their stooges while four citizens were mortally wounded before the black powder smoke cleared from the scene. The lives of four innocent men was a stiff price to pay for the elimination of such vermin but at least thereafter it was impossible for Southern Pacific detectives to blame the Daltons every time one of their express cars was knocked over and James B. Hume, Wells Fargo's energetic chief of police, slept better of nights.

A by-product of the railroad age in America which came into existence in the years of steam and is gradually vanishing in the Diesel era was the genus hobo, tramp or drifter. Once a familiar figure in rural regions, the old-time tramp long

MUSEUM OF MODERN ART

When the Edison Co., pioneers in the cinema, filmed *The Great Train Robbery,* a scene from which is reproduced here from the files of the Museum of Modern Art of New York, robbing the cars was already firmly established in the national literature of fiction. The exploits of the James boys, the Daltons, the Barrows gang and other railroad bandits both real and mythical were the matter of scores and hundreds of the paper-backed volumes such as those shown below that came to be known as dime novels even though many of them in those happy days retailed for five cents. Their moral tone was deplorable, for in them the wicked were as a troubled sea and virtue strictly at a discount, and an entire generation of youth delighted in them until the coming of the films rendered them to the discard.

N. Y. PUBLIC LIBRARY

Jessie James Achieved the Status of Legend

N. Y. PUBLIC LIBRARY

Jesse James, a moronic sadist and cowardly murderer, was elevated to a Robin Hood role by scores of maudlin sentimentalists in the public prints. One technique evolved by James and his thugs was to pile obstructions on the rails (*upper right*) frequently killing or injuring train crews before robbing the cars. On other occasions they boarded the cars in overwhelming numbers (*below*) murdering railroad employees without provocation and pillaging rich and poor alike among the passengers. No outlaw was ever more spuriously invested with the dubious role of stealing from the well-to-do to give to the needy.

LIBRARY OF CONGRESS

And Came to a Violent End in Fact and Poetry

The James gang's last train robbery, as depicted in this old-time woodcut, was of the *Fast Mail* on the Chicago & Alton Railroad at Blue Cut, Missouri, in 1881. Two railroad workers were murdered for the sum of $700.

The following year James was shot and killed by Bob Ford, a renegade associate, while living under the alias of Howard at St. Joseph, Missouri, a circumstance which gave origin to the rhyme about the "dirty little coward who shot Mr. Howard." A preposterous legend, perpetuated in the films, holds that James was shot from behind while adjusting a wall motto reading "God Bless Our Happy Home." The version of his last moments reproduced here is probably equally fictitious originating in a four sheet for the melodrama *Jesse James, the Missouri Outlaw.*

Violence and Treasure Rode the Wooden Express Cars

N. Y. PUBLIC LIBRARY

WELLS FARGO'S TREASURE CHEST WAS THE GOAL

The most expert train robbers aimed primarily at the express and mail cars rather than the passenger coaches. Here large shipments of valuables, bullion and currency might be expected in compact form in the Wells Fargo treasure chest or the express messenger's safe. The conventional routine (*above*) was for one or more members of the gang to overcome the engine crew while others assaulted the baggage car and tossed the safe on the right of way. If the cast-iron safes of the time resisted mallets and wrecking bars, giant powder was resorted to, as shown below. Locked steel express cars and heavily armed guards in the end reduced train robbery to a mere trace of its once profitable self.

CULVER SERVICE

CULVER SERVICE

In a daring holdup of the treasure car of the Texas Central, patriotically staged on Washington's Birthday, 1878, as shown above, masked miscreants made off with $2,000 in gold currency. In the picture below, a daring Pinkerton operative, having learned of a plot to rob a Burlington train near Ottumwa, Iowa, leaps from concealment upon a lone outlaw before he can overcome the messenger and admit his accomplices.

CULVER SERVICE

Resistance Was Seldom Encountered Among Passengers

LIBRARY OF CONGRESS

After the close of the Civil War bands of recently discharged soldiers of both sides, as shown above, made a practice of holding up passenger trains on a more or less amateur basis. Sometimes (*lower left*) they were bent more on disturbance than robbery. On other occasions (*lower right*) cowhands would board western trains and intimidate passengers by forcing them to drink or pretending to take their valuables. At such times watches and wallets might vanish but violence to persons was very rare.

CULVER SERVICE

The epidemic of train robberies which made news throughout the seventies and eighties was largely confined to the roads west of the Mississippi. Here four masked highwaymen are shown robbing the *Pacific Express* of the Chicago & Alton, a maneuver which they accomplished, according to a contemporary news account "expeditiously and without the slightest disturbance."

To believe the sensational journals of the era, the steamcars were no place for timid females. In 1891 the *National Police Gazette* was particularly fetched, editorially, by the event shown at the left in which "robbers made a rich haul on the night cars between Sacramento and Winnemucca, Nevada." As the distance between these points is 330 miles and the Central Pacific's trains averaged thirty miles an hour at this time, there was no need for haste on the robbers' part. In the scenes at the bottom of the page a brave maiden is putting up a game fight against an unchivalrous ruffian during a holdup on the Texas & Pacific cars. After the crisis is over she recovers her jewels which have been secreted in her reticule at the outbreak of hostilities.

(FIVE PICTURES) CULVER SERVICE

Robbing the Steamcars Ended in Nothing Good

Shortly after the gang dominated by John Reno and his brothers made train robbery an American institution by taking $96,000 from the express car of the Jefferson, Madison & Indianapolis Railroad in Indiana, five of their number were being taken to trial aboard a train of the Ohio & Mississippi when the train was stopped as shown here by a group of indignant citizens of Seymour and the prisoners removed. They were hanged (*below*) with neatness and dispatch from a gallows handy to the tracks and a few days later the four remaining members of the gang were executed under almost precisely similar circumstances. Such economy of time and effort beat anything the statutory courts had to offer and the practice enjoyed a considerable vogue thereafter.

N. Y. PUBLIC LIBRARY

Almost without exception robbing the cars led to a violent end for highwaymen. One of the last attempts to hold up a train was made in 1912 at Sanderson, Texas, where two misguided yahoos set upon the express messenger of a Southern Pacific passenger haul. One was instantly killed by a blow over the head from a bungstarter in the hands of the messenger who then picked up the fallen man's rifle and coolly eliminated his companion. Their bodies (*right*) were obligingly posed for a photographer on the depot platform at Sanderson and the messenger was voted a reward by Congress for protecting the mails.

AMERICAN EXPRESS CO.

ago became enshrined in the gallery of national characters along with the Negro minstrel, the itinerant printer and the bawdyhouse professor and was possessed of personal attributes no less well defined. The mobile vagrant took a dim view of manual labor and had a pronounced taste for travel. Traditionally he carried his worldly possessions all in a bundle slung over his shoulder on a stick and he fore-gathered periodically in well-identified tramp jungles throughout the land, the most notable of which were beside the tracks at Walla Walla, Dallas, Sacramento and Mattoon, Illinois.

The practiced 'bo traditionally carried his possibles in a bandanna-wrapped bundle or bindle, hence the appellation of "bindle stiff," and his communal stew, composed of whatever edibles the brotherhood might assemble, was mulligan, named for some long forgotten Escoffier of the brake beams. In time of severe fam-ine he might labor briefly for a handout of pork and beans, but the practice was frowned on by more exclusive members of the confraternity.

Common hoboes rode the car tops or empty boxcars of freight trains, sometimes paying the crews a small fee or "'bo money" to travel unmolested over their division. Aristocrats among the drifters boarded the vestibules of baggage cars or rode the brake rigging of passenger cars, a practice much abated with the coming of streamlined trains and hundred mile and more speeds. In this hierarchy of tran-sient thieves, thugs and drug addicts, top social rating went to car thieves, and the looting of warehouses and freight consignments cost the railroads untold sums. Ordinary 'bos or mere ride stealers received little attention from railroad police.

Eventually the hobo achieved immortality in American folklore comparable to that of the traveling salesman or Kentucky colonel. The tramp of the old school or Weary Willie has largely disappeared save in the Far West but his place has, to a certain extent, been taken by the migratory worker whose seasonal occupations call for extended travel at a minimum of expense. Railroad police estimated that during the depression years there were as many as 1,000,000 full-time vagrants riding the rods and blinds, but automobiles have made vast inroads on the hobo ranks and, like the Indian and boomer railroader, the professional drifter is a vanishing American.

The life of the drifter was not without its appeal to certain individuals with intelligence quotients far above the average car-top punk. The pressure and en-croachments of organized society from time to time induced men of notable talents to take to the open road for the sake of its freedom from responsibility and the easy shiftlessness it promised. During the nineteen twenties a shock-haired Irishman named Jim Tully attracted considerable literary attention with his stories of life among the tramp jungles while another, possibly even more authentic hobo, Albert Bein, wrote several plays concerning themselves with the existence of the brethren along the railroad rights of way. One of the authors of this book once knew a graduate of Dartmouth College who added academic distinction to the jungles which flourished along the Southern Pacific's Texas lines and could recite Verlaine's "Fetes Galantes" to confused fellow travelers aboard the gondolas, but he was regarded as something extra special in the fraternity, a sort of Baudelaire of the bindle stiffs.

A Gallery of Country Tramps and Drifters

The hobo was popularly believed to have a code (*left*) whose symbols chalked on a wall or fence indicated the type of reception he might receive within. The tramp at the right has not been warned of the housewife's broom.

Traditionally a handout of food (*left*) was purchased by drifters with an hour's work on the family woodpile. The hobo bracing the deacon on the right is already fortified with a bottle of something probably stronger than tea which bulges his pocket.

On Christmas Day (*lower left*) even the shabbiest hobo might expect a hospitable glass with the proprietor of a small-town tavern and perhaps a Christmas dinner, but at other seasons he came by his potables by scavenging (*lower right*) or outright pillage. The tramp in fact and legend was notoriously thirsty.

(ALL PICTURES) N. Y. PUBLIC LIBRARY

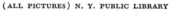

The city hobo, here depicted in his hour of repose on a park bench and at his morning ablutions at the municipal font, lends himself less to identification as an American type than did his cousin who rode the rods and blinds in the great open spaces. The drifter from city to city was usually a seasonal traveler rather than one who rode the cars for the air and scenery. Like the professional darky and the German waiter, the hobo gradually became an institution and a recognized stage character. Greatest of all tramp portrayers was Joe Jackson (*lower right*) who delighted a generation of theater audiences with his Weary Willie impersonations and vagabond humor. The folklore of the hobo and its association with the rails also received literary recognition. Albert Bein (*lower left*) himself a professional drifter who had lost a leg under the trucks on the Santa Fe, wrote the Broadway successes *Little Old Boy* and *Heavenly Express* in which the mythology of the "big rock candy mountain" and the drifter's heaven where there is always pie in the sky and no railroad police figured largely.

"NEW YORK HERALD TRIBUNE"
CULVER SERVICE

Hoboes and the Cars Formed an Immemorial Pattern

LIBRARY OF CONGRESS

"Even on the broad plains west of the Missouri," wrote *Leslie's* staff correspondent in the seventies, "in the shadow of the Wahsatches and in the desert of the Humboldt one comes with surprise upon the old familiar faces, and sees a dusty, slouching figure or two trailing beside the track, pipe in mouth, bundle on shoulder; or, as twilight is drawing over the desert, we rush past a group of them camping out beside their fire—a jovial-looking company with their pipes and bottles and cards to pass the time away." Travelers on trains in the West are still familiar from the car windows with the scene described by the reporter three quarters of a century ago. In those days of simple brake rigging it was possible (*lower left*) for the hobo "to dive unseen under the cars and coil himself in some complicated fashion along the iron-work between the wheels." Sometimes, too, in the days of open platforms (*lower right*) it was necessary for train crews to clear the rear platform of uninvited riders.

LIBRARY OF CONGRESS

Sometimes, in Force and Numbers, 'Boes Were Unruly

Sometimes, although not often, gangs of tramps boarded the cars *(above)* and terrified the passengers with riotous behavior and abuse. At other times *(lower left)* when in sufficient numbers they battled the crews of freight trains as in this scene where a well-dressed tramp in a tailcoat is going to the assistance of his companions. Always they walked the tracks *(lower right)* dusty players in the allegory of the iron horse.

(THREE PICTURES) CULVER SERVICE

LIBRARY OF CONGRESS

Although the greatest American railroad disasters were still to come, the year 1865 found even such conservative periodicals as *Harper's* in arms over the mounting death toll. In this fanciful drawing, although tribute is paid to other forms of mischance, the Grim Reaper pilots a locomotive to destruction over the prostrate forms of its victims. Death, even at this early date, rode the rails.

XVI

The Open Switch

Throughout the Nineteenth Century America was Horrified by a Series of Catastrophes to the Trains as Bridges Fell, Engines Left the Rails and Car Stoves Ignited the Debris

I NEVITABLY, along with their useful and valuable cargoes, the speeding cars were also freighted with disaster. Wrecks and other by-products of mischance began to appear early in the record and it is improbable that they will ever entirely be eliminated until the last carwheel stops rolling on the last rail. Safety

308

devices and improved operational practices have immeasurably decreased the incidence of railroad catastrophes until it has become the least perilous of all modes of travel, but derailments, ditchings and collisions still make news and the safety of railroading's mature years was purchased at a frightful cost in life and property in its less responsible youth. Throughout most of the nineteenth century the possibility of disaster when traveling by rail was a very real ponderable, and experienced travelers made a point of securing when possible places in cars located in the middle of trains, these being the least vulnerable either to head-on wreck or rear-end collision. Ticket clerks still occasionally encounter an old time traveler who demands the middle berth in the center car of the train consist, an instinct inherited from primordial times.

As long as the human element alone guided and guarded the passage of the cars the possibility of mischance was never altogether absent and quite aside from the major disasters which became part of the record for all time the press throughout the nineteenth century was almost daily filled with accounts of minor calamities somewhere in the land. The sensational illustrated papers were filled with blood-chilling artist's sketches "made at the scene" of demolished cars, overturned locomotives and human debris, and the culpability of railroad managements in such instances was stock matter for the sermons of indignant divines. To many Americans the place names of Ashtabula and Revere are to this day synonymous with railroad wrecks even though the occasions which lent them this bad fame are three-quarters of a century and more in the past. At about the turn of the century accidents were so frequent on New England's most famous railroad that, years later, in the Broadway sensation *Life With Father* one of the characters instantly set the date of the play's action by opening his paper and remarking: "Another wreck on the New Haven!"

Calamity appeared early in the annals of the cars. First in many other elements of fame, the Camden & Amboy in New Jersey was also the first to suffer a derailment which achieved space in the papers and one which was not without its prophetic overtones. For aboard the train brigade which went into the ditch and capsized its coaches upon the passengers was a "Captain Van Derbilt" of Staten Island who was later to be himself associated with railroading in the capacity of its greatest tycoon. Cornelius Vanderbilt was not seriously injured, but a couple of cracked ribs served to remind him unfavorably of the Camden & Amboy for some weeks to come.

The causes of the worst wrecks of the nineteenth century were defective bridges and the car stove. The possibilities for holocaust inherent in a red-hot cannonball stove in each wooden passenger coach that might go into the ditch were enormous. Wrecks with the greatest casualty list were almost invariably accompanied by fire.

The building of railroad bridges and trestles was, of course, as new as railroading itself. A few resolute engineers with doomsday as their objective might build such everlasting stone structures as the Erie's Starucca Viaduct and the New Haven's Canton Viaduct, both erected in the forties and still in use today, but where stone wasn't handy and roads were economy minded, wooden spans constructed along a variety of deplorable patterns were available to fire, stress and the elements. The so-called "Howe truss" was probably responsible for as many railroad deaths as any single agency.

Add to these hazards a whole catalogue of altogether lethal possibilities, the

E. S. HAMMACK

THE FIRST RAILROAD WRECK INVOLVED THE FIRST VANDERBILT

SCENE ON C—N AND A—Y RAILROAD.

BENEVOLENT EMPLOYEE—"*Does Mr. Jones live here?*"
MRS. JONES—"*Yes, but he's not in.*"
B. E.—"*Well, I rather guess not, seein' as I've got him here, a little mixed up with a few other fellows.*"

The first record of a railroad wreck in America was on the Camden & Amboy as its train brigade of coaches rolled across the New Jersey meadows near Hightstown in 1833. Aboard it, according to contemporary newspaper accounts was a "Captain Van Derbilt," who sustained two painfully fractured ribs. In the victim of this primal catastrophe it is possible to recognize the future Commodore Cornelius Vanderbilt, genius of the New York Central System and the most powerful railroad rajah of all time. By the middle fifties wrecks on the Camden road had become so frequent as to provoke what seems to be the first cartoon to attack a railroad management (*below*). It appeared in the *New York Illustrated News* and shows a widow receiving the remains of her husband who has perished in a crash on the C—— & A—— Railroad.

Mischance Rode the Rails from Earliest Times

GEORGE EASTMAN HOUSE

THE FIRST WRECK PHOTOGRAPH MADE NEWSPAPER HISTORY

What is believed by Beaumont Newhall of George Eastman House to be the first news photograph of a train wreck was taken on the main line of the Boston & Worcester Railroad near Pawtucket, Rhode Island, in August 1853. Thirteen people were killed and fifty injured and this daguerreotype was the basis for a facsimile engraving which appeared with remarkable enterprise for the time a fortnight later in the *New York Illustrated News*. Another railroad first, the first fatal accident, took place in England in the early thirties to an unfortunate Mr. Huskinson (*below*) who stepped onto the right of way during the trial run of the *Rocket* and was damaged beyond repair. This picture of the melancholy occurrence was published in an American magazine some years later in a feature story of railroad fatalities.

Disaster Vexed

The

Long Island

Then And Now

N. Y. PUBLIC LIBRARY

Wrecks on the Long Island Railroad, unhappy stepchild of the Pennsylvania, were nothing new when a series of shocking disasters transpired on its lines in the mid-twentieth century. The scenes on this page from contemporary news sources record a wreck when two express passenger trains collided near Jamaica in August 1865. *Leslie's,* where they appeared, was able to tell an awe-struck public that one of its own staff artists had been aboard one of the trains and to depict the horrors of the scene at the very moment the dust settled.

CULVER SERVICE

STYLE OF ADVERTISEMENT SUITABLE FOR
L. I. R. R. TRAVEL.

SOME OF THE SUMMER RESORTS TO BE
REACHED.

As far back as 1865 the Long Island Railroad was the object of savage abuse in the public prints on account of its multiplicity of wrecks, and such cartoons as these from the *New York Illustrated News* were commonplace. Nearly a century later, on the eve of Thanksgiving, the Long Island contrived to kill a record seventy-seven passengers in a wreck (*below*) at Richmond Hill in Queens, where a Manhattan to Hempstead local was rammed from behind by a Babylon express when block signals failed. Only the previous February a Long Island wreck at Rockville Center had eliminated thirty-two more commuters.

ACME

The

Ashtabula

Holocaust

Shocked

The

Entire

Nation

(THREE PICTURES) CULVER SERVICE

BETTMAN ARCHIVE

When, in 1863, a subordinate engineer on the railroad's staff protested to President Amasa Stone of the Lake Shore & Michigan Southern against the installation across a deep river bed at Ashtabula, Ohio, of a Howe truss bridge, pointing out that such a span was inherently dangerous, he was summarily discharged. The bridge was ordered and built by Charles Collins, chief engineer of the railroad and a brother-in-law of William Howe. For thirteen years the bridge stood. Then one December night in 1876 at the height of a fearful storm blown in from Lake Erie it gave way beneath the two locomotives and ten baggage, express cars and Pullmans of the crack *Pacific Express* and eighty-three persons were cremated in the wreckage as it burned on the frozen creek 150 feet beneath. The next day Chief Engineer Collins blew his brains out. A few days later the ailing Commodore Vanderbilt (the Lake Shore was a Vanderbilt subsidiary) died, the end perhaps hastened by shock. Five years later the once proud and arrogant Amasa Stone took his own life and the wheel of tragedy had come full circle. The Howe truss was never again incorporated in the construction of any responsible railroad. The graves of nineteen unidentified victims of the holocaust are cared for in the Ashtabula cemetery by the New York Central Railroad to this day. Above is an artist's conception of the very moment the locomotive *Columbia* plunged into the abyss, the *Socrates* having crossed in safety, while on the page opposite the scene is shown before, during and after the holocaust.

The "Angola Horror" Became a National Byword

LIBRARY OF CONGRESS

Because of the melancholy details of the accident, the wreck of the Lake Shore & Michigan Southern Railroad's *New York Express*, Buffalo bound, at Angola, New York, in 1867 came to be known as the "Angola horror." Because of improper maintenance of way, the rear coach of the fast train became derailed twenty-two miles west of Buffalo and plunged off a truss bridge forty feet above the water carrying the coach immediately in front along with it. The rest of the train continued some distance before the crew realized there had been an accident. The matchwood coaches of the period with their ornate furnishings were instantly fired by the car stoves and fifty persons were burned to death in the conflagration pictured above in *Leslie's*.

The victims of the "Angola horror" were removed to the town morgue (*top and bottom*) for identification but many were burned beyond that possibility. The following Sunday afternoon a huge throng turned out for a memorial service conducted at the Exchange Street depot of the railroad in Buffalo. Investigation of the wreck showed that evidence pointing to the culpability of the road master had been subsequently removed, and a national scandal resulted which shook the foundations of even the respected New York Central of which the Lake Shore was a subsidiary.

N. Y. PUBLIC LIBRARY

After Revere the Clergy Cried "Murder"

(ALL PICTURES) BROWN BROS.

While but twenty odd passengers were killed in the disaster at Revere, a few miles north of Boston on the Eastern Railroad compared to the scores at Ashtabula, Chatsworth and other celebrated wrecks, the prominence of several of the victims and the subsequent denunciations of the Boston press gained for it nation-wide attention. As a result of a veritable farrago of confusions in the Eastern's dispatching and operations that August night in 1871, the *Bangor Express* running out of Boston late with a heavy consist of Pullmans and coaches telescoped a local, stalled near Revere depot and the coal-oil lamps served in the function usually delegated to the car stove of firing the wreckage. Several well-known Bostonians perished in the flames including two divines, and the famed Phillips Brooks, who was usually more temperate, termed the disaster "deliberate murder" by the Eastern's management. The Eastern was nearly bankrupted by the ensuing lawsuits and Beacon Street viewed the affair in the light of an almost cosmic catastrophe until the following year when the Great Fire of Boston gave it something bigger to think about. Above is the scene at Revere depot and the page opposite shows an artist's view of the debris and the ministrations of neighbors to the wounded.

1887 Was a Banner Year for the Grim Reaper

CULVER SERVICE

The year 1887 witnessed a mounting toll of casualties along the nation's rails. It was the beginning of the age of speed, car construction was still in its most primitive stages, air brakes were in the future, the car stove was universal and the Howe truss, already guilty of scores of major catastrophes, was still in common use where it should never have been at all. The year was high-lighted by major disasters at Tiffin, Ohio, at White River, Vermont, at Forest Hills near Boston and the terrible Chatsworth wreck in Ohio. The scene above was sketched after an excursion train on the Old Colony, a rich and proud New England carrier, had been derailed near Wallaston depot with a loss of life which shocked the community to its foundations. Below is shown a wreck shortly afterward at Forest Hills, also a suburb of Boston, on the Boston & Providence, New England's oldest main-line railroad, in which forty passengers were killed and 120 injured when a Howe span collapsed over a suburban highway. Boston, a humane and articulate community, was torn by many catastrophes between a feeling of outrage and a desire to abate their mention as a city heavily interested in railroad securities.

CULVER SERVICE

The goriest chapter in the gory annals of the year 1887 and a carnival of carnage which topped all contemporary catastrophes was the wreck at Chatsworth, Ohio, on the main line of the Toledo, Peoria & Western Railroad. Near Chatsworth station a fifteen-car train of Pullman sleepers and coaches, double-headed by two fine locomotives and filled with cut-rate excursionists bound for Niagara Falls, ran through a burned-out trestle and promptly caught fire from the kerosene lamps suspended from car ceilings. Some notion of the frail car construction of the times may be gathered from the circumstance that although the train was running at less than twenty miles an hour and the trestle was only fifteen feet high eighty-two passengers out of a total of 950 were killed in the ensuing conflagration. The Chatsworth disaster aroused public indignation against the carriers as it hadn't flamed since the Ashtabula holocaust a decade previous and achieved a dubious immortality in folklore through the agency of a melancholy ballad whose lamentable structure was only equaled by its inaccuracy, since in it "a hundred lives were lost the night of the Chatsworth wreck." Nobody was ever called to account either for the wreck or the ballad. Above is an artist's version of the catastrophe and below scenes at the Chatsworth morgue.

BROWN BROS.

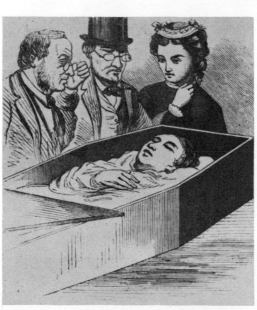

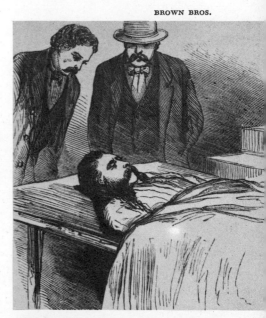

BOXING UP THE BURNT BODIES.

MRS. SNOW KILLED WHILE TRAVELING WITH HER SEVEN CHILDREN.

THE LAST DEAD BODY BROUGHT TO THE DEPOT

Even the Lordly Central Had Its Bad Moments

NEW YORK CENTRAL RAILROAD

BROWN BROS.

Before the era of the Twentieth Century Limited, the New York Central & Hudson River Railroad's crack train on the New York-Chicago run which it covered in thirty-six hours was the luxurious *Pacific Express* (*above*). When, therefore in February 1871, this fast varnish haul was involved in a catastrophic head-on collision with a train of tank cars loaded with petroleum it was sensational news all over the United States. At Wappinger's Creek a few miles south of Poughkeepsie a south-bound freight of tanks had become derailed on a narrow, two-track bridge, the wreckage covering the entire right of way. Into the debris the *Pacific Express* crashed at full speed, igniting the oil, and the whole shambles commenced to blaze on the frozen creek. The four rear cars, three Wagner sleepers and a coach, were uncoupled and pushed by crew and passengers to safety, but twenty-two persons were killed and the prestige of the proud Vanderbilt road suffered a sad blow. At the left the ruined engines are shown burning on the Hudson River ice.

The wrecking of the Central's famed *Pacific Express* was tremendous news in 1871 and provided a field day for pictorial artists such as those represented here from the pages of *Leslie's*. Above is the varnish train at the very moment of its plunge into Wappinger's Creek while below rescue workers are shown freeing the trapped from a flaming sleeper. In an age when ambulances were not universally available, private resources often aided the victims of such catastrophes until official relief could be procured, and the injured at Wappinger Creek were carried to a nearby town hall until the arrival of an ambulance train.

Hairbreadth 'Scap

Along The Rails

Thrilled

Nineteenth-Centur

America

N. Y. PUBLIC LIBRARY

The Fast Mail flagged in the nick of time and the *Limited* saved by a woman's daring became symbols of thrilling heroism in an age dominated by the concept of railroad travel. The collective pulse of America fluttered when a brave youth discovered a broken rail (*above*) and waved the thundering through train to a timely halt. To achieve the halt in an age innocent of air brakes, the engineer whistled for the rear-end crew to tie down the hand set brakes, reversed his power gear and stroked a rabbit's foot while the fireman set the hand brakes of the tender. Female heroines like those in the below reproductions from illustrated weeklies of the seventies frequently had their counterparts in real life. In the early eighties a figure of national fame was Kate Shelley, daughter of a Boone, Iowa, section hand on the Chicago & North Western who braved a hurricane and waved a passenger train to a photo-finish stop when a main-line bridge was washed out. To this day a Kate Shelley Memorial Fountain stands in a public square in Dubuque, and there is a Kate Shelley Lodge of the Brotherhood of Railroad Trainmen.

N. Y. PUBLIC LIBRARY

ASS'N OF AMERICAN RAILROADS

The reading public of the nineteenth century was intensely interested in every aspect of rail travel and none more than the evolution of new devices for the promotion of safety so that when the percussion torpedo fixed to the track (*above*) was put in use *Frank Leslie's Illustrated Newspaper* for June 20, 1874, gave it a full page with the caption "Down Brakes." This was a supplemental safety device to the red and green signal lights displayed in a control tower (*lower right*). Readers thrilled, too, to moments of crisis on the cars as when (*lower left*) a Pennsylvania locomotive cab caught fire but the brave engineer stuck to his post of peril and "thereby saved six hundred souls from death."

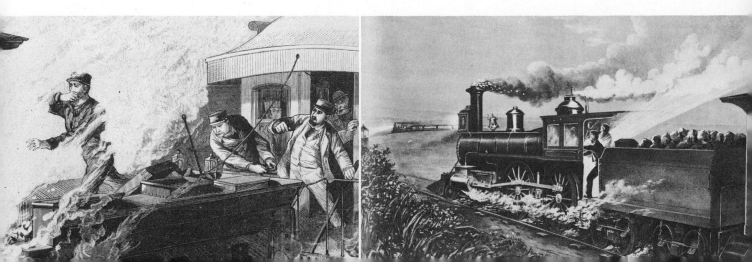

Loss of Life Was Often Picturesque

CULVER SERVICE

In an age of improvisation and evolution of a whole new science of transport freak accidents abounded. Shortly after the close of the Civil War, Alfred Nobel invented nitroglycerine, the explosive base of dynamite, and the result was found to be five times as powerful as black powder. The aging Henry du Pont of Wilmington, Delaware, refused to manufacture the compound, but his son, Lammot, would, did, and shortly thereafter blew himself and his plant to bits. Thereafter nitroglycerine accidents figured largely in the news, as when a trainload of the stuff exploded (*above*) and raised hell with the Lake Shore & Michigan Southern Railroad. Less drastic was the accident (*center*) when a train on the pastoral Rensselear & Saratoga Railroad drove through an open drawbridge. Still more picturesque (*below*) was the scene when a train on the Vermont & Massachusetts Railroad, now part of the Boston & Maine, fell through a covered bridge over the Merrimack River. A few covered railroad bridges survived into the mid-twentieth century in New England, six of them on the St. Johnsbury & Lake Champlain Railroad.

long hours, sometimes twenty-four on end, required of train crews in those prime-val times, the resistance to such rudimentary safety devices as air brakes by some roads until as late as 1893 when they were required by Federal law, the wooden construction of passenger cars and the system of dispatching by train orders which left ample room for human fallibility, and the wonder, from this remove, would seem to be that any train at all reached its destination unscathed.

For many years the possibilities of train wreck and the terrible fires which swept hotels of wooden construction constituted the occupational hazard of the traveling salesman.

Although the most fearsome pictures of destruction derive from the days of wooden passenger coach construction, when cars on leaving the rails disintegrated into heaps of expensive kindling or when subjected to the impact of collision simply flew apart like smashed packing cases, the potentialities of disaster did, in fact, keep pace with progress. As steel construction and heavier trucks came into use so did the speed of trains increase from the twenty and thirty miles of the sixties and seventies to the ninety and hundred mile speeds of the air-flow age. The death toll at Ashtabula, classic holocaust of its time, was eighty-three in 1876, but almost three-quarters of a century later in the era of all-steel cars and innumerable pre-ventative devices, the Long Island Rail Road contrived to kill a total of 110 passengers and trainmen in two wrecks within a year of one another. The toll in the great Revere disaster on the Eastern Railroad in 1871 which rocked the nation was only twenty-nine, but in 1918 two trains came together on the Nashville, Chattanooga & St. Louis Railway in Tennessee and ran up a grand total of ninety-nine killed and 171 injured, an all-time record in the annals of American railroad mismanagement.

Simply as car construction became more substantial the risks to which the cars were subjected were materially increased and as safety devices were perfected the speeds at which passenger trains operated were accelerated. The grim reaper has never been altogether outdistanced by progress.

For some reason not altogether apparent from the record, but probably deriving from the relative density of traffic and immoderate crowding of the trains, accidents in the East far overshadowed those west of the Mississippi during the latter decades of the nineteenth century. The holocausts at Revere, Angola, Ashtabula, Chatsworth, Tariffville and New Hamburg had no parallels on the western carriers despite the fact that the California press, always hostile to the Southern Pacific, made a practice throughout the Ambrose Bierce era of interviewing the "survivors" of every minor derailment or grade-crossing collision with a carriage. It must of course be remembered that during the seventies a single passenger train in each direction daily was sufficient for the transcontinental traffic on the Union Pacific and that elsewhere in the West passenger runs were quite as infrequent, a circumstance which almost entirely eliminated the possibility of collision.

Only in Colorado, where the narrow gages flowered so luxuriantly was there any multiplicity of mishaps, a majority of them resulting from the hazards innate in mountain operations. The little varnish trains not infrequently ran into one another in blind cuts or on abrupt curves, sometimes toppling from cliffs hundreds of feet above forest and river bed, but the casualty lists were astonishingly low. As recently as 1947 the Rio Grande's narrow-gage *San Juan* on the Durango-Alamosa run was carried nearly 2,000 feet down a cliffside on an avalanche without a single fatality.

LIBRARY OF CONGRESS

The vast operations of the Pennsylvania, from its inception a major rail system, have in the natural course of events produced some major catastrophes. Above is a wreck of the *Lancaster Express* near Lancaster, Pennsylvania, on the Pennsylvania Central in the late sixties. Below: a derailment at Woodbridge, New Jersey, in 1951, where eighty-five were killed on account of excessive speed over a temporary track.

"NEW YORK HERALD TRIBUNE"

The wrecking of freight trains, while seldom entailing loss of life and hence attracting less publicity, has always been vastly more frequent than mishaps to passenger runs. Freight equipment has never been as scrupulously maintained or subject to such close inspection and frequent repair as the passenger cars and the resulting derailments and ditchings have been fully as spectacular as the wreck of the fast varnish. In the days when Indians rode the western freights in considerable numbers they were about the only casualties when the Central Pacific or Santa Fe's manifest went into the ditch, and the newspapers briefly mentioned that the bodies of four or six Indians had been recovered, without further detail.

In general train wrecks, except when they achieve perpetuation through the agency of folklore such as "The Wreck of Old 97" or the collision on the Illinois Central which elevated Casey Jones to the ranks of American immortals, receive little attention in the chronicle of the high iron. The carriers themselves, quite understandably, do all within their power to abate the association of their names with catastrophe even though the accident in question may have taken place three-quarters of a century ago. Yet the disasters of the rails are quite as much a part of the record as the fast runs, train robberies or other events associated with the cars. Their fearful hold upon the public imagination in the days of their frequent recurrence is reflected in the newspaper and magazine accounts of the time. The big hook or wrecking crane which stands at all times with steam up in the railroad yards of the land is mute but lively evidence to the ever present possibility of disaster that has existed since the first train brigade of the Camden & Amboy left the rails.

Even the most modern freight and passenger operations sometimes end in the common ditch. Below left is a pile-up of a manifest freight on the Rock Island at Spickard, Missouri, while at the right the Santa Fe's crack streamliner *El Capitan* has come to grief at Azusa, California, on the Los Angeles-Chicago run.

ACME

ASSOCIATED PRESS

NEW YORK CENTRAL RAILROAD

XVII

The Fast Mail

The Romance of the Mails Carried Aboard the Speeding Cars Through Storm and Night Aroused the Imaginations of Men as They Had Not Been Fired Since the Pony Express

UNTIL the time of the Civil War incomparably the best mail service in the United States was conducted by private individuals or small firms and partnerships. In California and throughout the Far West the mail services of Wells Fargo & Co., were maintained by actual popular demand until the nineties and this in spite of their acknowledged illegality and the violent hostility of various postal officials, although elsewhere throughout the land the posts had largely been devoured by the inferior government monopoly.

330

Having their beginnings aboard the first train brigades which in the early thirties commenced radiating from Boston and gave it its name as the Hub of New England, private mail services combined with express agencies were organized and maintained by a number of enterprising individuals of whom William Frederick Harnden and the brothers L.B. and B.D. Earle are the best known to posterity. Shortly after this, Alvin Adams began executing commissions and carried letters for customers over the Boston & Worcester Railroad, thus setting off the career of the great Adams Express Co. which at one time operated in almost every state and territory in the Union. At first these swift couriers carried their letters in their capacious beaver hats or in carpet bags, paying fare to the railroads only as single passengers. Later they made arrangements to carry trunks on their daily journeyings and still later they rented entire baggage coaches for their business.

This sort of thing, conducted on a basis at once profitable and scrupulously honest, was of course an affront to postmasters whose own affairs were frequently neither. Postmasters, then as later, seldom had qualifications for their employment other than political activities at election times. The government mails were fantastically slow. Sometimes they didn't arrive at all. And at no time, naturally, were they expedited with the care and dispatch of private venture.

Now and then, however, to prove the exception to every rule, there came along an employee of the Federal mails possessed of the same initiative as individual entrepreneurs. One such was a clerk named W.A. Davis in the Post Office at St. Joseph, Missouri, who had charge of forwarding the mails brought to the railhead by the Hannibal & St. Jo Railroad in the year 1861 for transfer there to the flying *mochilas* of the great Pony Express. For the few months of its brief lifetime the Pony Express was the wonder of the Western World carrying the Overland Mail from St. Joseph to the Pacific Coast in a miraculous ten days, with a saving of some hours if messages were delivered to the Overland Telegraph at Carson City, Nevada, for even quicker transmission to Sacramento and San Francisco.

Until Davis came up with a better idea all mails were carried from post office to post office in locked pouches and sorted for distribution at focal points in the system. Davis proposed to his superiors that it would save a lot of time between the arrival of sealed mails at St. Joseph and the departure of the pony if the Overland Mail were sorted from the local on the run from Quincy, Illinois, instead of at the St. Joseph Post Office. Such good sense was impressive even in a government service and the railroad was commissioned to design and build a special mail car, the first ever placed in service, on this much publicized run.

The mail-sorting car was a huge success even in the comparatively short time it was allowed to function before the Pony Express was outmoded by the completion of the continental telegraph, and the Hannibal & St. Jo continued to use it for mails that required less dramatic urgency.

Three years later news of the innovation, presumably carried in the mails, percolated to Chicago where its merits at once became apparent to the Assistant Postmaster of that city, George B. Armstrong. Like Davis, Armstrong was a rarity in the U.S. Postal Service of the times, a man of imagination and resolution, and he advanced to Montgomery Blair, the Postmaster General at Washington, the daring idea of mail-sorting cars, not on isolated runs, but in a nation-wide pattern.

The idea came at the right time. The end of the Civil War was in sight; the mails were badly in need of revitalization and the railroads were looming large in the public imagination. Blair gave Armstrong his blessing and Armstrong speedily arranged with the Chicago & North Western, a far more consequential railroad than the primeval little Hannibal & St. Jo, to inaugurate mail-sorting service between Chicago and Clinton, Iowa.

Immediate opposition, according to Stewart Holbrook, was forthcoming from a familiar source. Joseph Medill, publisher of the *Chicago Tribune*, denounced the whole thing as a damned silly business. The letters, Medill asserted positively, would all be blown out of the car by the draft and it would be a hell of a job to pick them all up along the right of way. This dire possibility, suggested Armstrong temperately, might be obviated by closing the doors and windows of the car while it was moving, a novel concept which caused Medill to ponder profoundly.

When it had been demonstrated to the satisfaction of all the other newspapers except the *Tribune* that letters could be contained inside the mail car and even sorted with the greatest of ease and expedition, the United States Railway Mail Service came into being and the satisfactory and somehow romantic mail cars were speedily introduced on the fastest passenger runs of the Erie, the Burlington, the Alton, the Rock Island and the Pennsylvania.

Whether it was the public attention and interest the novel service evoked which had a stimulating influence on the officials and employees of the Post Office or the other way around, certain it was that the fast mail soon assumed almost as much glamor as had so briefly attached to the Pony Express. In the public imagination, already fired with the wonder of fast railroad operations and splendid luxury cars which promised within a few months to roll across the entire width of the continent, the thought of the brightly lit mail cars speeding through the storm and the night behind a locomotive trailing sparks and smoke as it threaded the iron highroad was implicit with unspeakable romance. The competent mail clerks going about their business as the cars sped along the moonlit Hudson or breasted the high passes of the Rockies assumed heroic proportions. The fast mail became the theme for melodramas and ballads, and the newspapers and illustrated weeklies devoted miles of newsprint to fine-set type and well-drawn engravings showing the interiors of the mail cars with their bearded and frock-coated clerks in the fashion of the age. The fast mail entered the realm of American folklore.

Gradually, of course, the mail-sorting cars were improved in comfort, safety and effectiveness. The first little wooden coach of the Hannibal & St. Jo could be contained in its entirety three times over in the rolling post offices that now run head-end on the crack passenger trains of the land.

From the concept of a mail car or several of them incorporated in the consist of a passenger train it was an easy step accomplished in the mind of George S. Bangs, who succeeded Armstrong as head of the Railway Mail, to the idea of an entire train devoted to the carriage of the posts both in sorting and in locked storage cars. The obvious run on which such a train should be inaugurated was between New York and Chicago, a thousand-mile stretch of heavily trafficked right of way between East and West, and Bangs took his shining idea to William H. Vanderbilt of the New York Central & Hudson River Lines.

Vanderbilt, fully as shrewd a railroad man as his father, the old Commodore, saw the promotional value in the idea right away and ordered the construction of a number of fine, cream-colored mail cars with ornamental trim and the coat armor of the United States engrossed in colors on their sides. The train, which was run on express train schedule with a cleared track something the way the *Twentieth Century Limited* was later operated, was known as *The Fast Mail*. It was a huge success and shortly after its inaugural, the Pennsylvania, ever eager to match any performance by the Central, put into service its own flyer, *The Limited Mail*, also on the New York-Chicago run. The schedule for both trains was a flat twenty-four hours, about the speed of local trains on the same run today, but a fabulous rate for the middle seventies.

For a time, due to the envy of postmasters not benefiting from the fast train deliveries, Congress suspended payment for the special handling of the posts and *The Fast Mail* and *The Limited Mail* were pulled out of service. They were shortly resumed, however, and the service extended to the Pacific over the lines of the Union Pacific, the Santa Fe and Northern Pacific.

In the twentieth century speedy mail runs between the principal cities of the land are established and profitable functions on all main-line railroads, but the romance conjured throughout an entire generation by the words "the fast mail" has never entirely disappeared from the American awareness.

IN THE DAYS OF THE PRIVATE MAILS

The earliest carriage of mails to the farmsteads and hamlets of New England was by horseback over the corduroy roads (*above*) which traversed the forests. Later, when the trains made steamship connections on Long Island Sound for traffic between Boston and New York, William F. Harnden, shown here in a modern impersonation, earned for himself the title of "Father of the Express" by executing commissions between the two cities and carrying letters and small parcels in his carpet bag. As Harnden enlarged his services to cover New England as far west as Albany, he hired as his Albany agent a Yankee named Henry Wells who, as one of the founders of Wells Fargo & Co., was to become one of the greatest firms of private mail carriers of all time.

The Mails Were

First Sorted

On The St.Jo

(ALL PICTURES) BURLINGTON RR.

U.S. Railway Post Office No. 1 (*above*) was a converted baggage car of the Hannibal & St. Joseph Railroad whose western terminus was the jumping-off place for the brief-lived but exciting Pony Express. In its interior (*below*) the first of all mail was sorted en route. Thirty-five years later the Burlington, which had absorbed the little Hannibal & St. Jo, was running its own *Fast Mail* (*bottom*) between Chicago and Council Bluffs on a split-second schedule for connection with the Union Pacific at Omaha.

At St. Joseph the mails from the East were ferried across the Missouri to Elwood, Kansas, aboard the steamer *Denver* (*above*) and thereafter went forward in the mochilas of the Pony Express, shown below in the version of an imaginative French artist. Mails for the Rocky Mountain regions were sometimes stalled for weeks at a time (*bottom*) crossing the Great Plains in dead of winter.

Mail on the Fly Lent Romance to the Rails

"TRAINS"

The idea of picking up mail on the fly had its inception in the mid-sixties shortly after the inauguration of the Railway Mail itself and never failed to delight successive generations of countryfolk. High speed and heavy equipment feature the Chicago & North Western Post Office shown above. Letter drops on Post Office cars (*lower left*) came into vogue for last-minute missives. If a railroad was too poor to install mail cranes (*lower right*) the postmistress herself held the pouch for the pickup.

CULVER SERVICE

LIBRARY OF CONGRESS

THE MAIL GOES THROUGH

Delivery of city newspapers in rural districts (*above*) became a function associated with the mail cars as these drawings made on the Long Island Railroad in the seventies show. In that age of innocence the idea of a careless platform lounger being caught up in a mail crane (*center*) was hilarious. Posting a late letter (*below*) in the car slot was a treat for a nineteenth-century moppet.

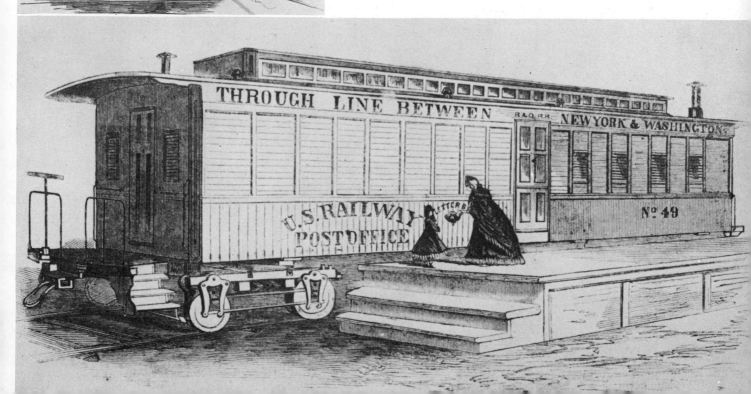

BROWN BROS.

Postal Superintendent George S. Bangs (*center*) first suggested a train of all mail cars on the New York-Chicago run, and the idea was translated into action by William Vanderbilt who inaugurated a fine service in specially built cream-and-gold cars on a twenty-four hour schedule. Above is the interior of the first R. P. O. to run over the New York Central and its connecting lines and below the first train on its arrival in Chicago.

Rival Roads Competed for the Mail Contracts

PENNSYLVANIA RR.

The public imagination was instantly captivated by the New York Central's *Fast Mail* (*page opposite*) and the rival Pennsylvania shortly inaugurated a parallel run with its *Limited Mail* shown above and below. The entire idea met with the resolute disapproval of Joseph Medill (*center*) whose *Chicago Tribune* declared in firm editorial tones that the whole thing was chimerical and would never work.

Mails East and West Rode the Pacific Railroad

WESTERN COLLECTION

AN EXCHANGE OF MAILS SOMEWHERE WEST OF OMAHA

"And here upon the very outskirts of the Great Plains, there rushes upon us the long train of eastward-bound travelers, and the two locomotives pause to pay their respects, as one may fancy, to each other. Here takes place a grand transfer of mail bags and their contents, the immigrants and tourists on their way to the still further West, seizing an opportunity to send back a budget of letters on the Eastern train, and vice versa, and there is a great deal of running to and fro and swinging of long leathern bags from car to car and much deft catching and throwing on the fly as the engines part and their wheels and piston rods take up their motion again."

And Went Forward Through Storm and Gloom of Night

"UP, UP THROUGH THE NIGHT GOES THE OVERLAND MAIL"

Kipling

Sometimes the fast mail trains of the Union Pacific and its Central Pacific connections rolled on too tight a schedule to pause at whistle stops in Nebraska and Wyoming and the bags were picked up on the fly (*above*) but at water stops or depots of consequence they paused briefly on their appointed rounds. The artist for *Leslie's* identifies the horseman as posting his letter at Palisade, Nevada, possibly a report from the mines of Hidden Canyon that has missed the daily up-train of the Eureka & Palisade.

CULVER SERVICE

A FRONTIER POST OFFICE.

The mail trains of the Northern Pacific bound for Bismarck, Dakota Territory, with letters from the States were sometimes stalled in winter snowdrifts for days at a time, giving the railroad's cultured president, Henry Villard, cause for concern. On such occasions grizzled frontiersmen called in vain at the village postoffice for the weekly mail edition of the *New York Tribune*.

CHICAGO HISTORICAL SOCIETY

Although parcels post was many years in the future, the Railway Post Office at the time of the Great Fire of Chicago in 1871 (*above*) handled thousands of tons of food and clothing for the destitute through regular mail channels. Below contributions are shown being loaded at the Erie Railroad ferry at Twenty-third Street in New York for transfer to the cars on the Jersey shore.

The Word

Emergency

Was In The

Postal

Lexicon

An index of the hazards of employment in Railway Post Offices in their early years is the fact that there were between 1875 and 1917 no fewer than 9,400 wrecks involving postal cars. In such wrecks as this on the Erie where rescue workers are shown removing mail sacks, mail cars spotted head-end (next the engine) were death traps. Other contingencies of peril included train robbers, against whose activities the Union Pacific cars were veritable arsenals (below) and such massive investigations of occasional irregularities in the service as the Congressional probe held in the New York Post Office in 1877 shown at the bottom of the page.

N. Y. PUBLIC LIBRARY

Ninety Years Have Seen the Mail Cars Roll

LUCIUS BEEBE

Sometimes, as on this train of the St. Johnsbury & Lake Champlain in deepest Vermont, the R. P. O. combined with a passenger coach is the only car on the run. Until 1950 when service was abandoned, the narrow-gage mail cars of the Denver & Rio Grande Western's *San Juan* (*below*) on the Alamosa-Durango run brought letters to the desolate Colorado Southwest.

CHARLES CLEGG

CHARLES CLEGG

During the Second World War so heavy were movements of military mail west-bound that solid trains of mail-storage cars such as this on the Texas & Pacific (*above*) rolled on all transcontinental trunklines. Modern Railway Post Offices such as that shown below on the Chicago & Eastern Illinois are a far cry from the simplicities of the first mail run on the Hannibal & St. Joseph.

CHICAGO & EASTERN ILLINOIS RR.

N. Y. PUBLIC LIBRARY In the age of which the Saratoga trunk was the symbol, every domestic resource was required to get squared away for a holiday at Pinehurst, Bretton Woods or The Vineyard. The seasonal trains had a clientel all their own.

XVIII

By the Seashore, in the Mountains

Once Seasonal Resort Trains Ran in Many Sections to Palm Beach, to Bar Harbor, to Saratoga and All the Mountains and Spas Beloved by Three Generations of Holiday Seekers

A FEATURE of railroad travel in the Saratoga-trunk-and-Florida-water age was the heavy traffic attracted by seasonal trains serving the then popular resorts of New England in summer and Florida during the winter months. Palm Beach had yet to establish its imperial social supremacy on the shores of Lake Worth, but older and more conservative spots, Jacksonville, St. Augustine, St. Petersburg and Orlando flourished mightily each winter in a generation that required women to wear cotton stockings on the bathing beach and sat down to ten-course table d'hôte dinners in the mammoth dining rooms of a thousand American plan resort hotels dotting the map from Key West to Bar Harbor.

The Florida season started in December and closed up with an abrupt bang and a score of monster balls and galas promptly at Washington's birthday. Throughout the months of December, January and February the Pullman Company drew heavily on its pool of sleepers and room cars for assignment to the Atlantic Coast Line, Florida East Coast and Seaboard Air Line and even the little Live Oak, Perry Gulf blossomed grandly with through sleepers for an enormous resort hotel located near its western terminus. In later years when Wilson Mizner and Mrs. Stuyvesant Fish had established Palm Beach as the winter capital of American society, the Seaboard and Florida East Coast rolled their through Pullmans from New York, Boston and Washington across a now vanished trestle from West Palm Beach and spotted them on the house track of the fantastically immense Royal Poincianna Hotel.

King of the Florida resort business was Henry M. Flagler who built the Florida East Coast Railway and financed a chain of magnificent resort hotels along its right of way. With a shrewd eye to the sales possibilities of tropical climate he directed that "the main line shall go out to sea" and engineered the construction of the great causeway spanning thirty-seven miles of the Gulf of Mexico between the tip of Florida and the island of Key West. With the aid of fast steamers across the remaining ninety miles of the Caribbean he planned to make Havana a suburb of New York. When it was finished, the line of the Florida East Coast across the Florida Keys was known as "the eighth wonder of the world," but hurricanes caused great havoc along it and in 1935 the causeway was rebuilt as a motor highway.

In the middle years of the twentieth century Florida is served by scores of seasonal trains having their origins in Chicago, New York and Washington operating over such remote lines as the Chicago & Eastern Illinois, the Pennsylvania, the Nashville, Chattanooga & St. Louis, the Frisco and the New Haven. The season is longer today and the through equipment is apt to be streamlined and Diesel powered, but old-timers remember when the first wood burners chuffed smokily into Miami in 1896 and visitors from the Back Bay and Chicago's Gold Coast first descended from the wooden sleepers to spread the fame of Florida's sunshine, citrus fruits and the long shady verandas of its resort hotels in an age innocent of urgency or tight-locking draft gear.

Throughout the latter decades of the nineteenth century proper Bostonians turned their faces determinedly toward their villas at Buzzards Bay, Cape Cod, the White Mountains or the stern and rockbound coast of Maine and the railroads radiating from the Hub were their natural and almost only means of egress from the shadow of Beacon Hill. Aboard the green-and-gold cars of the Old Colony & Newport Railroad they headed for Newport and its implications of social elegance; behind the locomotive *Highland Light,* most beautiful of all Taunton-built eight wheelers, they rolled past the cranberry bogs adjacent to the right of way of the Cape Cod Railroad or they brought their shoebox lunches aboard the Eastern if headed for Portland or took the Boston & Maine as far as Concord where they changed to the cars of the Northern New Hampshire Railroad for Franklin, Enfield and West Lebanon. The Troy & Boston and the Western Vermont took them gratefully to Bennington, Manchester, East Dorset and Rutland or they boarded the Grand Trunk Railroad of Canada between Portland, deepest New England and Montreal.

There was for many years at the end of last century a fine summer train which went on promptly the first of every June between Portland and Niagara Falls via Rouse's Point at the northern extremity of Lake Champlain. It was operated over the Portland & Ogdensburg Railroad as far as St. Johnsbury where it passed to the iron of the St. Johnsbury & Lamoille County and the round-trip ticket business was brisk with happy newlywed couples in curly brimmed bowler hats and long skirts and chatelaine watches. There was even a through sleeper for Chicago by a Wabash connection. The P. & O., when first its diamond-stack locomotives panted over what is now the Mountain Subdivision of the Maine Central, claimed that its trackage through Crawford Notch in northern New Hampshire was the steepest standard-gage railroading in the world. In the Green Mountains this luxury varnish threaded narrow defiles and thundered through the covered wooden bridges of the St.J.&L.C. (known in later years as the St. Jesus & Late Coming) with Pullmans, diners and brassbound observation cars, a sight which would surprise the residents along what is today little more than a dairy products short line.

Cream of all the seasonal railroad travel in the seventies and eighties was, of course, to and from the celebrated precincts of Saratoga Springs. New Yorkers took Mr. Vanderbilt's pleasantly routed cars along the ever fascinating Hudson as far as Albany or, after its completion in 1883, they might ride stylishly in the cars of the Hudson River & West Shore Railway as far as the New York capital. There everybody of consequence stayed aboard their New York Central parlor cars while they were shifted to the tracks of the Rensselaer & Saratoga Railroad (now the Delaware & Hudson) for the short hour's ride to Saratoga and the opulent fascinations of the United States and Grand Union hotels. In those halcyon days the West Shore, which is today maintained as a freight haul and commuters' branch by the New York Central, was a very fine railroad indeed. Solid trains of Pullmans arrived and departed daily from its Weehawken terminal.

The Rensselaer & Saratoga during the racing season late in the summer ran ten or twelve trains a day into Saratoga awash with dudes and the sporting fraternity in patterned suits and white top hats and the private cars of the millionaires of an age when millionaires were a commonplace, jammed its sidings and house tracks at America's most celebrated spa. Upon one occasion, late in the century, the comedian De Wolf Hopper was trying vainly to catch forty winks in his suite in the United States Hotel while the R. & S. noisily shifted cars all night under his bedroom and a gentle rain of soot was wafted through the lace curtains of the hotel's French windows. Finally in desperation Hopper reached for the bedside telephone, a Babylonish luxury of those times, and demanded pettishly of the night clerk: "My man, can you tell what time this hotel reaches Chicago?"

Bostonians headed for the cures and carouses of Saratoga, the setting for each being handily adjacent to the other, took an all-parlor car train run by the Boston & Maine during the summer months and made the trip in five and a half hours. Only the very best equipment was assigned this de luxe flyer and travelers of the nineties compared it favorably with the cars of the Central's *Saratoga Express* on which New Yorkers rode. The Forbses, Peabodys and Higginsons of the age were used to the best of everything.

348

By the middle years of the twentieth century the cream had been skimmed from the once rich seasonal resort travel. Only a memory were the mile-a-minute runs with which the Philadelphia & Reading trains between Camden and Atlantic City used to astound the nineties. Saratoga was served by a single first-class train daily, the Delaware & Hudson's *Laurentian* between New York and Montreal. *The Blue Comet* operated by the Central of New Jersey between Jersey City and Atlantic City lasted into the thirties and then became one with the New York & New England's "Ghost Train" and the *Pennsylvania Flyer*. The once populous trains over the New York Central to the Adirondacks have been replaced with single through cars carried in milk and newspaper runs and many of the through trains to Florida had ceased to be seasonal luxury hauls and were regular daily, year-round services.

Only New England still knows a ponderable representation of summer trains to its beaches and mountains. *The East Wind, The North Wind, The Bar Harbor Express* and *The Neptune* still maintain the old tradition combined with more modern equipment and operations. In Michigan too both the Pennsylvania and the Central of recent years have found it profitable to run week-end summer trains between Chicago, Detroit, St. Louis and Mackinaw City. But in general the once colorful and festive trains whose names appeared in *The Official Guide* for only four or five months of the year have disappeared as completely as the bearded engineer, the frock-coated conductor and the colored-glass transoms in the clerestories of palace cars.

STYLE AND SERVICE AT STOCKBRIDGE STATION

At Stockbridge, in the Massachusetts Berkshires, a coach and four met all New York trains to transport arriving guests to the comfortable premises of the Red Lion Inn.

Long Before Palm Beach, Aiken Was Well Established

N. Y. PUBLIC LIBRARY

For many years before Florida's emergence as the winter playground of the nation's well-to-do, Aiken, South Carolina, enjoyed the patronage of visitors from the North who descended from the trains of the South Carolina Railroad from Charleston and Augusta (*above*) to put up at its only hotel (*center*) and promenade in its town square (*below*) in an age of simple pleasures and tranquil living.

Things Were Simpler in Florida's Early Days

N. Y. PUBLIC LIBRARY

After the close of the Civil War Southerners from the Carolinas and Georgia began to hear of the healthful properties of various primitive spas and watering places in Florida. The first tourists arrived at Jacksonville and St. Augustine aboard wooden coaches drawn by wood-burning engines which stopped frequently while darkies sold regional specialties to the passengers (*above*). The very first railroad in St. Augustine, the St. Johns Railway, provided horsecars riding over wooden rails (*below*) which rolled serenely through forests of live oak and palmettos. They stopped often for the crew to grease the wheels. Twenty years later Florida tourists were riding south in rococo splendor aboard Pullman-built sleepers (*right*) on the *Florida Special*, the first luxury train to be fitted throughout with electricity.

THE PULLMAN CO.

At Flagler's Fiat, Florida Became the American Riviera

FLORIDA EAST COAST RR.

Although older Florida resorts still commanded the conservative winter tourist trade, the splendid Royal Palm (*above*) which Flagler opened in 1897 together with a Flagler-financed waterworks and electric system put Miami on the map. His rival who had done much to develop the Florida West Coast, Henry B. Plant once wired Flagler facetiously: "Where is Miami?" Flagler wired back: "Just follow the crowd."

DECEMBER, 1894.

The St. Augustine R

Jacksonvi
St. Augustine
And Indian Rive
Railway

JOSEPH RICHARDSON,
General Passenger A

J. R. PARROTT,
Vice-President.

ST. AUGUSTINE, FLA.

When the first train was run over Flagler's mighty causeway across the keys to Key West (*above*) vast crowds were on hand to greet it and honor the aging millionaire who more than anyone else had made Florida the American Riviera. Flagler foresaw the need of northbound freight traffic to compensate for the seasonal lag in passenger travel to Florida, and the Jacksonville, St. Augustine & Indian River Railway, whose insignia is shown at the left, was built to tap the citrus fruit groves and pineapple trade along the Indian River.

COLLECTION OF MAE E. ANDREWS

IN WINTER RARE BIRDS OF TROPIC PLUMAGE HEADED SOUTHWARD

Both the State of Florida and the legend of Ponce de Leon existed before the coming of Henry M. Flagler, but neither were exploited to any notable degree until that pioneer capitalist perceived the promotional possibilities of pecans and palmettos and built a chain of luxury hotels in their midst. The Hotels were the Alcazar at St. Augustine, the Ormond at Ormond Beach, the Royal Poinciana and the Breakers at Palm Beach and the Royal Palm at Miami and after they were completed he set about operating a railroad to serve them. He evolved the great Florida East Coast Railway and started the profitable business of ferrying millionaires and heliophiles from the wintry north to Florida's now glorified resorts. The first train into Palm Beach over the trestle from West Palm Beach spanning Lake Worth arrived in March 1896 and posed picturesquely on the private car siding in front of the Royal Poinciana Hotel, a mammoth caravansary of mile long corridors and superlative clientele. On the first train was a gathering of celebrities to bug the eyes of any society editor and shown posed here before a graceful Florida East Coast eight wheeler are Philip M. Lydig, Helen Morton, Gladys Vanderbilt, Amy Townsend, Captain A. T. Rose, Mrs. Cornelius Vanderbilt, Edith Bishop, Thomas Cushing, Edward Livingston, Dudley Winthrop, Graig Wadsworth, Gertrude Vanderbilt, Lispenard Stewart, Harry Payne Whitney, Sybil Sherman and Cornelius Vanderbilt. Palm Beach was to know the mighty of the world for years to come, but seldom in greater concentration. For many years the favored train to Florida resorts over the Flagler System was the steam-powered Florida Special (*above right*) which often rolled south with twenty Pullmans until the coming of the *Henry M. Flagler* (*lower right*) in the age of Diesels.

LUCIUS BEEBE

From Earliest Times New England Summers Beckoned

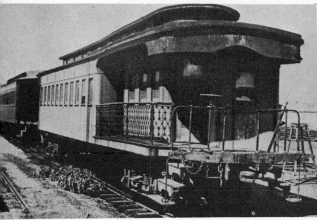

The first observation car in America (*above*) was operated on the White Mountain Express by the New Haven Railroad in the early seventies, and tourists in deer-stalker caps and pork-pie bonnets rode its open platform to happy days in the resort towns of New England. A thrill by no means to be missed was the ascent of Mt. Washington to the Summit House aboard the cogwheel railroad (*right*) which slowly raised the bug-eyed tourists above the clouds. Its first locomotive was the *Peppersass*.

Typical of the hundreds of Notch, View and Profile Houses which came to people the New England countryside from Narraganset to Seal Harbor and from Rye to Lake Champlain is the vast New Ocean House at Swampscott, Massachusetts, famous for its shore dinners and vast dining rooms, dormers and cupolas, porches, gazebos, lawns and shrubbery in opulent profusion.

NEW OCEAN HOUSE

N. Y. PUBLIC LIBRARY

An eminent divine who regularly summered in the White Mountains of New Hampshire was the Rev. Henry Ward Beecher whose amorous activities were to be the scandal of the generation, when aired in court. Here he is shown kissing an infant from the window of a Western Railroad coach and in a spirited game of croquet on the Notch House lawn in Franconia. A more appreciative generation of vacationists took pleasure in the pastoral pursuits of Yankee farmers they saw in summer, making hay (*below*) while the patient horses waited and the barley water cooled under a convenient apple tree.

Newport's Grandeurs Had Simple Beginnings

Although Newport was accessible over the rails of the Old Colony Railroad and the private cars of the nabobs bore them there in style, many visitors preferred the pleasant approach by water as shown at the top of the page. Its street scenes (*right*) were decorous and its Viking tower a celebrated landmark (*right*) and a source of much speculation as to its origins. But later-day dowagers would have been surprised to know that in the fifties the august precincts of Bailey's Beach were the scene of greased pig chases (*bottom right*). Visitors at that time (*bottom left*) sometimes found the New England climate less than advertised.

N. Y. PUBLIC LIBRARY

MOTORS DISPLACED RAIL TRAVEL TO NEWPORT AT AN EARLY DATE

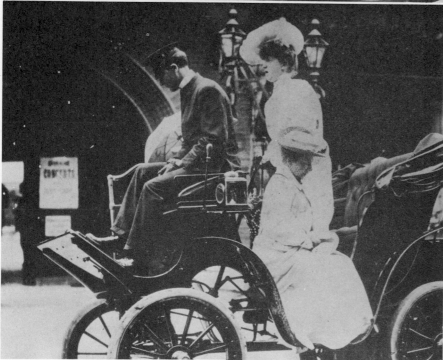

Newport cottages in 1875 (*above left*) possessed "all that taste and money could make them," as a chronicler wrote at the time, but soon gave way to such enormous imitations of French chateaux as Ogden Goelet's "Ochre Hall" (*above right*) and the stately carriages of fashion were replaced by the new-fangled automobile. In the center Ogden Goelet drives a horseless buggy down Bellevue Avenue and at the bottom Miss Kate Brice and Miss Maude Wetmore pose in their car at the entrance to the Casino. "There is an air of unmistakable gentility about Newport," wrote the same reporter, "that few watering places have. There are no horse-jockeys, blacklegs, billiard markers, no cozeners masquerading in the ill-fitting garments of gentlemen, no ballet dancers, clairvoyants or demi-reps. Bathing in the sea is not fashionable."

(ALL PICTURES) BROWN BROS.

Fashionable Long Branch Played for High Stakes

In the nineties, Americans, always indignant about gambling and willing to risk their all in any game of chance that offers, were intrigued by the reportedly fast way of life at Long Branch, the fashionable New Jersey watering place. This is the game at an expensive Long Branch clubhouse, a spectator at which is Evander Berry Wall, long the best-dressed man in the world (*foreground*) and famed for his wing collars and exciting waistcoats. In the oval insert a gambler lures a dude to fiscal undoing. Below, ex-President Grant takes a dip at Long Branch whose attractions were available from New York by steamer (*lower left*) or the trains (*lower right*) of the Central Railroad of New Jersey.

N. Y. PUBLIC LIBRARY

While Bourgeoise Coney Island Pleasured Hoi Polloi

IN THE SEVENTIES, AS NOW, CONEY WAS FOR THE MILLIONS

It took forty minutes aboard the steamcars to reach Coney Island from downtown Manhattan by either the Long Island or the Brooklyn, Flatbush & Coney Island Railway. The Brighton Hotel at Brighton Beach (*above*) was once mounted on rails and towed to safety by ten locomotives when threatened by the waves. After a cooling dip from the bathing pavilion (*center*) holiday makers crowded aboard the Long Island's cars (*below*) to return to New York, sunburned, fatigued and suffering gastric disturbances from too much salt-water taffy.

HOWARD FOGG

"TRUE ROUND WHEELS" TO SARATOGA

Probably the first railroad to serve a resort of consequence in the United States was the Rensselaer & Saratoga running between Troy and Saratoga Springs which, by 1836 when the railroad was constructed, was well established as a spa of both fashionable and therapeutic overtones. The railroad started off with the best of everything, two beautiful locomotives, the *Erie* and the *Champlain,* and twenty-four cars, "at once spacious, elegant and convenient, being twenty-four feet in length and sufficiently high within for the passengers to stand erect." These compartment cars were miracles of the coach builder's art, painted fawn color on the exterior, with buff shading, painted-in picture panels with rose, pink-and-gold borders and deep lake shading and small moldings of delicate stripes of vermilion and opaque black. The car panels contained reproductions of "ancient and modern masters: Leonardo de Vinci, Horace Vernet and Gilbert Stuart." As each car was illuminated with ten paintings the total number must have been in excess of 240 and the subjects included Napoleon Crossing the Alps, Byron's *Mazeppa,* Gilbert Stuart's George Washington, the Dying Tiger and the Rail Road Bridge Near Philadelphia. "The *tout ensemble* is more like a movable gallery of the fine arts than a train," wrote one traveler. "The circle of the car wheels is perfect from the center, which is a great desideratum, and the road, I venture, will become the most fashionable as well as interesting to 'The Springs!'" Howard Fogg painted this scene of early railroading in upper New York.

E. S. HAMMACK

When, in the middle thirties, the grandfather of Samuel Hopkins Adams, the historian, had occasion to take the cars from Troy, New York, to Balston, a matter of twenty-five miles which he would have covered by canal except for the urgency of his mission, he took passage aboard the Rensselaer & Saratoga Railroad. Progress on the train brigade of what was destined to be America's first notable resort railroad since it served the spa of its title, was retarded on that particular day. On the train's previous trip, while passing through a thick woods, the locomotive engine had been attacked by a she-bear and her two cubs, causing consternation and panic among passengers and crew alike. Thereafter a boy was sent ahead at all curves to ascertain if there were bears in waiting. The Rensselaer & Saratoga had no monopoly; when the first train was run over the St. John's Railroad in Florida many years later it was stopped while the crew removed "two little brown bears asleep on the track path."

Saratoga Glittered in the Crystal and Madeira Years

N. Y. PUBLIC LIBRARY

Through the portals of the depot of the Renssalaer & Saratoga Railroad (*above*) was achieved for a full century the wealthy social life that identified Saratoga with names of substance and fashion as well as with mineral waters, trunks and potato chips. A favored resort of well-heeled Southerners before the Civil War, Saratoga was at its social zenith when the Boston & Maine Railroad introduced the Edison electric light aboard the parlor cars of the *Saratoga Limited* out of Boston (*center*) to establish a new pinnacle of luxury. Proper Bostonians read the *Atlantic Monthly* or the *Transcript* reclining in spacious ottomans or armchairs upholstered in red-and-gold brocade with hassocks handy in the same color scheme.

By the mid-twentieth century, however, the glory had departed from Saratoga and the only first-class daily train was the Delaware & Hudson's *Laurentian* (*bottom*) on the run between New York and Montreal. The great hotels had vanished or were socially unthinkable, the game rooms and racing colors gone. The D. & H.'s carloadings were less concerned with millionaires than with garden produce and diary products.

ACME
CHARLES CLEGG

N. Y. PUBLIC LIBRARY

Saratoga social life in the Edith Wharton years centered around the fabulous United States Hotel, whose shaded and pilastered verandahs reminded Southerners pleasantly of Savannah and New Orleans. The drawing (*above*) was made in the middle eighties. A few years previous one of the sights of the spa had been William H. Vanderbilt (*center*) out for the air with his fast pair, "Small Hopes" and "Lady Mag." The facade of the Grand Union Hotel (*below*) reflected the spaciousness, tranquility and ease of Saratoga's great days in a world of cold bottles, fast horses and blue chips.

BROWN BROS.

CULVER SERVICE

Every afternoon during the "season" Saratoga's Congress Street was thronged with carriages of the fashionable bound for the race track with its implications of social grandeur and distinction. On the way they passed "The Club," maintained by gambler Richard Canfield (*above*) where such notables as Lillian Russell, John W. "Bet-a-Million" Gates and Senator Edward O. Wolcott of Colorado played poker, dice games and roulette for what were invariably described as "blue chips." On the porch of the Grand Union Hotel (*lower left*) folk liked to point out William H. Vanderbilt as he gave instructions to his betting commissioners as to how much to wager on his beloved "Maude S" in the third. Everybody (*lower right*) took the healthful and therapeutic waters at Congress Spring.

BROWN BROS.   BROWN BROS.

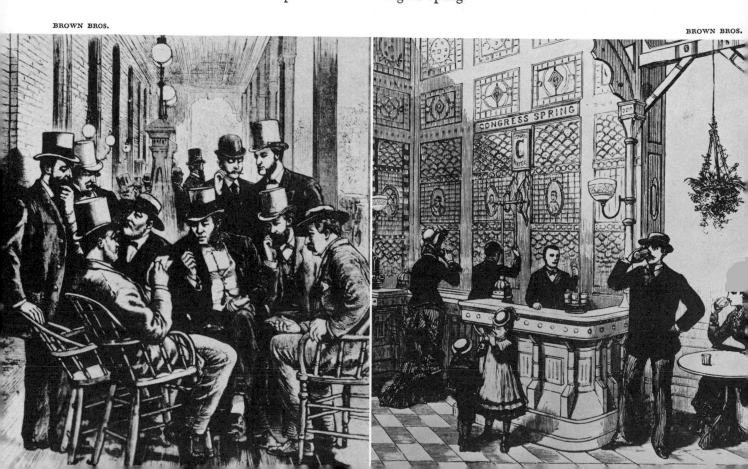

Then as Now, New Yorkers Ventured Afar or Stayed Home

N. Y. PUBLIC LIBRARY

New Yorkers of the seventies, as now, were sharply divided between the venturesome vacationists passionately convinced that health, recreation and the good life lay somewhere else, presumably at Lake Champlain, the White Mountains or the Catskills, and every summer thronged Grand Central (*above*) with their departure, and the home guard. The latter (*below*) swore and still believe that New York is the finest of all vacation spots and wouldn't change it for all the country pleasures listed in Thomson's *Seasons*. Of a hot evening in 1878 they thronged Manhattan's rooftops with such solaces as literature, a thermometer and field glasses with which to penetrate the curtains of the neighbors. Three quarters of a century hasn't served to sell the mountains or the seashore to the home guard.

WESTERN COLLECTION

In the days when the Baltimore & Ohio's seventy-five cent dinner included diamond back terrapin a la Maryland, broiled quail and filet mignon, eating en route was both sumptuous and substantial. There was no lack of good things on the menu.

XIX

Amenities of the Cars

Riding the Red-Plush Cars Opened New Vistas to a People Who Had Long Tarried at Home, It Made Them Aware of Far Places, of Strangers and Changing Ways

I T IS probable that no aspect of terrestrial travel of yesterday or today, neither leisured progress aboard the "canawl" boats nor the thorough-braced Concord coaches of Western plains, has ever laid so compulsive a hold upon the American imagination as the delights and mysteries of sleeping and eating on the cars. Perhaps their peer in the realm of mobile splendors existed in the cream-and-gold

366

Mississippi River steamers of the mid-nineteenth century, the memory of whose crenelated smokestacks, towering upper works and dangerous skirt-coated gamblers will haunt the national consciousness forever. A meal eaten or a night spent on the cars has been within the common experience of millions, yet the enchantment of dining as the summer landscape flows by the windows in an endless succession of meadows and farmsteads or the security of a snug berth while threading the wintry high passes of the continental cordillera has no counterpart anywhere save in the recollections of the nation's vanished yesterdays.

Two men more than any others translated the dream of secure, comfortable and luxurious long-distance overland travel into a reality. They were George Mortimer Pullman who gave his name to the standard sleeping car of the world and brought the dining car into being, and Frederick Henry Harvey, a Scotch-Englishman of fastidious tastes, who raised dining en route from a gustatory catastrophe to an almost sybaritic art.

The name of Pullman has come to be of international significance since many of his patents were adopted on English and European railways, while that of Harvey is more local in its association with the American Southwest and, specifically, with the Santa Fe Railroad, but his influence was actually of far wider scope than his activities, for the fair renown of his diners and hotels was such as to raise the standards of railroad dining all over America. A traveler who had dined with Fred Harvey was apt to be in no mood to put up with the diners on other roads which earned for them the name of "The Swillpail Route" or "The Ptomaine Limited."

In the golden age of free enterprise when worlds yet offered themselves to be conquered by men of foresight and resolution, Pullman was a titan of inventions, promotion and organization. Sleeping cars were, in point of fact, not unknown long before he appeared on the scene. As early as 1829 an inventive Yankee, R.F. Morgan of Stockbridge, Massachusetts, who had already won notice by his highly practicable survey of a railroad route from Albany to Springfield which was shortly to be the Western Railroad, designed a sort of land yacht for railway travel. In Boston's Faneuil Hall, where he displayed a model of it at a railroad exhibit held under the famed grasshopper weather vane of that august premises, it attracted a great deal of attention to its two spacious decks surmounted by a gazebo or cupola for the occupancy of the train captain as well as by its sleeping compartments on the lower deck. Morgan's land yacht dropped from serious consideration when it was discovered that its inventor had taken no account whatsoever of such matters as clearances and that no bridge or tunnel yet designed could accommodate its spacious proportions.

In 1837 a sleeper named *Chambersburg* was built by the firm of Embry & Dash at Philadelphia and placed in service the following year between Philadelphia and Baltimore on the Cumberland Valley Railroad, now a part of the Pennsylvania system. The *Chambersburg* was in actuality a coach with four compartments at one end screened off from the aisle by curtains and innocent of any toilet facilities, storage space or other conveniences, and historians since then have taken a dim view of their resources of comfort. In 1843 the New York & Erie Railroad had in service two overnight cars with makedown berths, the *Erie* and *Ontario* which came to be known as Diamond Cars from the shape of their windows. Perhaps the earliest sleeping car which should be read into the record as a successfully functioning piece of rolling stock was designed by Webster Wagner, a former carriage builder, for Commodore Vanderbilt and the New York Central & Hudson River Railroad. Wagner's drawing-room cars embodied the best of everything known to carriage makers and interior decorators of the year 1865. They were rolling miracles of plush, marquetry, beautifully matched woods, plate-glass mirrors, gold trim and rich Turkey carpets. As the Central was at that period the standard railroad of the world, a superlative which has since been challenged by the Pennsylvania, and since operations on it were apt to be the pattern for operations on every other road in the land, the Wagner car came within an ace of being the accepted sleeping car of universal design and manufacture.

There were also half-a-dozen less successful companies of the time: the Flower Sleeping Car Company, the Knight Company which built cars exclusively for the Baltimore & Ohio, and the celebrated if fanciful Mann Boudoir Car Company. Colonel William D'Alton Mann, later to achieve fame as editor and publisher of *Town Topics* and a blackmailer of florid and dressy proportions, divided his car into compartments or "boudoirs" in the European manner with doors opening directly onto a running footboard outside the car instead of onto a central car corridor. The Mann cars found considerable favor for a time but were of cheap and meretricious construction so that, as is described elsewhere, Mme Nellie Melba's private car, built by the redoubtable Colonel, was found to be almost entirely made of papier-mâché. Although Mann's patents were eventually bought up by Pullman and disappeared into the economy of the Pullman car, it was he who was almost solely responsible for the adoption of sleepers in Europe where he organized the Companie Internationale des Wagons-Lits, which flourishes mightily to this very day.

George Pullman appeared on the railroad scene in Chicago in 1858 and, being a man of direct action and given to the frontal approach to all problems, he presented himself one day to the master mechanic of the Chicago & Alton with a prospectus for a sleeping car which should be available to daytime occupancy as a coach and to conversion after dark into a dormitory car.

The master mechanic had the good sense to see the possibilities of the proposition and gave Pullman a couple of flat-roofed coaches that had seen better days and were destined for the rip track. Pullman hired an assistant named Leonard Seibert and, without so much as a blueprint to follow, they set out to build a sleeper that was to make its inventor a millionaire and itself an American institution comparable to baseball and Congress.

The first run of the converted cars was between Bloomington, Illinois, and Chicago on the night of September 1, 1858, a night that should be epic in the annals of a nation's humor since it saw the first use and occupancy of an upper berth in a center aisle sleeping car, an arrangement that has since been the basis of countless witticisms, unnumbered burlesque situations and incomputable comedies of errors, misunderstanding and mistaken identities. Reason recoils from the thought of what three generations of music-hall eminenti of the De Wolf Hopper school would have done without the upper berth.

In the first Pullmans the upper was suspended from the ceiling by an arrangement of ropes and pulleys which hoisted it out of the way when not in use. The device by which the lowers were evolved from facing seats was basically the same as it is today and the company provided blankets, pillows and porter or conductor service. The cars were a success after a fashion, but their inventor presently tired of them and for four years went helling off to Colorado to follow the boom in precious metals which was opening up the diggings of Idaho Springs, Georgetown, Central City and Blackhawk in Gilpin County, "the richest square mile on earth."

In 1863 Pullman returned to Chicago and, with a boyhood friend, Ben Field for partner, took out two patents that were to be the basis of the Pullman fortunes. One covered a hinged upper berth which folded up against the ceiling much as the first had done on its ropes and pulleys only with greater ease and economy of space, and the other the hinged back and seat of the lower which made a bed by night and a coach section by day. These mechanical novelties were first incorporated into a car named *Pioneer*, which again had been provided by the interested Chicago & Alton, and with them, at the then unheard-of cost of $20,000, went a wealth of fine woodwork and upholstery whose mere contemplation caused admiration and vertigo among the peasantry of the Illinois countryside. To be sure, the *Pioneer* had its drawbacks for, like the land yacht of the optimistic Morgan back in the Boston twenties, it was far too wide for any of the existing clearances along the Alton's right of way.

And here fate stepped in and dealt Pullman and Field a full house. The assassination of President Lincoln required the return of the martyred statesman's body to his native Springfield. Mrs. Lincoln had seen and admired the *Pioneer* a short time previously and nothing would do but that it must be incorporated in the funeral train for her personal occupancy. The whim of Lincoln's widow was a command and, to get the train over its tracks, the Alton added two feet to the clearance of every bridge, depot platform and other installation over its entire right of way. The publicity attracted by Mrs. Lincoln's insistence on the Pullman car was, of course, enormous and was in no whit diminished by the trouble and expense to which the Alton was put to facilitate its progress.

Shortly after this, General Ulysses S. Grant expressed a desire to ride the *Pioneer* to his home town of Galena, Illinois, a community which was happily served by the Chicago & North Western. To refuse the least whim of the hero of Appomattox Court House was unthinkable and now the North Western was put to it to widen all its clearances just as the Alton had done.

Pullman was now set for his main chance. In 1867 he incorporated the Pullman Palace Car Company with works first at Palmyra, New York, and later in Detroit, and set about turning out sleeping cars in quantity and of a beauty and luxury exceeding anything yet known. His cars cost $25,000 apiece to build and were now in service on the Michigan Central and a number of other western roads including the Burlington and the Great Western. It cost four bits more to ride with Pullman than in any other company cars but nobody complained of the expense. Americans were getting a taste of a de luxe life and loved it. The expense could be damned.

From that date forward the success of Pullman and his sleeping car were assured. A promoter and publicist far in advance of his age, the inventor toured the country aboard his own sumptuous cars *Pullman* and *Monitor,* displaying their luxurious appointments to the press and pouring a Niagara of champagne and rare liquors into railroad presidents and directors to whom he wished to sell a bill of goods. Distinguished foreigners, royalties and the nobility scarcely considered a tour of the United States complete unless it had been accomplished aboard the clever Mr. Pullman's personal private car, and when his daughter married Frank

Lowden, later Governor of Illinois, their wedding trip aboard the *Monitor* in its every rococo detail was front-page news throughout the nation.

Pullman never missed a customer. When, during the seventies, the Central Pacific was reluctant to allow its Palace cars to run over the lofty trestles and precipitous fills of the Virginia & Truckee Railroad in Navada, Pullman was quick to arrive in Virginia City aboard his own massive car just to show it could be done. He was always just a little ahead of the competition. When everyone else was using Pintsch gas lamps, Pullman had electricity. When fine bed linen and crystal table services were commonly the equipment only of the most de luxe hotels, Pullman equipped his cars with the best of these articles that money could buy.

Competition withered before him. He bought out Knight, Woodruff, Flower and the shady Colonel Mann and made life miserable for Webster Wagner with one lawsuit after another until, ironically enough, Wagner was cremated in one of his own sleeping cars in a wreck on the New York Central in the early nineties.

Having launched the sleeping car on its career of immortality, Pullman then turned his attention to the problems of eating while riding the cars.

There was nothing new in the idea of a dining car. As far back as 1838 when the *Baltimore Chronicle* for October 31st was hymning the praises of the new sleepers introduced by the Cumberland Valley on its Baltimore to Phiadelphia run, it had remarked parenthetically that "nothing now seems to be wanting to make railroad travel perfect and complete in every convenience except the introduction of dining cars, and these we are sure will soon be introduced." But it remained for George Pullman to build the first diner, *Delmonico* nearly thirty years later.

Until 1867 two expedients had been open to the voyager whose travels took him on the road for longer than the conventional time between meals. He might carry the shoebox lunch that became an American institution in the early years of railroading, or he might depend upon railroad eating houses along the way where, at meal times, the trains stopped for twenty minutes while the passengers descended and engaged in losing skirmishes with avaricious managements, atrocious table fare and eventual dyspepsia. The railroad eating house became a standard item of music-hall humor and the belief that its proprietors were direct descendants of the Borgias gained wide credence.

Now and then some railside lunch room achieved a fair renown for its antelope steaks, its buckwheat cakes or its homemade pies, but generally only terror and dismay lurked on the gastronomic horizon.

Saddened by such conditions, Pullman designed and placed in service in 1867 on the Great Western Railroad of Canada the hotel car *President*, a sleeper fitted with a kitchen and staff prepared to serve all meals to passengers in their sections. Its success was so immediate that it was followed by the cars *Western World* and *Kalamazoo*, and the year after this the first car devoted entirely to the preparation and service of food en route made its appearance on the Chicago & Alton, appropriately named *Delmonico*.

It was at once apparent that dining on the cars possessed a fascination for the American public. Newspaper reporters were assigned to write detailed reports of what was toward aboard the rolling restaurants. Platform lecturers dwelt upon their marvels and travel directors and tourist managers, who were as frequent then as now, wrote at length and reassuringly on how to conduct oneself when dining or lunching at a perilous twenty-two miles an hour.

WESTERN COLLECTION

YOUNG EDISON, THE GENIUS NEWS BUTCHER

In the age when the last word in daytime luxury was aboard such reclining seat parlor cars as this, Thomas Alva Edison and his brass water can *(below)* were familiar sights aboard the Grand Trunk trains running between Port Huron, Michigan, and Detroit. Edison started life as a water boy, later rising to full-fledged news butcher with a stock of candy, periodicals, tobacco and novelties. He also set up a small chemistry laboratory in a corner of the baggage car, but was discharged by the conductor when the train was derailed and his acids ate holes in various company properties.

ASS'N OF AMERICAN RAILROADS

Trains Stopped

For All Meals

Before diners were installed on Chesapeake & Ohio trains, darkies did a brisk business at way stations such as Gordonsville, Virginia (*above*) selling coffee, fried chicken and hot cakes to hungry travelers. When the Columbus, Hocking Valley & Toledo Railroad arrived at Logan, Ohio, the depot hotel there (*right*) was the archetype of hundreds of such hostleries located beside the tracks or upstairs from the station throughout the land. Eight trains a day, some of them with 300 passengers, stopped at Logan for meals and their arrival was a major social and economic event. Road companies of New York successes, salesmen of a thousand commodities and simple countryfolk peopled the lobby of the Depot Hotel. The Golden Hotel at Promontory, Utah, where the transcontinental trains stopped in the seventies advertised (*below left*) that its fare was top notch, but accounts differ. The lady in midair (*below right*) according to the picture's original caption was in such a hurry to reach the lunch counter at the Delavan House at Albany that she illustrated the sip-between-cup-and-lip proverb.

THIS TRAIN

STOPS

20 Minutes for Supper at the

Golden ┃ Hotel

PROMONTORY, UTAH.

FIRST-CLASS MEALS, 50 CENTS.

THE GOLDEN SPIKE

Completing the first Trans-continental Railroad was driven at this point May 10, 1869. Don't fail to treat yourself to a first class meal at this celebrated point.

T. G. BROWN, Prop.

N. Y. PUBLIC LIBRARY

THE PAUSE AT DEPOT RESTAURANTS WAS NEVER DULL

Cartoonists for popular periodicals made a standing joke of depot restaurants, but travelers remembered many with pleasure and excitement. Yankees still recall the station lunch counter at White River Junction, Vermont, once the scene of incredible gastronomic tumults as passengers were fed and departed on three different railroads. Small fry were bought green glass switchmen's lanterns filled with hard candy and the Boston & Maine stocked its counters with a brand of extra strong checkerberry wafers whose flavor lingers yet in the New England memory.

Ornate Luxury Characterized the Age of Grant

(FOUR PICTURES) N. Y. PUBLIC LIBRARY

The two scenes above are from the parlor and smoking cars respectively on the Pennsylvania's 1876 version of today's "clockers" which run on the hour between New York and Philadelphia. The Pullmans of the period (*right*) were an amazement of inlaid woods and marquetry, plate-glass mirrors, velvet drapes and ornate lighting fixtures. As overnight travel became commonplace occupants of gentlemen's washrooms (*below*) learned to use even a straight razor with a minimum of carnage.

And the Sleepers Opened New Vistas of Wonderment

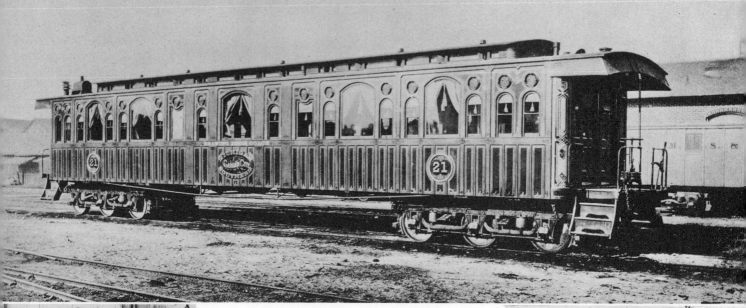

Throughout the sixties and seventies the detail and ornamentation of passenger equipment was constantly refined as is shown by the de luxe drawing-room day-coach *Garden City* (*above*) in service between Chicago and Cleveland on the Lake Shore Railroad. George Pullman (*left*) was inordinately proud of his beautiful sleepers and the details of their servicing (*right*) and their resources of linen closets, uppers and lowers and porter service, as shown below, never failed to fascinate a public which was rapidly accustoming itself to luxurious ways of life hitherto available only in the homes of the well-to-do.

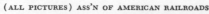

(ALL PICTURES) ASS'N OF AMERICAN RAILROADS

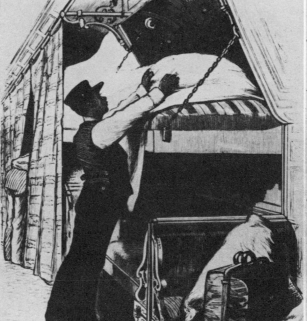

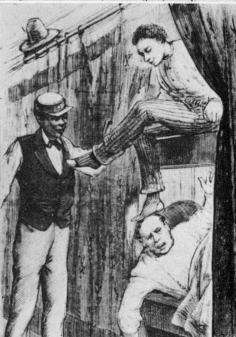

Dining on the Cars Has Delighted Three Generations

AMERICANS BECAME ACCUSTOMED TO DINING AS THE SCENERY PASSED BY

The first diner, the *Delmonico* (*above*) was placed in service on the Chicago & Alton in 1868, and was an instant success. Ten years later they ran on all main-line railroads, but the traveling public never ceased to be fascinated by their diminutive but efficient kitchens (*below*) the mysteries of their servicing (*right above*) and their clever pantries (*right below*) where skilled servants performed their functions.

N. Y. PUBLIC LIBRARY

BROWN BROS.

In a generation that took six-course dinners for granted and when roast partridge at four bits was a commonplace, Americans did well by themselves aboard the diners (*above left*). The lockers of the wine steward (*above right*) were generously stocked with Burgundies and Bordeaux, Hocks, Champagnes and Madeiras in the vintages then current, and Crug's Private Cuvee (a Champagne) was universally listed as refreshment on dining-car breakfast menus. The Rock Island diner of the seventies (*lower left*) reflected the taste of the period, while the abundance of the six-bit dinner menu on the Baltimore & Ohio (*lower right*) which included Saddle Rock oysters, pheasant, filet mignon and lobster, was by no means unique. The United States was still a good place to live in.

BALTIMORE & OHIO RR.

⇥ MENU. ⇤

Saddle Rock Oysters on Shell.

Green Turtle.   Brunoise.   Chicken Gumbo.   Crab Bisque.

Boiled Lake Trout, a la creme.   Baked Blue Fish, Madeira Sauce.
Broiled Spanish Mackerel, Saratoga Potatoes.
Brook Trout, Breaded a la Anglaise.

Leg of Mutton, Caper Sauce.   Buffalo Tongue, Piquant Sauce.
Chicken, Celery Sauce.   Turkey, Oyster Sauce.

Loin of Beef. Saddle of Southdown Mutton. Stuffed Loin of Veal.
Spring Lamb, Mint Sauce. Turkey, Cranberry Sauce. Ham, Champagne Sauce.
Spring Chicken, Giblet Sauce. Rib ends of Beef.

Beef Tongue.   Pheasant Larded aux Truffes.   Lobster Salad.
Mayonnaise of Chicken.   Spiced Oysters.   Pate de Foie Gras.

Fillet de Bœuf Pique, aux Champignons. Lamb Currie with Rice.
Sweetbreads Larded, aux Petits Pois.   Fresh Mushrooms, Stuffed.
Fillets of Chicken, aux Truffes.   Timbal of Macaroni.
Apple Charlotte, a la Parisienne.
Mutton Kidneys, Grille, Madeira Sauce.

Punch a la Romain.

Saddle of Venison, with Jelly.   Young Prairie Chicken.
Canvas-back Duck.   Loin of Antelope,   Vin d' Oporto.   English Snipe.
Broiled Woodcock on Toast.   Quail, Stuffed and Larded.
Broiled Teal Duck, with Olives.

Boiled Potatoes.   Mashed Potatoes.   Baked Sweet Potatoes.
Stewed Tomatoes.   Fried Egg Plant.   Lima Beans.
Green Corn.   Cauliflower.   Green Peas.
Turnips.   Squash.   Asparagus.

English Plum Pudding, Brandy Sauce.   Lemon Meringue Pie.
C. B. & Q. Pudding, Hard Sauce.   Latour Blanche Jelly.
Apple Pie.   Cranberry Pie.   Omelet Souffice.   Italian Cream.
Fruit Cake.   Macaroons.   French Kisses.   Fruit Jelly.

Vanilla and Strawberry Ice Cream.   Neapolitan Cream.
Figs.   Apples.   Oranges.   Nuts.   Raisins.   Grapes.   Bananas.   Pears.

Tea.   Coffee.

BREAKFAST AND SUPPER TO ORDER.

ALL MEALS 75 CENTS.

NOTE— Choice Wines, Liquors and Cigars imported direct by the Burlington Company always on hand in the Dining Cars.

Charles Nordoff wrote in *Harper's Monthly* in 1872:

From Chicago to Omaha your train will carry a dining car, which is a great curiosity in its way. I expected to find this somewhat greasy, a little untidy and with a smell of the kitchen. It might, we thought, be a convenience, but it could not be a luxury. But in fact it is as neat, as nicely fitted, as trim and cleanly as though Delmonico had furnished it. . . . You sit at little tables which comfortably accommodate four persons, you order your breakfast, dinner or supper from a bill of fare which contains quite a surprising number of dishes, and you eat from snow-white linen and neat dishes, admirably cooked food and pay a moderate price. It is now the custom to charge a dollar per meal on these cars; and as the cooking is admirable, the service excellent and the food various and abundant, this is not too much. You may have your choice in the wilderness eating at the rate of 22 miles an hour off buffalo, elk, antelope, beefsteak, mutton chops and grouse. Breakfast wines are claret and sauterne; Champagne wines, Heidsick and Krug.

But, while dining cars on the Chicago & North Western such as the one described here and a few other restaurant cars and buffets may have been nice in their refinements of food and service, the average in the depot restaurants where the great majority of travelers obtained their meals in transit was of a very low order indeed. A diner represented an investment of anything from $25,000 up and was patronized by persons of influence and importance, but the flyblown hash houses where the non-extra fare trains stopped at morning, lunch time and the dinner hour were something else again. And the something else, if one believes the reports of contemporaries, was abysmal.

The story of Fred Harvey is the American success story in quintessence. An emigrant who arrived from Liverpool with ten dollars in his pocket and a stock of indomitable resolution which would have shamed the hero of a Horatio Alger novel, Harvey worked in New York and then New Orleans in menial capacities in restaurants and finally came to the world of railroading as western freight agent of the Burlington. Being a man who liked good food he was first revolted and then acquired stomach ulcers as a result of the necessity for eating in railroad restaurants. Through a lucky acquaintance with a Santa Fe division superintendent, he secured permission to open a railroad restaurant of his own in the Topeka depot. The only memorandum of agreement between the high contracting parties to this arrangement was a handshake, and for many years the Santa Fe and Fred Harvey did business on a basis of mutual trust and admiration without a document or signature between them.

Harvey acquired a reputation at Topeka that caused drummers to get themselves routed through his district and travelers to write home about it. He then moved on to Florence, Kansas, where he started out with a chef imported from the Palmer House in Chicago at a salary of $5,000 which was about $2,500 more a year than was made by anyone in the county including the banker. Harvey always outfitted his eating houses with the best of everything: silver from England, Irish linen for the tables and raw food products of a superlative order. Kansas, Oklahoma and New Mexico had never seen anything like it and generally regarded Fred Harvey as a benefactor to the regions he served equal with if not superior to the Santa Fe itself.

Harvey didn't mind, and the Santa Fe backed him up, whether he made or lost money so long as his food, service and reputation were second to none. James Marshall, official biographer of the Santa Fe, deposes that on one occasion he discharged a restaurant manager because he didn't lose as much on his operations as Harvey thought his restaurant ought to lose. The West ate up this sort of thing both literally and metaphorically and by 1901 when Fred Harvey died the system he had founded and brought to perfection owned and operated fifteen hotels, forty-seven restaurants, and fifteen dining cars. It has been growing ever since.

For his waitresses Harvey eschewed the Gold Tooth Tessies and Dirty Girties of the hash-house tradition and employed neat and respectable young women of unimpeachable morals, an impressive proportion of whom married handsomely, and the Harvey House girls became celebrated in song and verse, on stage and, eventually, on the screen. To secure prompt service for all patrons of his restaurants without holding up trains longer than the twenty minutes allowed by immemorial practice he had the train conductor wire ahead the number of prospective customers and the steaks, eggs and chops were put on the fire when the engineer whistled for the yard limit a mile out of town. The waitresses put out the hot plates, biscuits and coffee as the train slowed to a stop and the manager in person, in the pleasant manner of an older tradition, passed around the meat platter with all the patron wished to take for the universal Harvey tariff of four bits. It is part of the legend that no Harvey patron ever missed his train or ever had to bolt his food.

The fame of the Harvey Houses eventually, of course, led the Santa Fe to have him take over their ever crescent fleet of diners.

With the passing of time other railroads besides the Santa Fe came to understand the promotional possibilities of restaurants on the rails. The legend came into being, and it is part of the American credo to this day, that "real railroading" didn't begin until the traveler got west of Chicago. What this actually meant was that, generally speaking the food on the western diners was incomparably superior to that east of the Mississippi and that, since how he ate on the cars made more impression on passengers than any other aspect of railroad operations, "real eating" became synonymous with "real railroading."

In some cases food was associated by railroads in their advertising slogans. The Northern Pacific described itself as the "Road of the Great Big Baked Potato." The Great Northern was known as the "Route of the Big Red Apple." The Union Pacific, with much Idaho trackage, also traded on the fame of Idaho potatoes and at one time President William Jeffers distributed thousands of bags of Idaho spuds among shippers and business associates as a symbol of the road's choicest freight. The Bangor & Aroostook also shared in potato promotion since the Maine potato is and always has been its largest single item of revenue merchandise. The Boston & Maine loudly proclaimed the superior merits of the Boston baked beans served on its diners and a short line in the Deep South, the Atlantic & East Carolina, achieved fame as "The Mullet Line" from the quantities of fish it handled.

The golden age of gastronomy aboard the cars was also the age of the dollar dinner which flourished grandly on a number of railroads at the turn of the century. The florid profusion of game in the form of grouse, quail, partridge, antelope, venison, bear meat, plover and buffalo that had characterized the menus on the first diners in the West of the frontier was beginning to disappear. The Santa Fe had been in the habit of paying six bits a dozen for Mexican quail and $1.50 a dozen for fine plump prairie hens. Pheasant and antelope steaks had been fixtures on the earlier bills of fare on the Burlington and the chefs of the Great Northern were celebrated for their knowing ways with sage hen and mountain sheep. Terrapin and canvasback appeared on some of the more elaborate menus of the Pennsylvania and Rocky Mountain trout, then as they are still, were ornaments on the first menus of the Rio Grande and Colorado & Southern.

But by the end of the nineties the diminishing availability of game and regulations governing its sale and transportation began curbing its service in public restaurants. It was then that the dollar dinner, usually with steak, chicken or lobster, emerged as the wonder and glory of the age. Western railroads carried thousands and millions of heads of stock annually in the direction of Chicago, Omaha, Kansas City or Denver. Their purchasing agents had access to the finest beef, lamb and pork produced anywhere in the world. The sirloins, T-bones, New York cuts and tenderloins of American dining cars became proverbial. Its low price at the stockyards in the quantities bought by the railroads made it practicable if not profitable to include on the dollar dinner and the institution became one of the best advertised assets of such roads as the Baltimore & Ohio, the Burlington, the Southern and the Atlantic Coast Line. And the dollar dinner included all the trimmings, soup and dessert, hot breads, olives, nuts, preserves, mounds of vegetables and water ices with the meat course, pickles, chowchow and the elaborate and spectacular salads dear to the heart of the vegetable chef.

Regional dishes were, of course, featured by railroads everywhere. There was scrapple on the Reading, pompano on the Louisville & Nashville, scrod on the New Haven, shrimp Creole on the Illinois Central and sand dabs and California figs on the Southern Pacific. Out-of-season strawberries and green peas from old Mexico were common currency on the Texas & Pacific and Florida melons of prodigious size and wonderful Georgia peaches were stocked in the iceboxes of the Atlantic Coast Line and the Seaboard.

Now and then dining car stewards have emerged to more than local fame for their personalities or the superior food and service on their cars. On the Santa Fe's Chicago-Kansas City run there was Bill Gardner, creator of a special salad dressing which found vast favor with the railroad's patrons. To passengers who commented on it Gardner made a practice of presenting a bottle of the non-such with his and the Harvey system's compliments. On the *Twentieth Century Limited* two genial Irishmen named Tommy Walsh and Tommy O'Grady were for years celebrities in their own right and much esteemed by such notables on the New York-Chicago luxury run as Ogden Armour, Colonel Robert McCormick, Rufus and Charles G. Dawes and Charlie MacArthur, the playwright.

Perhaps the most famous of all diner managers west of the Mississippi was Wild Bill Kurthy who, for many years, fed and sluiced the great of the world aboard Southern Pacific trains such as *The Forty-Niner, Overland Limited* and *City of San Francisco.* Kurthy had been brought up in the hotel tradition by Oscar (of the Waldorf) Tchirky and he believed in solid food and its service in mammoth quantities. During the Second World War travelers to the West Coast went to some pains to travel with the noisy and indeed uproarious Kurthy, because, in some manner or other, he contrived to stock his car with gratifying resources of steak, hams, butter and heavy cream when these articles were at a great premium and available in only the most reduced quantities.

T-bones swimming in melted butter, pheasants from the Nevada ranges and elaborate whipped-cream desserts appeared as though by magic in the diners of the *City of San Francisco,* and Kurthy pressed them urgently upon his patrons. Frilly old ladies who were accustomed to breakfast off tea and melba toast found themselves confronted with towering stacks of little thin hot cakes garlanded in wreaths of sausages. Two-inch-thick steaks appeared on the most casual luncheon table and late at night, if the indomitable Kurthy felt you hadn't done justice to his table at dinner, a grinning waiter was apt to appear in your drawing room along bedtime with a couple of quarts of milk and an assortment of ham and cheese sandwiches of monstrous proportions. Any refusal of this bounty caused the boy to assume an expression of remarkable concern and apprehension. "The wild man will be terrible cross if I bring them back," he would mutter darkly. "You better eat them for sure." Usually the passenger ate them.

The decor of diners has undergone many changes since George Pullman's *Delmonico.* The looped and fringed draperies, ornate lighting fixtures and elaborately inlaid panels of Victorian taste gave way to simpler interiors and more chaste ornamentation although the fundamental overall design has remained much the same. With the coming of the air-flow age diners began to run to functional steel furniture, severe decorations or none, fluorescent lighting and printed chintz curtains. On main-line roads with great density of traffic, double-unit diners with kitchens in one car and the entire length of another unit devoted to tables made their appearance. Some railroads such as the New Haven and the Pennsylvania devised café cars with counter lunches and snack bars. Composition fuels and briquettes supplanted the traditional coal in ranges, and devisings of modernity in the form of dish-washing machines, electric refrigerators and even electric stoves appeared. In time of war mass feeding became a highly organized technique and the Santa Fe contrived to feed 350 persons at one meal, a crisis which necessitated the frying of 1,004 eggs in a single batch in a single frying pan.

Change too appeared in the design and structure of sleeping cars. Late in the forties a decision of the Supreme Court separated the activities of the Pullman Company as a car builder and as the operator of its sleeping-car services, and these are now conducted by two separate corporations. The demand for economy in continental travel declined until railroads found it difficult to sell space in upper berths and there was a vast increase in the demand for private room accommodations. Single rooms, roomettes, drawing rooms, staterooms and compartments became in greater requisition, and at length such crack trains as the *Broadway Limited* and the *Century* carried room cars only. Private suites with showers and enclosed toilet space became commonplace instead of, as formerly, encountered only on private cars and extra-fare runs. By the mid-twentieth century the Pullman upper berth was disappearing from the consciousness of American travelers although it was destined for a bright immortality in the legend and folklore of the nation.

Entire Trains for Private Hire Were Sumptuous Indeed

(ALL PICTURES) BROWN BROS.

At the turn of the century parties of travelers with the means at their disposal might engage entire trains of Pullman built luxury cars such as those shown on these pages and cross the continent or sojourn in Florida in upholstered privacy. The lounge car *(upper left)* was designed for social intimacy while the observation parlor *(upper right)* was a turmoil of fringes, draperies and inlaid woods.

There was also a library car for the sober-minded and solvent. Patrons of the Santa Fe's trains to California in the age before streamlining and cocktail lounges remember with pleasure the library cars with their courteous attendants which also contained the barber shop and shower bath on the *Chief* and the *California Limited*.

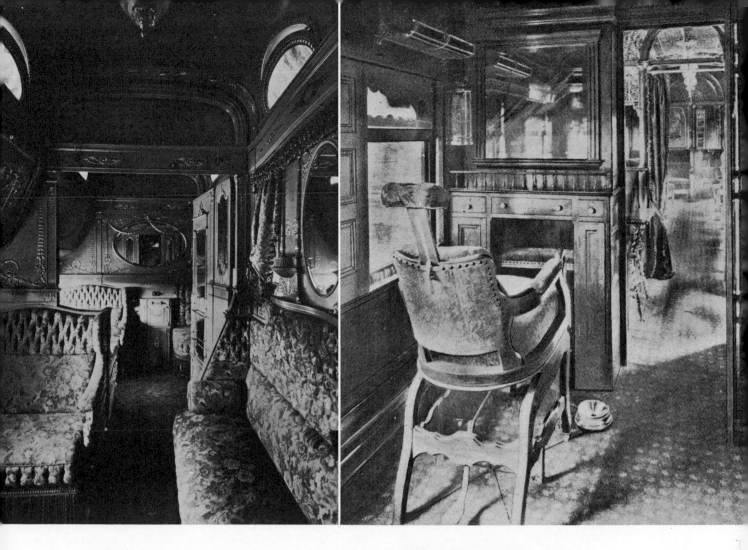

Sleeping apartments included drawing rooms with connecting staterooms *(above left)* in stylish fabrics and rich brocades, while a barber shop with attendant tonsor and manicurist *(above right)* was a masculine convenience. Barber shops first appeared on the *Twentieth Century* and *Broadway Limited* at about this time.

The taste of the period decreed divans with a multiplicity of cushions, hassocks and brocaded chairs *(left)* while the dressing rooms and lavatories *(right)* bristled with commodes, bevel-edge mirrors and ball-fringed draperies.

Fred Harvey Gentled the Frontier With Choice Viands

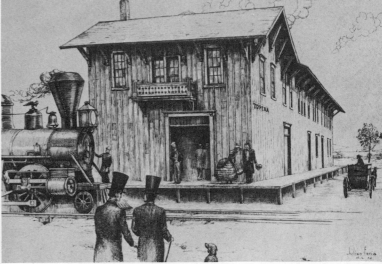

(THREE PICTURES) FRED HARVEY

"THE SAME LIKE YOU CAN GET IN HIGH-TONED RESTAURAWS DOWN EAST"

Eugene Field

The final panache to the pacification of the Southwest, which had begun in the days of the Taos trade, was supplied when Fred Harvey (*left*) a resolute prophet of good living, opened a series of superb depot restaurants along the main line of the Santa Fe Railroad. The first of these at Topeka (*above*) set a pattern of excellence which started the Harvey House legend. The one at Newton (*below*) popped the eyes of cowtown waddies in what was reputed to be the gastritis capital of the West. The demitasse came to the range before ever Marie Dressler sang about their peril for the woiking goil.

Soon Fred Harvey was order-
ing the affairs of the Santa
Fe's dining cars in a manner
that patrons compared favorably with Delmonico's, then
the national standard of gastronomic excellence. Fine wines
and game appeared at table
(*left*) in bountiful profusion.
Elderly folk (*below*) winter-
ing in Pasadena or Phoenix
took the Santa Fe cars on the
strength of Fred Harvey whose
stewards remembered their
preferences year after year.
For many years the only agreement of partnership between
Harvey and the railroad was
an annual handshake.

BROWN BROS.

"BEASTS FEED, MEN EAT, THE MAN OF DISCERNMENT ALONE DINES"

CULVER SERVICE

N. Y. PUBLIC LIBRARY

Until the coming of Fred Harvey the social status of waitresses in depot restaurants left something to be desired. So outrageous was the conduct of the staff in the union station lunchroom at St. Louis that upon one occasion the police rounded them all up for a night in the municipal calaboose and forced them to listen to a moral exhortation by an eminent divine the next morning (*above*). All inducements by the clergy, it was reported in the public prints, to get the girls to take a temperance pledge were unavailing. The waitresses at Harvey restaurants and lunch counters were of impeccable morals and large numbers of them made advantageous marriages. The lunchroom at Somerville, Texas, was typical in the Gibson Girl age.

FRED HARVEY

SANTA FE RR.

GENERAL MOTORS

Following in Harvey's footsteps, other railroads took measures to establish their dining facilities more nearly on a level to gratify Brillat-Savarin. Above are the galley-pantry and a private dining compartment with flowered wallpaper aboard the General Motors *Train of Tomorrow,* bought by the Union Pacific for use on its western lines. Below is the Harvey managed private dining apartment, the *Turquoise Room,* on the Santa Fe's *Super Chief* where, presumably, the shade of the founder hovers solicitously over the service of the sole Marguery and the decanting of the Romanée Conti for the railroad's extra-fare guests.

SANTA FE RR.

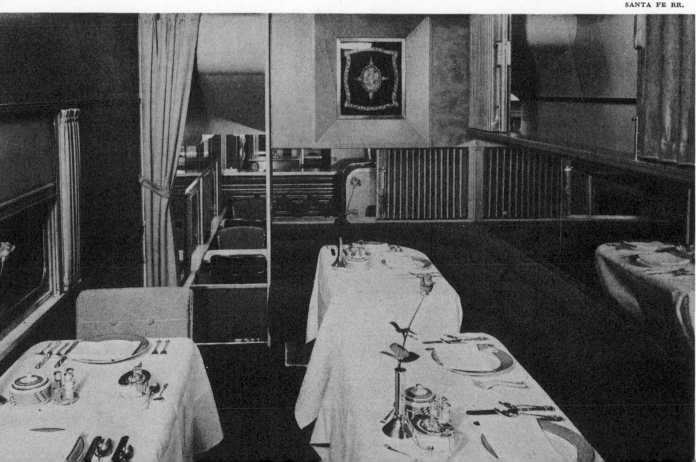

CAL PHOTOS

The finest flower of the car-builder's art was the private railroad car with the brass-railed platform of the grand tradition. It added a dimension of grandeur to an age of wealth and well-being.

XX

Private Varnish

Once the Private Railroad Car Was the Hallmark of Financial Importance and Social Success, Its Implications as Spacious as the Times of Which It Was an Ornate Part

To two full generations of Americans the private railroad car was the supreme symbol of success, luxury and the enviable way of life. It was synonymous with social exclusiveness, financial importance and the de luxe order of things, and into its design, construction and decor went the ultimate devisings of

388

skilled craftsmen and artists. It was the finest flower of the golden age of passenger equipment and, although a degree of its luxury and some of the refinements of its appointment and maintenance are now more generally available, no perquisite of wealth and importance will ever achieve the distinction of the dark green private varnish car that for half a century rolled splendidly over the nation's railroad system.

In the earlier days of railroading there was little or no distinction drawn, as there later came rigidly to be, between the Pullmans and varnish cars owned by private individuals and those maintained by railroads for their officers and executives. In the middle nineteenth century well-to-do individuals were very often also railroad directors and the distinction meant nothing. A later generation of railroaders prefers to refer to their executive varnish as "business" or "official" cars and they are carried in the books as railroad property rather than personal assets of their proprietors.

The first record of anything resembling a private car in the United States appears in the tariff rates of the Boston & Providence Railroad for 1834 among whose items appears a round trip rate between Boston and Dedham Township, "private cars holding twenty passengers: $15." Their next mention would seem to be when, in 1841, William H. Harrison went to Washington as President-elect of the United States, and the general manager of the Baltimore & Ohio asked his superiors if he should supply this dignitary with "a distinct car." Twenty odd years later the military carshops at Alexandria built for President Lincoln the first armored car designed in this country for a chief of state, and, although Lincoln never had occasion to use it in his lifetime, it did carry his body to Springfield, Illinois, after his assassination.

From these first beginnings, the private car rose rapidly in general use and in the public imagination until, in the eighties and nineties, the millionaire, society figure or railroad or industrial nabob who did not own at least one private car and in many instances two or three, simply had not arrived socially or financially speaking. William H. Vanderbilt's favorite private varnish car was named, somewhat redundantly, *Vanderbilt* and another, *Duchess,* was available if his guests were numerous. George Pullman had two cars, *Pullman* and *Monitor,* and General William Jackson Palmer was outraged at the infringement upon his privacy when the Colorado press reported that his *Nomad* on the Denver & Rio Grande, a narrow-gage drawing-room car, rejoiced in a bath with both hot and cold running water. Life in a later generation of railroad tycoons was even less austere. In his diaries, published many years later, Count Boni de Castellane told how, when he was courting Anna Gould, guests aboard the private train of her brother George Gould were expected to wear full evening dress at dinner.

Among the first-known private cars of railroad executives—the austere pretentions of later years would call it a business car—was that of Daniel Torrence, general superintendent of the New York Central in the seventies. It was called the *Shoo Fly* after a popular Negro dialect song of the Civil War times, painted a very dark chocolate with gilt trim and scrollwork, and its name was whimsically represented by the word "Shoo" in gold letters followed by a picture of a fly in bright red.

With the turn of the century when railroad executives became increasingly inhibited about the use of private equipment the custom became general among railroad officials to remove fanciful or colorful names from their business cars and substitute plain and functional numbers, so that to this day a railroad president may travel in comparative anonymity aboard *Car 100* or *Car 1,* numbers widely favored by railroaders of presidential rank. Although comfortable, well-staffed with servants and unavailable to any but qualified persons, the modern business car is, by comparison to its ornate and orchidaceous predecessors, a paradigm of Spartan simplicity.

Private varnish of the nineties and early nineteen hundreds reached an all-time high in luxurious appointments, ornamentation and physical conveniences. Pipe organs, solid gold and silver dinner services, period furniture, costly upholsteries, rare paintings and air conditioning long before it was commonly available to stand-ard railroad equipment were the merest commonplace. *Loretto,* the celebrated Pullman-built car of Charles M. Schwab, boasted marble plumbing fixtures, plate-glass mirrors of heroic dimensions, brass beds and ceiling murals in its master bedroom executed by an Italian artist specially imported to Chicago for the commission. *Ranger,* belonging to Cissie Patterson, publisher of the *Washington Times Herald,* was kept fully staffed twenty-four hours a day in the Southern's Washing-ton yards and possessed seven complete sets of slip covers for its furniture so that its passengers might not become fatigued with the same decor on successive days.

Jomar, the car inherited from his uncle John Ringling by John Ringling North, owner of the Circus, has in its dining salon a series of circus murals by Charles Baskerville, a fashionable painter of animal life. The personal car of Brigham Young, President of the Latter-day Saints, had a frieze of heavily gold-plated angels around the transoms in its clerestory, and the car of Arthur E. Stilwell, a railroader of religious leanings, had a pipe organ installed as an adjunct to divine services which were held every Sunday wherever the car might be spotted. When Estelle Manville, the roofing heiress, married the Count Folke-Bernadotte of Sweden a few years ago, Mrs. Edward F. Hutton, a friend, took two of her own private cars from Grand Central to Pleasantville, New York, a distance of thirty-one miles for the wedding. Charles Clark, son of famed Senator William F. Clark of Montana, re-portedly commissioned the Pullman Company to build *Errant* for his wife so that she might travel with her pet dog, forbidden in public conveyances. The first air-conditioned railroad car in the world was *Edgewood* the property of Major Max Fleischman, the yeast tycoon, and Mrs. J. P. Donahue's *Japauldin,* perhaps the most costly private car ever outshopped by Pullman, had solid gold lighting fixtures, quartered oak beams running the length of the drawing room ceiling and a wood-burning fireplace equipped with an electric blower for draft.

In the easygoing days of the nineteenth century a private car was a factual convenience as well as a luxurious property. Regulations governing the movement of private cars by public carriers were practically nonextant and what there were were spaciously interpreted. Almost any director of a short line in Arkansas or Georgia was permitted, by the terms of universal business courtesy, to attach his personal car to trains of main-line transcontinental railroads. Directorates and other official positions in obscure railroads were in widespread requisition solely to secure the benefits of free transport over the nation's rails. Occasionally there were so many requests for the inclusion of private or semi-private Pullmans in trains of the Pennsylvania, the Central and other important carriers that head-end revenue cars and even paying passengers had to be eliminated for their accommodation. What had started as a gesture of courtesy became a major abuse and, shortly after the turn of the century, the I.C.C. imposed stringent regulations governing the inclusion of private cars and the transportation of railroad executives everywhere.

In the years between the company's formation and 1930 when it outshopped its last private railroad car for Harry Payne Whitney, the Pullman Company, according to its records, built a total of 350 such items of equipment. Many others were built by American Car & Foundry and the carshops of individual railroads. Today there are but two privately owned and operated railroad cars maintained for the pleasure and convenience of their owners, *Helma*, once the property of A. C. Burrage, a Boston millionaire, and now the rolling home of Bruce Dodson, a Kansas City insurance magnate, and *The Gold Coast*, owned and operated by the authors of this book.

As a result of the Second World War when rail equipment of all sorts was in great demand for the military, the private cars of yesterday were largely turned back to the railroads for official or government use. *Curley Hut*, the handsome varnish car of Franklyn L. Hutton, is now business car No. 25 of the Chesapeake & Ohio. Barbara Hutton's car with its elaborate Tiffany silver service and spacious bedrooms is the business car of the president of the Western Pacific.

Henry Ford's *Fair Lane* is reserved for the president of the Cotton Belt. *Atalanta* the sumptuous car built for Jay Gould in the eighties at a cost of $50,000, a fabulous sum for the times, ended its days as a yardmaster's shack on the Missouri Pacific in Overton, Texas. Joshua Cosden's Pullman, on which the then Prince of Wales toured the United States in 1924, is now grounded as the residence of a coal-stripping gang at Hazleton, Pennsylvania. For private cars, the paths of glory lead but to the rip track.

As part of its function of public service, the Pullman Company still maintains a number of drawing-room cars with kitchens and observation salons which can be rented for a fixed daily sum with a staff of two attendants. Rental is in addition to the eighteen full first-class railroad fares required by law, taxes, parking and sanitation charges. But the private varnish car that once rolled over the nation's rails is one with the passenger pigeon and the canal boat, only a legend.

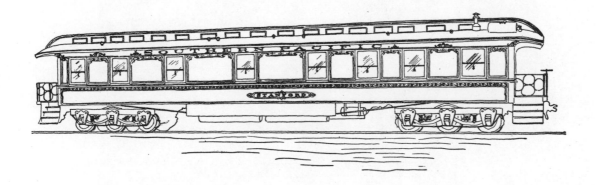

The
Presidents
Harrison

CULVER SERVICE

BROWN BROS.

Heads of State Voyaged in Private Splendor

N. Y. PUBLIC LIBRARY

A PRINCE ARRIVES IN THE DE LUXE STYLE OF 1870

CANADIAN NATIONAL RAILWAYS

When in 1841 President-elect William B. Harrison journeyed to Washington for his inaugural over the Baltimore & Ohio Railroad the general manager inquired if he should be accorded a "distinct car." He was, and at the top of the page opposite is shown as the "distinct car" was surrounded by admirers at Baltimore depot. In the picture below another President Harrison—Benjamin (*seated*)—is shown aboard a presidential special en route for a state function half a century later. Another personage of importance, H. R. H. Prince Arthur of England is shown at the top of this page arriving in New York in 1870 on a private car of the Hudson River Railroad. Below is the sleeping car specially built by the Buffalo & Lake Huron Railroad to accommodate the prince's entourage.

For Princes,

Princely Decor

In the plush and ormolu eighties, when the distinguishing hallmark of affluence and social position was the ornate privately owned railroad car, George Gould, inheritor of a vast railroad empire, maintained an entire private train. Guests aboard this stylish conveyance were expected to appear for dinner in full formal evening attire, a detail which favorably impressed the French Count Boni de Castellane, here depicted by the artist E. S. Hammack, when he was a suitor for the hand of Gould's sister, Anna, most eligible American heiress of the moment. In its glittering noontide the private car carried with it implications of wealthy elegance: Scotch grouse on gold dinner service by Tiffany and Jockey Club coronas with the vintage cognac when the ladies had left the table. Private cars in the age of luxury embraced costly appointments: turkey carpets, pipe organs, marble bath tubs, wine cellars, silver plumbing fixtures, crystal chandeliers and rare inlaid woodwork. But while their decor and appointments have been as widely various as the times and tastes they served, the functional economy of the private car has changed little with the years. Almost invariably their floor plan has included a lounge or observation drawing room opening onto the brass-bound platform of tradition, a series of sleeping apartments, a dining salon seating from eight to ten, forward of which have been the galley, pantry, store rooms, ice boxes and sleeping quarters for the crew which usually numbers two. In some cases, as in Doris Duke's *Doris,* observation room space has been sacrificed in favor of more ample sleeping compartments. In *The Gold Coast* pictured on the page opposite there are but two master bedrooms while the drawing room is twenty-four feet long. Its Victorian decor, awash with crystal lighting fixtures, Venetian mirrors, antimacassars and looped and fringed draperies is designed to recreate the interior of Leland Stanford's private car *Stanford,* built in the seventies.

E. S. HAMMACK

CAL PHOTOS

VICTORIAN DECOR RECREATED ABOARD THE CAR *THE GOLD COAST*

CAL PHOTOS

Private Cars for Presidents Are an Official Tradition

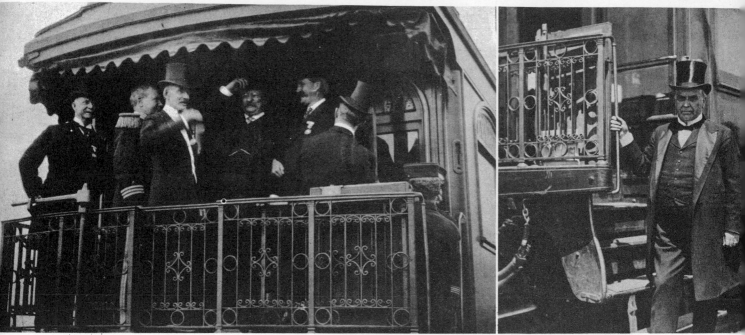

BROWN BROS.

CLEARANCES ONCE ACCOMMODATED SILK HATS

Although American presidents of the top hat and Prince Albert frock-coat era such as McKinley *(upper right)* and Theodore Roosevelt surrounded by his staff and advisors *(upper left)* rode grandly on campaigns and official tours aboard private cars of contemporary vintage, no chief executive has ever maintained a private car so completely *moderne* in decor as the one *(below)* built for Fred Gurley, president of the Santa Fe Railroad. Its stainless steel construction, roller-bearing trucks and faired-in roof have been copied by ranking executives of the Great Northern and Rio Grande roads, but few railroaders have been able to resist retaining the open observation platform of classic tradition, here skirted with steel plates for protection at high speeds from flying bits of roadbed.

SANTA FE RR.

THE *MAGELLAN* IS SEVERE, UTILITARIAN AND SECURE

United States Railroad Car No. 1, named the *Magellan* after a world traveler of earlier vintage, is the rented property of the Federal government, leased from the Association of American Railroads for a dollar a year for the use of the President when he travels on public business or private pleasure by rail. It was built during the tenure of office of Franklin Roosevelt, a confirmed railroad habitue, whose trains over all roads had a ruling speed of thirty-five miles an hour because the President liked the scenery and enjoyed leisurely ways. Built of armor plate and weighing nearly twice as much as a standard Pullman, the *Magellan* is elaborately proofed against intrusion, molestation or accident. Its decor is a far cry from the ornate interiors deemed suitable for heads of state only a generation ago, and when the Chief Executive lounges (*top*) sits down to dinner (*center*) or retires to bed (*bottom*) it is in surroundings of almost Spartan simplicity and conventional comfort.

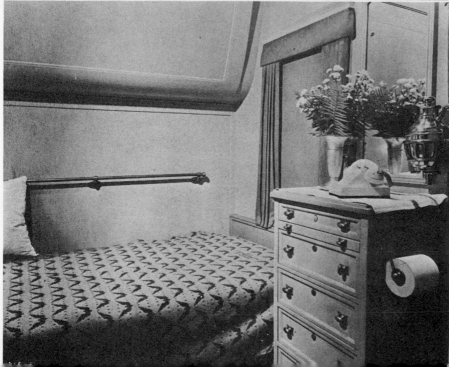

ASS'N OF AMERICAN RAILROADS

Private Cars Were The Symbol Of Spacious Times

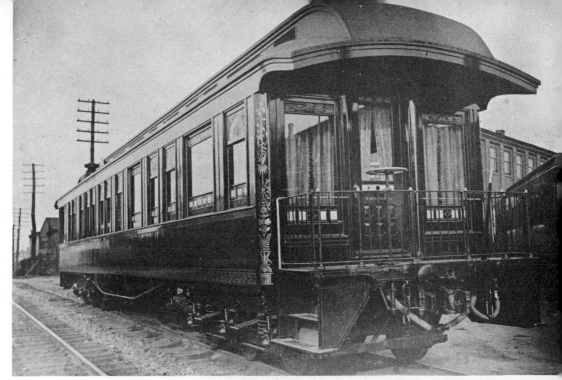

AMERICAN CAR & FOUNDRY

The private cars of the golden age of railroading in America were things of beauty, conceived in terms of rare woods and sumptuous decor and known as varnish cars because their finish was the satin sheen of perfection. The car shown above was out-shopped by American Car & Foundry in the eighties for the Long Island Railroad's more affluent patrons on a rental basis and was christened *Manhattan*. Below at the left is the main salon of the *Loretto* No. 2 built by Pullman in 1917 at a cost of $75,000 for the steel magnate and now the property of Colonel Elliott White Springs of South Carolina. Adjacent is the interior of the car of Arthur E. Stillwell, builder of the Kansas City, Pittsburgh & Gulf Railway. A religious man, Stillwell admired to have Sunday services held aboard his car and for this purpose an organ, visible here, was built in. Later when the car became the property of Bet-a-Million Gates, the gambling, barbed-wire salesman, its atmosphere was somewhat less inhibited by decorum.

THE PULLMAN CO.

Styles in Presidential Travel Changed With the Years

EAST BROAD TOP RAILROAD

SOUTHERN PACIFIC RR.

Grover Cleveland liked to travel in a flower-decked narrow-gage private car (*upper right*) with ferns and looped portieres. With a plainer decor (*upper left*) it is the property today of the East Broad Top Railroad in western Pennsylvania. President Theodore Roosevelt wore a top hat and Prince Albert when he stepped down from his car (*center*) to view the Denver & Rio Grande Western's hanging bridge in the Canyon of the Arkansas. Below, President McKinley speaks from the observation platform of a private car of the Southern Pacific at Stockton in 1901. Colored-glass transoms and ornate railings were the order of the day.

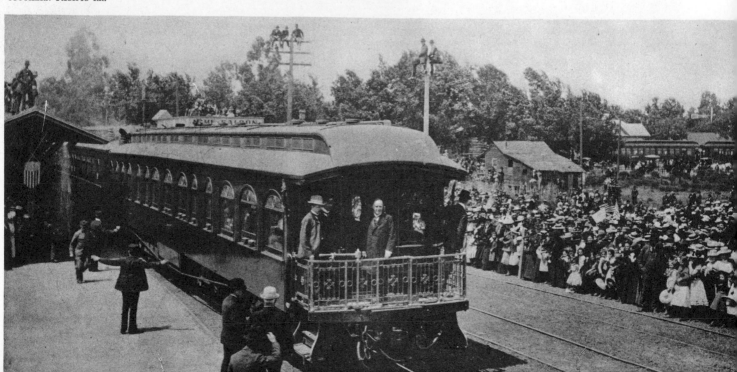

BROWN BROS.

For decades the private car was an indispensable for headliners of the stage or music worlds. Paderewski's car the *General Stanley* (*above*) contained, in addition to conventional facilities, an upright piano and cabinet for the owner's silk hat. Below is the music room aboard the private varnish of Fritzi Scheff, built when the diminutive singer and toast of two continents was singing *Mademoiselle Modiste*. The Dillingham office advertised that she bathed in champagne as a beauty aid aboard the car, but years later Miss Scheff told one of the authors of this book that the bath was more prosaically drawn with tap water and that in order to bathe without inundating her apartment she was forced to time her ablutions to train stops of twenty minutes duration whatever the hour of day or night.

M. B. WAKEFIELD

Henry Flagler Lived in the Golden Age of Private Cars

AMERICAN CAR & FOUNDRY

The dream of Henry Flagler was to create in the state of Florida a resort empire that should take advantage of its natural resources for health and relaxation and at the same time bring traffic to his Florida East Coast Railroad. To achieve this he built a chain of magnificent resort hotels at Jacksonville, Palm Beach and Miami and served them with luxury trains from the North throughout the winter months. As a hotelier and railroad man in one, Flagler had his own ideas of luxury and his private car, out-shopped to his special order by the American Car & Foundry Co., is shown in the pictures on this page. Below is an earlier private car of the rail magnate, *Moultrie*, which in later years slipped several rungs down the social scale to become the business car of the president of a short line in Virginia. The photograph shows it as a property of the Georgia Northern.

MIKE RUNEY

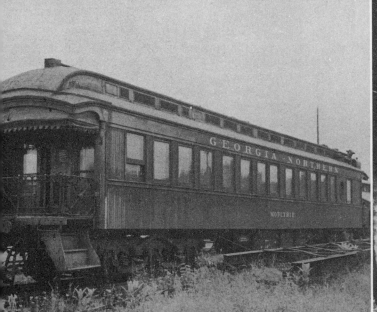

Business Cars Come in Assorted Styles and Sizes

When executives of the Central Pacific (*top*) rode their line in the seventies they took their families and braved the elements from the observation platform attired in deer-stalker hats and rat-catcher suits of daring design. Directors of the Delaware & Hudson on inspection trips could ride in swivel chairs at either end of Car 80 (*center*) or, if the weather was inclement, in its snug compartment. The president of the Southern Railway rides a duplex suite of two Pullmans named *Carolina* and *Virginia* of which only *Virginia* is shown below. Duplex was built to carry the road's aristocratic and scholarly president, Fairfax Harrison (*above*) who sometimes bewildered division superintendents with learned discussions of Santa-yana's sonnets or asked traveling engineers their opinions on Ming ceramics.

SOUTHERN RAILWAY

A distinguished example of modern car building is the private Pullman *Helma* originally built for the Boston financier A. C. Burrage and more recently the property of Bruce Dodson, a Kansas City insurance magnate. The initials of the Florida East Coast Railway above its rear window indicate that the owner has arrangements with that railroad to handle the charges of its transportation and storage. The center photograph shows a railroad president's business car parked beside a private pleasure car: the business hack indicated by its track lights and sober decor, the private varnish by its ornamental brasswork, Venetian blinds and gaily striped awning. Typical of interior decorative schemes of a slightly earlier period than *Helma* is Mrs. Schwab's bedroom on the second *Loretto*, shown at the bottom of the page. Below will be found a brief list of private car owners and their choice of names for their cars:

Mrs. John Mackay: *Corsair*
John Ringling: *Wisconsin*
William H. Vanderbilt: *Vanderbilt* and *Duchess*
Adelina Patti: *Adelina Patti*
Adolphus Busch: *Adolphus*
Ignace Jan Paderewski: *General Stanley*
George Pullman: *Pullman* and *Monitor*
Charles M. Schwab: *Loretto* and *Loretto No. 2*
Leland Stanford: *Stanford*
Harry Payne Bingham: *Pawnee*
Harry Payne Whitney: *Wanderer*
Alfred P. Sloan, Jr.: *Pheasant*
W. F. Kenny: *St. Nicholas*
Charles W. Clark: *Errant*

Lucius Beebe and Charles Clegg: *Gold Coast*
John Ringling North: *Jomar*
Cissie Patterson: *Ranger*
Charles Gates Jr.: *Bright Eyes*
Paul Block: *Friendship*
Andrew and Richard B. Mellon: *Vagabondia*
Harry F. Sinclair: *Sinco*
Henry Ford: *Fair Lane*
Henry Flagler: *Moultrie*
Otto Mears: *San Juan*
Jay Gould: *Atalanta*
Franklyn L. Hutton: *Curly Hut*
John J. Raskob: *Skipaway*
William F. Woodin: *Berwick*
Joseph Widener: *Lynnewood*
Mrs. Harry Payne Whitney: *Adis*

THE PULLMAN CO.

OIL INDUSTRY INFORMATION

Spindletop, discovered in 1901 and shown here two years later, was the first big Texas oil field and its derricks cast a long shadow over the destinies of railroading.

XXI

Fin de Siécle

The Steam-Driven Wheel Came Full Circle With the Internal Combustion Engine. Oil Marked the End of an Era, the Fulfillment of a Cycle, Finis to the Age of Steam

THE PETROLEUM industry in the United States had existed since the year 1859 when Drake's well at Titusville, Pennsylvania, commenced commercial operation, so it would be too pat to remark that Spindletop marked the beginning of the end of the cycle of steam railroading. But Spindletop was the symbol, and when it put Beaumont, Texas, on the map in 1901 as the mightiest oil field the world had ever seen a new dimension was given to transportation and the emergence of the internal combustion engine was at hand.

404

The technique, practice and fullest expansion of steam railroading required roughly three-quarters of a century for their mature achievement. But by the middle of the twentieth century the internal combustion engine was to inhibit entirely the expansion of railroading, eliminate its operation on thousands of miles of established branches and short lines and so to alter operations on the main lines which survived highway competition at all as to leave it almost unrecognizable as the agency which had brought the nation to its fullest industrial and geographic being.

Railroading lost much of its significance in the everyday life of the United States when the automobile began to divert a ponderable proportion of its freight and passenger traffic. It lost all of its character of wonderment and vitality when steam motive power was supplanted by Diesel locomotives, and it will disappear altogether from the general consciousness when it is wholly Dieselized, an eventuality that is already in sight. In the aspects in which it achieved its ascendency in the life and imagination of America, the railroad is already with the ages and can be objectively viewed by the historian as a completed cycle along with continental expansion, the Yankee domination and the independence and individualism that were once a part of the American character. Railroading, to the perceptive intelligence, is a feature of the profile of the past.

The disappearance of the cars from the universal consciousness began in the 1920's, approximately a century after their first emergence.

Passenger travel by railroad began to revert to its original estate, disappearing almost in its entirety from the daily experience of a majority of people. They no longer rode the cars short distances to neighboring cities, to picnics, ball games or fairs. That the national economy still depended in a very large measure on rail transport of merchandise became less apparent with the growth of cities and the removal of the cars and engines from public view.

Except for a limited population along the upper reaches of Park Avenue where the New York Central's tracks are located, no nontraveling resident of the nation's largest city need see, hear or smell a railroad train from one year to the next. Only a railroad strike or wholesale disaster which achieves the front pages ever brings the railroad to his attention at all.

In only slightly differing degrees the same thing was being achieved all over the United States as short-haul passengers deserted the cars and the short runs disappeared from the *Official Guide*. The once familiar local ceased to whistle at the town limits at breakfast and supper times. Even the mails, which had once endeared the trains in far places and lonely crossroads, now come in by truck. Short lines and independent railroads that had once carried millions annually in red-pulsh comfort now maintained freight service only or gave up the ghost altogether. When the management supplanted steam with Diesel power it gave up all claim to public interest or hold on public affection.

Thus passenger traffic reverted evermore to its primal status: an agency for transport for limited portions of the public bound on predetermined journeyings over considerable distances. The distance and its implications in 1950 between, say, Boston and Chicago, were no greater comparatively than those of a trip in 1850 between Boston and Stonington, Connecticut. Either was a substantial journada requiring preparation and economic resources. Rail travel became once more a facility within the experience of comparatively few. The cycle was complete.

That railroading is assuming something of the charm and patina of antiquity is demonstrable through a number of agencies, but none more vivid than the ever growing cult of amateurs of its art and mystery, especially in their more outmoded aspects. It has been estimated by competent authority that fully a million Americans in no professional way associated with the industry are interested in some angle or aspect of the progress of the flanged wheel along the steel rail. Railroad historical societies, clubs, fan organizations, collectors of memorabilia and photographic aficionados exist in impressive numbers and the impassioned devotion of their faith is fanatic. Scores of chartered trains are run over obscure or forgotten routes every year for votaries whose blood pressure is aroused to perilous heights by obsolete equipment and souvenirs of the old days generally. The model railroad industry grosses sums of money running into the millions annually and there are specialized railroad periodicals ranging from the *Bulletin* of the scholarly and austere Railway and Locomotive Historical Society with headquarters at Harvard University to the mimeographed feuilletons of fan groups devoted to the annals of short lines. Aside from the official organ of the industry, *Railway Age* and the various house organs of individual lines, union publications and similar periodicals there are two monthlies, *Railroad Magazine* and *Trains*, devoted altogether to the lore of the high iron from the purely amateur viewpoint. Books on railroading are known by publishers to be assured of a certain sale conditioned by their type, author and degree of expensiveness, and the writing of official histories of railroads themselves is a not unremunerative activity of a small but specialized group of corporate camp followers. Railroad museums pure and undefiled by other antiquities exist in half a score of communities and there is hardly a museum or historical society in the land but possesses its share of railroadiana. Any photographic specialty shop proprietor will depose that a ponderable number of the negatives he develops commercially are concerned with railroad subjects. Indeed railroad photography is so well established and recognized an activity that the Pennsylvania Railroad issues annual identification cards to practitioners who wish to photograph its properties.

Railroading, a part of the national folklore from its inception, has also achieved the estate of a cult for antiquaries.

Railroads have contrived to retain their long haul and transcontinental passenger traffic and to derive substantial revenue from name trains by heroic efforts, as many of them in the field of promotion and advertising as in actual practice and operations. Much that is spurious has been fobbed off by adroit advertising as progress in passenger comfort and convenience. Neither Diesel motive power, for example, nor the air-flow train design known as streamlining are possessed of any least inherent passenger advantage over the steam motive power and standard weight cars of the preceding generation. Steam locomotives were precisely as fast and perhaps slightly more reliable than modern Diesel engines. Standard weight Pullmans, given the advantages of air conditioning, roller-bearing trucks and tight-lock draft gear, could be as luxurious as and perhaps safer than the lightweight cars of alloy metals and prefabricated design. But lightweight rolling stock and Diesel power were characterized by operating advantages and economies for the carriers and were therefore sold as a bill of goods making for increased passenger comfort and convenience. So far as the passenger was concerned, these in fact represented change but no conceivable progress.

Railroad food, in common with the standard of public dining everywhere, has declined pitifully. Diners always operated at some loss, but with the fantastic rise in the cost of labor their deficits mounted in such astronomical proportion that the railroads passed on the grief to the public in the form of drastic curtailment of every aspect of dining en route. Luxury dishes were almost universally eliminated, portions were grossly reduced and shabby devices resorted to ranging from the elimination of finger bowls to the substitution of paper napkins. With a few notable exceptions, mostly on name trains that serve their companies as show windows, dining on the cars is a vanishing amenity of travel.

The greatest factors in retaining passenger traffic in the entire picture of twentieth-century railroading have been air conditioning and improvements in dispatching and operations which have cut time from long-haul schedules and elevated reliability to a point where it is taken for granted. The on-schedule performance of American passenger trains is phenomenal and air conditioning added decades of usefulness to the cars. Without them the air routes and motor cars would long since have divided between them all but a trace of rail passenger traffic.

Speculation as to the possible future status of railroading in the American economy and industrial scheme is profitless. As a military implement it is the most important single factor in the defense of the continent and in the conduct of campaigns beyond the continental limits as well, and its destinies are certain to be conditioned by the circumstance no matter what the turn of international events. Nothing within the fore-imaginable future can ever obviate the fast and certain land transport of men and the materiél of war.

But railroading as an institution in the American consciousness, save as an aspect of the facade of yesterday, has passed its grand climacteric and nothing has been evolved even to approximate the dominance it once held, least of all the airplane. Reduced to basic realities, it is a matter of pure esthetics. There is nothing about the internal combustion engine, admirable though it may be from almost every technical and economic aspect, that fires the imagination as did the visible guts and glory of the reciprocating steam locomotive. Neither is a generation of youth inspired by the calling of a military mechanic whose field of activities is almost wholly beyond human access and as remote as the sidereal galaxies from common human experience. The dynasty of the locomotive engineer has never yet been dethroned by the mere boy aviator, although his prestige and wonderment has been immeasureably diminished by demotion to control of a machine whose progress he guides in a business suit from a cabin as antiseptic as an operating room. It must be remarked parenthetically, however, that his demotion to the effete ease of Diesel motive power has been cheerfully accepted by the generality of railroad enginemen who were glad to surrender the splendors of the smoky past along with its dangers and discomforts.

In taking leave of steam railroading and the ineffable legend of the high iron, America is taking leave of an old friend, whose successor it could not find even if it would. The locomotives and the cars have conditioned every aspect of its life and progress toward the unforeseen future. It has been good riding, profitable beyond all historic experience to a nation which has never seen anything but virtue in taking a profit. For the historian, the amateur of departed splendors, the wheel has come full circle and from the vantage point of its completed cycle he can see the pageant of railroading and see it whole.

Oil Spelled An End To Steam

America's first commercial oil well at Titusville, Pennsylvania, (*near photo*) penetrated seventy feet to reach oil sands under a derrick but thirty-five feet high, compared to modern operations which erect derricks 220 feet tall to drill 15,000 feet into the earth. The great oil fields of the Gulf States were inaugurated when Spindletop (*far photo*) came in. In a few years many railroads near oil supplies were using it as fuel in their steam locomotives, but in time the internal combustion engine displaced even these.

At first oil was transported from the wells—they were called petroleum farms—to refineries in tank cars each mounting two wooden tuns, and many accidents, such as the terrible wreck of the New York Central's Pacific Express at Wappinger's Creek on the Hudson in 1871, resulted. The oil industry, when young had about it the excitement and jungle-warfare aspects which characterized cattle raising and mining and created more but less colorful millionaires than both combined.

(ALL PHOTOS) OIL INDUSTRY INFORMATION

The two scenes shown below depict boom times when oil was discovered at Ranger, Texas, and shack towns, hastily laid spurs and branch line railroads, and blue sky speculation recreated the scenes of bonanza days and silver booms in Nevada only a few years earlier.

Internal Combustion Brought a Travel Revolution

In the early years of the horse-less carriage automobile clubs everywhere promoted races and exploratory trips across the continent. When city streets were clogged with snow, motorists found it convenient (*above*) to follow the streetcar tracks. In Nevada, if the pioneers got that far which was comparatively infrequent, they discovered that the railroad right of way (*center*) provided a better highway, despite the corduroy effect of the ties, than the desert. From the very beginning the motor car was an intruder on the railroads.

The flying machine, eventually a contender for the railroads' passenger business, was not a serious rival when a New York inventor proposed this arrangement in the seventies, but its resemblance to a helicopter was prophetic.

(THREE PHOTOS) LIBRARY OF CONGRESS
N. Y. PUBLIC LIBRARY

Airflow Design and "Streamlining" Are not so New

BALTIMORE & OHIO RR.

Uninformed persons incline to believe "streamlining" is something conspicuously up-and-coming, one of the ultimate contrivings of modernity and progress. The Adams "airsplitter" train shown above had most of the aspects—fluted sidewalls, faired-in trucks, a cruiser stern and one-piece roof— that are characteristic of the *Denver Zephyr* (*right*) and it was discarded by the Baltimore & Ohio in 1900 as serving no valid purpose. The oval end compartment (*lower left*) of the Great Northern's *Red River* was first incorporated into the rear-end passenger car (*lower right*) of the Old Colony's train between Boston and Fall River in 1865.

LUCIUS BEEBE
GREAT NORTHERN RR.

What Progress?

WABASH RAILROAD   GENERAL MOTORS

The vista-dome, widely hailed as a triumph of modern engineering design as represented by the Wabash *Blue Bird* (*above*) and Union Pacific *Train of Tomorrow* (*upper right*) was first suggested by a car builder from Winnipeg in the pages of *Scientific American* (*right and bottom*) in 1891. Unlike the Baltimore & Ohio's "windsplitter," it was never actually built or put in service until half a century later when vista-domes began to turn up throughout the West, notably on the *California Zephyr* where they scared the daylights out of passengers as they headed into the multiple tunnels on the approach to the Moffat out of Denver.

CULVER SERVICE

Back in the dark ages of railroading, as the champions of progress would like to think of the eighties, telegraphic communication from the moving cars (*above*) to shore was achieved by induction, and silk-hatted businessmen (*left*) were able to transmit orders to their brokers from trains of the Lehigh Valley through the agency of a member of the crew with a portable instrument. Telephone communication (*below*) between the engine crew and caboose on long freights is today a commonplace on the Erie and other carriers and train-to-shore phones are carried on some de luxe passenger runs. Its equivalent was in operation three quarters of a century ago.

ERIE RR.

Steam, the King Whose Kingdom Ebbs and Flows Each Day

LUCIUS BEEBE

While modern and highly effective steam motive power was still performing with maximum efficiency and about a quarter the initial investment required by Diesel engines on such runs as the Union Pacific's climb of Sherman Hill west of Cheyenne (*above*) lightweight Diesel-electric units were usurping the place of steam on many short lines and branch runs. Heading a freight consist through one of the few remaining covered railroad bridges in Vermont (*center*) is an Alco-built road Diesel of the once pastoral and uncomplicated St. Johnsbury & Lamoille County Railroad.

Other railroads, such as the once prosperous Virginia & Truckee (*bottom*) which had served Nevada for eighty years, found themselves operating parallel to state-financed trucking highways and simply ceased operating, leaving the communities they had once served faithfully at the mercy of irresponsible stagers.

ALCO
LUCIUS BEEBE

GENERAL MOTORS

IF YOU AT LAST MUST HAVE A WORD TO SAY,
SAY NEITHER, IN THEIR WAY,
"IT IS A DEADLY MAGIC AND ACCURSED,"
NOR "IT IS BLEST," BUT ONLY "IT IS HERE." *

John Brown's Body

Over the rails of the Monon in Southern Indiana, where once Horace Greeley propelled himself through the night aboard a handcar to keep a lecture date, 5,000 Diesel horses roll the tonnage of the venerable Hoosier line.

* Copyright 1927, 1928 From *John Brown's Body*, by Stephen Vincent Benet.

CHARLES CLEGG

As the star of railroading dimmed, the steamcars that had been good familiar things for seven generations of American life and movement began to recede from the general awareness, never to return. They rolled, obedient to the rails, through woodlands and meadows, over lofty trestles and in the high passes of the hills toward the final coach-yard of forgetfulness, their locomotives, proud in the ancient ritual of reciprocating side rods, housed for all time in the last roundhouse. The cars went freighted with happy memories of a nation's bearded youth and of the brave years, of destinies beyond the horizon and a good time on the way. They had quickened the pulse as only the ships of the ocean-sea had done before them, and they were unseated from the wonder and admiration of men by the melancholy uses of progress and discomforts of modernity. The age was happy that had ridden the red-plush seats and watched the coal smoke roll over the windowed farm lands. The generation which followed and was going conspicuously nowhere was to ride with more expedition surrounded by the decor of an operating room. Fortunate was the world that had heard the train blow.